USING DATA
TO IMPROVE
TEACHER EDUCATION

USING DATA
TO IMPROVE
TEACHER EDUCATION

Moving Evidence Into Action

EDITED BY

Charles A. Peck
Kristen Cuthrell
Désirée H. Pointer Mace
Tine Sloan
Diana B. Lys

Foreword by G. Williamson McDiarmid

TEACHERS COLLEGE PRESS

TEACHERS COLLEGE | COLUMBIA UNIVERSITY
NEW YORK AND LONDON

Published by Teachers College Press,® 1234 Amsterdam Avenue, New York, NY
10027

Copyright © 2021 by Teachers College, Columbia University

Cover image of lecture hall by ozgurcankaya / iStock by Getty Images.

Library of Congress Cataloging-in-Publication Data

Names: Peck, Charles A., editor. | Cuthrell, Kristen, editor. | Pointer Mace, Désirée
    H. (Désirée Hood) editor. | Sloan, Tine F., 1965– editor. | Lys, Diana B., editor.
Title: Using data to improve teacher education : moving evidence into action /
    Edited by Charles A. Peck, Kristen Cuthrell, Désirée H. Pointer Mace, Tine
    Sloan, Diana B. Lys ; Foreword by G. Williamson McDiarmid.
Description: New York : Teachers College Press, Teachers College, Columbia
    University, [2021] | Includes bibliographical references and index.
Identifiers: LCCN 2020054593 (print) | LCCN 2020054594 (ebook) |
    ISBN 9780807764718 (hardcover) | ISBN 9780807764701 (paperback) |
    ISBN 9780807779248 (ebook)
Subjects: LCSH: Teachers—Training of—Research. | Teachers—Training of—Data
    processing. | Teachers—In-service training—Research. | Teachers—In-service
    training—Data processing. | Education—Research.
Classification: LCC LB1707 .U85 2021 (print) | LCC LB1707 (ebook) |
    DDC 370.71/1—dc23
LC record available at https://lccn.loc.gov/2020054593
LC ebook record available at https://lccn.loc.gov/2020054594

ISBN 978-0-8077-6470-1 (paper)
ISBN 978-0-8077-6471-8 (hardcover)
ISBN 978-0-8077-7924-8 (ebook)

Printed on acid-free paper
Manufactured in the United States of America

Hannah♡

Contents

PART IV: NEW DIRECTIONS

Foreword

For decades, university-based teacher educators have routinely collected evidence on their preservice teachers (PTs) and graduates. Exit surveys of candidates and graduates and their supervisors' interviews and surveys were fairly common. Campus-based faculty members, supervisors, and cooperating teachers also provided evaluations of PTs. Advisory boards typically included educators from surrounding districts who offered their impressions of graduates' preparedness. To what extent and how data from all these sources were used to evaluate and improve educator preparation program (EPP) effectiveness is not clear. Although accrediting authorities required programs to report these data, little attention appears to have been paid to how the data were used—if at all—for program improvement.

So, what has changed over the past few decades? For one, EPPs, like other human service–oriented organizations, have come under unprecedented levels of scrutiny and criticism. Although critical, occasionally scathing, reviews appeared periodically in the past, few authorities questioned the profession's right to police itself (Bestor, 1953; Conant, 1963; Mencken, 1928). This has changed dramatically over the past 3 decades. Not only have policymakers required EPPs to collect and publish data on the performance of their graduates, the primary accrediting authority—the Council for the Accreditation of Educator Preparation (CAEP)—has instituted standards that require both the collection of performance data as well as evidence that data are being used to inform program improvement (CAEP, 2020).

This change has occurred within a broader shift in attitudes toward various services—health, social, and educational—in the last 2 decades of the 20th century (Dalton, 2005; Drake et al., 2001; Miller & Borrelli, 1991; Mullen et al., 2008). A 2010 Pew Research Center report begins, "By almost every conceivable measure Americans are less positive and more critical of government these days" (Pew Research Center, 2010). Pressure on agencies and institutions to produce evidence of effectiveness has steadily increased. "Evidence-based" policies and practices have become the watchword across various professions (Dyck, 2010; Jenicek, 1997).

Under pressure to demonstrate efficacy as well as their longstanding commitment to better serving their clients, multiple professions sought to improve the research base for their practices (Biglan & Ogden, 2008). In education, beginning in the mid-1980s, the standards and accountability movement brought a new level of scrutiny for public schools. Disaggregated data from standardized state assessments revealed the persistent gap between test scores for majority-culture students and those from marginalized groups (Lyons, 2004). Predictably, politicians fingered university-based EPPs as a major part of the problem. Secretary Duncan's well-publicized comment a decade ago reflected the views of his immediate predecessors and many policymakers, commentators, and charitable foundations: "By almost any standard, many if not most of the nation's 1,450 schools, colleges, and departments of education are doing a mediocre job of preparing teachers for the realities of the 21st century classroom. America's university-based teacher preparation programs need revolutionary change—not evolutionary tinkering" (Duncan, 2009).

University-based EPPs were vulnerable to attack, in part because of what their critics saw as a weak evidentiary basis for their curricula, pedagogy, and practices (Walsh, 2001, 2006). Although teacher education scholars attempted to counter this attack (Darling-Hammond, 2002), critics used this vulnerability to pressure EPPs and push for alternatives to traditional university-based EPPs (Humphrey et al., 2008).

A major hurdle to providing more convincing and useful evidence on the effects of EPPs was the lack of reliable tools to measure program impact on PTs and their practice. As the pressure to demonstrate effectiveness mounted, statisticians were refining their methods—value-added models, specifically—for isolating teacher effects on student performance from other factors (Raudenbush & Bryk, 1986; Sanders & Rivers, 1994). These tools had immediate appeal to policymakers who were searching for ways to identify and remove ineffective teachers. Applying these tools to determine the quality of EPPs was a logical next step (Noell et al., 2014). States initially lined up to adopt value-added measures (VAM) of teachers, as well as of EPPs. Despite questions about the use of VAM data to evaluate individual teachers, 34 states continue to use student scores as part of their teacher evaluation systems—down from 43 in 2015 (Ross & Walsh, 2020). The tide appears to have turned.

Researchers and teacher educators who are committed to program improvement have long questioned the value of such data, especially in isolation from other measures, in moving the field forward (American Statistical Association, 2014; Bill & Melinda Gates Foundation MET Project, 2013; Schochet & Chiang, 2013). The limitations of the data generated by the statistical models lent urgency to the development of alternative approaches to measuring PT class performance. To improve their programs, teacher educators need more actionable evidence that faculty find credible and motivating. As a dean colleague remarked, "value-added data provide a 30,000-feet-view of programs—which has some value in knowing where to look. But what we need is ground-level information on what our candidates can and cannot do in the classroom before they leave us."

The quotation above highlights the conflicting goals of policymakers and teacher preparation leaders (McDiarmid, 2019). The former's goal is to identify and, if justified in their eyes, shutter low-performing programs. In addition, the possibility of closure represents a Damoclean sword suspended above EPPs: improve or die. Making achievement data on the students of program graduates publicly available also allows consumers—students and their families—to choose among programs. Consequently, as market-think goes, low-performing programs would lose enrollment and, eventually, wither away without direct intervention from policymakers.

In contrast, teacher educators value evidence that will help them better prepare their students to succeed in classrooms. Surveys of PTs, graduates, and principals, with response rates often in the range of 20% to 30%, frequently lack the type of information that motivates and guides substantial change. Knowing that PTs feel inadequately prepared to work with non-native speakers provides important information but is inadequate to help address the problem. Whose issue is this—foundations or subject-matter methods or both? Or is it an issue for university supervisors or cooperating teachers—or both? Is it a lack of information or adequate practice—or both? Is the problem the placement schools for student teaching? Commenting on value-added and survey data, another reform-minded EPP leader said: "It's like if you were to go to the doctor and say, 'I don't feel well,' and, after examination, she says, 'Yep, you're sick. Hope you feel better soon.'"

The need for program impact evidence that is more fine-grained, more ground-level, and more compelling drove, in part, the development of performance assessments—in particular, the educative teacher performance assessment (edTPA; Darling-Hammond & Hylar, 2013). Tracing this history is beyond the scope of this foreword, but, for the first time, the field has available evidence on PTs' classroom performance that is empirically sound, actionable, and compelling (Bastian, Fortner, et al., 2015; Bastian, Henry, et al., 2015). Encountering firsthand evidence of the classroom performance of their own students has the power of disruption. After reviewing his students' edTPA-like portfolios that included descriptions and self-analysis of their teaching, a renowned methods instructor who prided himself on his courses declared, "This is a syllabus-shredding moment. I need to start over."

Other improved tools to inform and motivate improvement have also appeared. Some programs are adopting empirically sound observational instruments such as CLASS™ (Center for Advanced Study of Teaching and Learning, n.d.). The Teacher Effectiveness Initiative project, funded by the Bush Family Foundation, has produced exit, entry, transition, and supervisor surveys that meet psychometric standards that instill confidence in the data they yield (Bush Foundation, 2015). Designed, in part, to strengthen the evidentiary base for EPPs, the Teachers for a New Era Project enabled participating institutions to develop and test new tools for evaluating program impact (McDiarmid & Caprino, 2018). For instance, Boston College scholars created a well-researched instrument for gauging PTs' preparation as social-justice educators (Cochran-Smith et al., 2009). In short, today's teacher educators have tools, however imperfect each may be, not available in the past.

With faculty motivated by both external pressures and their internal commitments to improving their programs and the availability of multiple, higher-quality evidence, the remaining issues are the organizational structures, cultures, and norms in which improvement work occurs. This is where the chapters in this book are invaluable. As Sarason (1990) taught us 3 decades ago, educational reforms historically have failed to ~~disrupt existing organizational social and power relations and cultural norms~~. Organizations prove remarkably resilient to genuine change, bending under the force of reforms and then snapping back to the *status quo ante* when the reform momentum dissipates. As a result, reforms come and go, only skimming the organizational surface and leaving the subterranean relations, culture, and norms undisturbed.

The project for leaders, in particular, is how to challenge these norms and relations and disrupt the existing culture. As the chapters herein describe, the power to do so may well reside in the evidence generated by the newly available tools in the hands of educators who are collectively committed to program improvement.

—G. Williamson McDiarmid,
University of North Carolina–Chapel Hill

REFERENCES

American Statistical Association. (2014). *ASA statement on using value-added models for educational assessment.* Retrieved from http://vamboozled.com/wp-content/uploads/2014/03/ASA_VAM_Statement.pdf.

Bastian, K., Fortner, K., Chapman, A., Fleener, J., McIntyre, E., & Patriarca, L. (2015). *Data sharing to drive the improvement of teacher preparation programs.* Education Policy Initiative at Carolina.

Bastian, K. C., Henry, G. T., Pan, Y., & Lys, D. (2015). *Evaluating a pilot of the teacher performance assessment: The construct validity, reliability, and predictive validity of local scores.* Education Policy Initiative at Carolina.

Bestor, A. (1953). *Educational wastelands: The retreat from learning.* University of Illinois Press.

Biglan, A., & Ogden, T. (2008). The evolution of evidence-based practices. *European journal of behavior analysis, 9*(1), 81–95.

Bill & Melinda Gates Foundation MET Project. (2013). *Ensuring fair and reliable measures of effective teaching: Culminating findings from the MET Project's three-year study.* https://secure.edweek.org/media/17teach-met1.pdf

Bush Foundation. (2015). *Using data to improve teacher preparation.* https://www
.bushfoundation.org/learning/bush-papers/using-data-improve-teacher
-preparation

Council for the Accreditation of Educator Preparation (CAEP). (2020). *Standard 4:
Program impact.* http://caepnet.org/standards/standard-4

Center for Advanced Study of Teaching and Learning. (n.d.) *Classroom Assessment
Scoring System™.* https://curry.virginia.edu/classroom-assessment-scoring
-system

Cochran-Smith, M., Reagan, E., & Shakman, K. (2009). Just measures: Social justice as a teacher education outcome. *Teacher Education and Practice 22*(3),
237–263.

Conant, J. (1963). *The education of American teachers.* McGraw-Hill.

Dalton, R. (2005). The social transformation of trust in government. *International
Review of Sociology, 15*(1), 133–154.

Darling-Hammond, L., & Hylar, M. (2013). *The role of performance assessment in developing teaching as a profession.* Rethinking Schools. https://
www.rethinkingschools.org/articles/the-role-of-performance-assessment
-in-developing-teaching-as-a-profession

Darling-Hammond, L. (2002). *Research and rhetoric on teacher certification.* Education policy analysis archives. https://epaa.asu.edu/ojs/article/view/315/441

Drake, R., Goldman, H., Leff, H., Lehman, A., Dixon, L., Mueser, K., & Torrey, W.
(2001). Implementing evidence-based practices in routine mental health service
settings. *Psychiatric Services, 52*(2), 179–182.

Duncan, A. (2009). *Teacher preparation: Reforming the uncertain profession.*
https://www.ed.gov/news/speeches/teacher-preparation-reforming-uncertain
-profession

Dyck, J. (2010). Political distrust and conservative voting in ballot measure elec-
tions. *Political Research Quarterly, 63*(3): 612–626.

Humphrey, D., Wechsler, M., & Hough, H. (2008). Characteristics of effective alternative teacher certification programs.*Teachers College Record.* http://policy-
web.sri.com/cep/ publications/AltCert_finalTCversion.pdf

Jenicek, M. (1997). Evidence-based medicine working group. Evidence based medicine. A new approach to teaching the practice of medicine. *JAMA, 268*(17),
2420–2425.

Lyons, R,. 2004. Measuring the gap: The state of equity of student achievement in
Kentucky. *Educational Research Quarterly, 27*(3), 10–21.

McDiarmid, G., & Caprino, K. (2018). *Lessons from the teachers for a new era
project: Evidence and accountability in teacher education.* Routledge.

McDiarmid, G. (2019). Competing theories for improving teacher preparations: The
case of North Carolina. *ECNU Review of Education, 2*(2), 117–136.

Mencken, H. (1928, December 31). The war upon intelligence. *Baltimore Evening
Sun,* p. 5.

Miller, A., & Borrelli, S. (1991). Confidence in government during the 1980s. *American Politics Quarterly, 19*(2), 147–173.

Mullen, E., Bledsoe, S., & Bellamy, J. (2008). Implementing evidence-based social work practice. *Research on Social Work Practice, 18*(4), 325–338.

Noell, G., Brownell, M., Buzick, H., & Jones, N. (2014). *Using educator effectiveness measures to improve educator preparation programs and student outcomes* (Document No. LS-1). CEEDAR Center. https://ceedar.education.ufl.edu/wp-content/uploads/2014/09/LS-1_FINAL_08-27-14.pdf.

Pew Research Center. (2010, April 18). *Distrust, discontent, anger and partisan rancor.* Pew Research Center: U.S. Politics & Policy. https://www.people-press.org/2010/04/18/distrust-discontent-anger-and-partisan-rancor/

Raudenbush, S., & Bryk, T. (1986). A hierarchical model for studying school effects. *Sociology of education, 59*(1), 1–17.

Ross, E., & Walsh, K. (2020). *State of the States 2019: Teacher and principal evaluation policy.* National Council on Teacher Quality. https://www.nctq.org/pages/State-of-the-States-2019:-Teacher-and-Principal-Evaluation-Policy#TStudentGrowth

Sanders, W., & Rivers, J. (1994). *Cumulative and residual effects of teachers on future student academic achievement.* University of Tennessee Value-Added Research and Assessment Center.

Sarason, S. (1990). *The predictable failure of educational reform: Can we change course before it's too late?* Jossey-Bass.

Schochet, P., & Chiang, H. (2013). What are error rates for classifying teacher and school performance using value-added models? *Journal of Educational and Behavioral Statistics, 38*(2), 142–171.

Walsh, K. (2001). *Teacher certification reconsidered: Stumbling for quality.* The Abell Foundation. http://www.abell.org/sites/default/files/publications/Teacher-%20Certification%20Reconsidered.pdf

Walsh, K. (2006, March 16). Teacher education: Coming up empty. *Fwd: Arresting insights in education, 3*(1). https://files.eric.ed.gov/fulltext/ED493850.pdf

Acknowledgments

Where to begin? So many people have contributed to this work. The work of program improvement is quintessentially collaborative work, so we gratefully acknowledge the many colleagues who have contributed to our collective work and to this volume. We thank in particular the colleagues in the 10 institutions we visited in our original data use study, who graciously shared what they learned in their own efforts to make data matter to decisions about program improvement. We are grateful to the Spencer Foundation, which funded the study (Project No. 201200045), and to the American Association of Colleges of Teacher Education for their collaboration in developing and carrying out the research that forms the foundation for much of the work that appears in this volume.

There are many individuals who collaborated with us, helped us, and inspired us to undertake the present work. Three must be called out specifically:

- Morva McDonald worked with Cap (Charles Peck) on the initial proposal to the Spencer Foundation, and on the conceptualization, design, and early phases of the study;
- Linda Patriarca *showed* us how institutional transformation can take place, how hard it is, and how rewarding the work can be;
- Sarah Byrne Bausell supported and improved the work immeasurably with her scholarly knowledge and editorial skill.

None of us can imagine undertaking this work, or any other serious professional endeavor, without the patient and loving support of our respective families. We are very fortunate in so many ways.

And, it was fun.

—Cap, Kristen, Désirée, Tine, and Diana

CONCEPTUAL AND EMPIRICAL FOUNDATIONS

CHAPTER 1

Introduction and Overview of the Book

Charles A. Peck

Well, the main thing I remember about that first meeting was that I'd pretty much been up most of the night worrying about it. The state was breathing down our necks with its new performance assessment mandate, and the faculty were hopping mad. And not just the ones that were always mad about something . . . but also many of the folks who I respected most deeply as teacher educators—the ones that worked hardest to make the program better. Many of them had actually left the P–12 world because of this kind of thing . . . and they were really angry about their sense that the state was now intruding into what had historically been the protected space of the university. Many faculty members felt that complying with the mandate would undermine the integrity of the program. But if we did not comply, we would lose our accreditation. I felt very much overwhelmed by this dilemma, and I had no idea how to deal with it.

—Associate Dean for Teacher Education

Teacher preparation programs in the United States, as elsewhere in the world, are currently faced with increasing levels of bureaucratic oversight, regulation, and evaluation by state and federal policymakers—policy developments that reflect increased public skepticism about the value and effectiveness of the programs themselves. Program accountability policies developed in the context of these concerns reflect two general purposes. One clearly has to do with identifying and eliminating ineffective programs (Crowe, 2010). The other purpose, however, has to do with using data to improve programs. In this context, state and federal policy mandates, new professional program accreditation standards, and the dramatic expansion of technologies for collecting and analyzing program outcome data have all converged to create unprecedented possibilities, and unprecedented pressures, for teacher education programs to become more "data-driven." At the same time, for teacher education practitioners, it is easy to be over-whelmed by the intensifying policy requirements around "data use"—and easy to experience these as mandates for increased accountability rather than opportunities for inquiry, learning, and program improvement. In this volume, we describe how some programs of teacher education have found ways to manage these tensions and leverage new demands for accountability as opportunities to improve their individual and collective practice.

This is not simple work. Teacher educators in positions of leadership—and by this we really refer to all teacher educators in one way or another—contend with a complex and highly dynamic set of issues and concerns emerging from both within and outside institutions of higher education. As one dean wryly put it, "our program's data are now out there . . . in the pa-pers, in the public . . . in front of God and everybody else." Engaging public perceptions, misperceptions and reactions to program outcome data can be extremely challenging. At the same time, program faculty can be very reac-tive to the requirements and impacts of new accountability policies—and "opt out" movements, union appeals, and more passive forms of resistance often constitute another set of challenges to making these policies "work" for the improvement of programs. Just to be clear, we do not suggest that the concerns of policymakers, the public, faculty, program graduates, or other stakeholders lack substance. There is indeed much to be concerned about with regard to the organizational structure, curriculum priorities, and efficacy of teacher education programs—as evidenced by a nearly continu-ous stream of critical appraisals of the field that have emerged over the last several decades (Conant, 1963; Goodlad et al., 1990; Levine, 2006). The paradox we have observed, however, is that the meanings of new account-ability mandates as interpreted by many teacher educators often function to demoralize their work and undermine the motivational conditions needed to undertake the difficult and complex work of improving programs. Peck, Gallucci, and Sloan (2010) articulated the core dilemma, noting that "com-pliance with prescriptive state mandates is often interpreted by faculty to signify a demoralizing loss of program autonomy and integrity, whereas noncompliance may result in loss of program accreditation" (p. 451). The programs and practices we describe in the present volume represent exam-ples of thoughtful and strategic responses to this dilemma, in which the re-quirements of program accountability policies are leveraged to achieve local goals for program improvement.

THE POLICY LANDSCAPE

It is worth noting that teacher educators are hardly alone in facing public skepticism, new accountability mandates, and intensifying pressures to be-come more "evidence-based." Indeed, over the past 2 decades the logic and rhetoric of "data use," "evidence-based" decision making, and related con-structs has become a dominant discourse across national and international policy contexts (Young et al., 2002) and across diverse fields of professional practice. These include medicine (Sackett et al., 1996), social work (Thyer, 2002), nursing (Estabrooks et al., 2007), mental health (Achenbach, 2005), and others. In higher education, historically intense pressures for change are driven by a complex and often conflicting set of dynamics related to expand-ed expectations for access (the "massification of higher education") coupled with reduced resources, particularly in public institutions (Alexander, 2000; Zeichner, 2010). These changes may in turn be understood to be related to massive social and economic shifts related to globalization, expanding information technologies, and ideological change. Some observers have commented on the ways in which these changes have constrained discourse around public value and social equity in higher education, and contributed to an increasingly corporatist approach to defining the goals and operating policies of the academy (Gaffikin & Perry, 2009). The dark side of this shift in zeitgeist, and the ascendancy of market principles with which it is associ-ated, is reflected in this commentary by Gaffikin and Perry (2009):

> [This corporatist approach] is reflected in the appropriation of business language and practice, with the associated elevation of efficiency and cost-effectiveness within institutional imperatives. Partly, it can be represented in the reduction of collegial consultation and participation in favor of more managerialist lead-ership and decision making, a related rise in central administrative staff, and the importation of an audit culture and ritualistic performance measurement. (p. 119)

These dynamics, and others, have produced a policy climate character-ized by increased skepticism regarding both the willingness and the capacity of institutions of higher education to undertake reforms that policymak-ers consider important to meeting rapidly changing and expanding public need (cf. the "Spellings Report" [U.S. Department of Education, 2006]). Consequently, state and federal policies in teacher education now include a variety of mandates related to outcomes-based evaluation, accountability, and program improvement (Cochran-Smith, 2003; Wineberg, 2006). For example, during the Obama administration, to successfully compete for fed-eral Race to the Top funds, states were required to develop accountability systems that linked student test scores to both teachers and the programs and pathways through which they entered teaching. The specific directions these policy initiatives may take in the context of the current federal admin-istration are not clear yet, but the accountability discourse that has taken hold among policymakers appears unlikely to abate.

The emphasis on outcomes-based accountability has also been embraced to some extent within the teacher education profession itself, particularly by accrediting bodies. For example, the Council for the Accreditation of Educator Preparation (CAEP) accreditation standards emphasize demonstration of evidence-based program improvement using a broad array of data sources (CAEP, 2013). A key construct underlying the Council's stance is the notion of a "culture of evidence":

> For CAEP, the culture of evidence is summed up by the language of the Commission's Standard 5: *Provider Quality Assurance and Continuous Improvement*, but the concepts reappear throughout the supporting rationales from the Commission. These identify several inter-related roles for educator preparation providers. They:
>
> - Maintain a quality assurance system comprised of valid data from multiple measures.
> - Gather evidence of candidates' and completers' positive impact on P–12 student learning and development.
> - Support continuous improvement that is sustained and evidence-based.
> - Evaluate the effectiveness of their completers.
> - Test innovations to improve completers' impact on P–12 student learning and development.
> - Use the results of inquiry and data collection to establish priorities, enhance program elements and capacity. (CAEP, 2015, p. 5)

Unfortunately, social science research from multiple fields of human service suggests that the challenges of making data both *useful* and *used* involve much more than creating policies and related information technologies to support collection, archival, and analysis of information about program outcomes (Estabrooks et al., 2007; Mandinach & Gummer, 2019; Sudsawad, 2007; Weiss et al., 2008). Rather, the most significant challenges for achieving systematic use of data for decision making lie in what Brown and Duguid (2002) have referred to as "the *social* life of information" (author's emphasis). Particularly at issue are the ways in which organizational policies and practices shape opportunities for deliberation, learning, and action (Nicolini et al., 2003). Spillane and Meile (2007) have been particularly articulate in expressing this viewpoint:

> For those in the trenches, our take home message is this: work practice is where the rubber meets the road in the schoolhouse. Understanding how information becomes evidence, and how this evidence gets used or goes unused requires attention to work practice. Work practice can be difficult to assess, and even more difficult to analyze. We often gloss over these difficulties by focusing on simplified strategies for evidence-based decision making. But to understand evidence use, we must attend to practice, which necessitates attention to interactions

between people, as well as to how these interactions are mediated by aspects of the situation (such as organizational routines and tools). (p. 68)

We believe this kind of practice-oriented perspective on data use is seriously underrepresented in current policy discourse.

THE PURPOSE OF THIS VOLUME

Viewed together, it is clear that state and federal policy mandates, increased public scrutiny of teacher preparation, accreditation standards, and the dramatic expansion of technologies for collecting and analyzing program outcome data have converged to create unprecedented pressures for teacher education programs to become more "data-driven." In the context of these pressures, Zeichner (2010) makes this observation:

> In many teacher education programs across the country, a clash has been created by current accountability demands between authenticity (doing what one knows is in the best interest of the learning of one's students) and performativity (doing what one needs to do to meet accountability demands even when one knows it is not in the best interest of one's students). (p. 1548)

This interpretation of the current policy context is understandable, albeit one that leads naturally to efforts to deflect accountability policies that are viewed to be in tension with the integrity of local program values and practices (e.g., see Kornfeld et al., 2007). In this book we examine how a select group of teacher education programs around the country have productively navigated the tensions Zeichner (2010) describes between "authenticity and performativity." We describe the local policies and practices these programs have developed that have allowed them to respond strategically to contemporary policy pressures in ways that align with their own values and goals. Our hope is that teacher educators will find these practical examples useful in their own efforts to use emerging data sources as resources for improving their practice in ways they find meaningful in the context of their values and the integrity of their practice.

The volume is based in large part on a 3-year field study of 10 teacher education programs around the country. Each program was selected for their commitments to developing organizational policies and practices related to using data for program improvement. The data we have collected in these programs suggest that in many cases their efforts have shifted the focus of engagement from "compliance" or "performativity" toward an emphasis on using data to achieve local goals related to program improvement (Davis & Peck, 2020). Our data further suggest that this shift has

in many cases been associated with an increased sense of shared responsibility among faculty and an increased sense of individual and collective
agency with respect to their work as teacher educators. We believe the
case examples we present in the present volume, as well as data from the
broader sample of programs in the study, offer the field a sense of possibility for how programs may navigate the complex and dynamic tensions
between state and federal accountability policies and the local work of
program improvement.

THE PROGRAMS:
HOW WE SELECTED THEM AND HOW WE LEARNED FROM THEM

In the early phases of our work we developed a list of 43 teacher education
programs identified as potential examples of high data use practice on the
basis of survey data collected annually through the American Association
of Colleges of Teacher Education (AACTE), as well as nominations collected through contacts with other national organizations involved with
teacher preparation (e.g., SCALE, NCATE). From this list we selected 16
programs representing a variety of institutional characteristics (size, mission, funding) and state policy contexts. We were particularly interested
in including programs located in states that used value-added measures
(VAM) for assessing the impacts of teacher preparation on standardized
tests of P–12 student achievement, and others sited in states involved in
implementation of standardized teacher performance assessments (e.g.,
the edTPA). We conducted follow-up telephone interviews with program
administrators (deans and directors of teacher education) in each of the
16 programs, inquiring in more detail about the extent to which each
program was engaged in regular data use activities related to program
improvement.

Based on these initial phone interviews we selected 10 programs that
reported particularly vigorous efforts to develop organizational policies
and practices supporting the systematic use of outcome data for program
improvement. We included programs situated in a variety of institutional
contexts, including large public universities, research-intensive universities, small private colleges, and an alternative route program administered
by a nonprofit agency. In an effort to learn more about how the programs
supported data use activities, we then conducted 1- to 2-day on-site visits
for each of the 10 programs. On-site visits included interviews of program
faculty and administrators and collection of artifacts reflective of program
practices. From these data we selected 3 of the 10 programs for more
extended study. These programs were chosen both for the depth of their
investment in using data for program improvement and also because they

represented important variation in both institutional size, mission, and state policy context. One program was situated in a large regional public university that produced over 700 teachers per year. Another program was in a small private liberal arts college. The third program was based in a midsize public research-intensive institution. Over the following 2 years, we conducted 2–3 additional on-site visits for each program, as well as multiple phone interviews and email exchanges with program faculty and administrators in an effort to more fully document the ways in which each of the programs supported systematic and ongoing activities in which outcome data were used to improve program policy and practice. A more detailed description of our methodology and our cross-case findings from the study are presented in Chapter 2 of the present volume.

We felt it was important to include a strong sense of practitioner "voice" in presenting this work to the field. Following formal analysis of our data, we invited a team of faculty and academic leaders from each of the three extended case study programs to collaborate with us to develop a set of brief resource documents that might be useful for those engaging the challenges and dilemmas of responding productively to mandates for "data use." These resources were subsequently distributed by the American Association of Colleges of Teacher Education (see https://secure.aacte.org/apps/rl/resource.php?resid=504&ref=rl). The present volume represents the further efforts of this collaborative group to share what we have learned about navigating the challenges of making data *useful* and *used* in programs of teacher education.

THEORETICAL PERSPECTIVES

In undertaking the study that forms the basis of the work reported in the present volume, we were not naive about the complex, layered, and transactional nature of factors affecting data use practice. Our earlier work in this area (Peck et al., 2010; Peck & McDonald, 2013, 2014) had convinced us that making sense of the ways teacher education programs, as organizations, do (or do not) use data for program improvement would require an orienting framework to help us attend to important aspects of their policies and practices. We knew that teacher education programs were organized the way they were for reasons rooted in history; and we assumed that appreciating this history would be key to understanding the struggles they underwent in attempting to engage new accountability policies in a way that was consonant with their established values and commitments.

We also assumed that people's understanding of their individual and collective work was affected by the kinds of conceptual and material tools they used to carry out that work. Most specifically, we assumed that the kinds of data-related tools people used to evaluate their programs would affect what became visible, and actionable, about their work. These tools included the measures of candidate learning and performance used to monitor and evaluate program outcomes, as well as ways in which data from those measures were stored and accessed, often via electronic platforms. We recognized that formal and informal rules about who had access to these tools and who had standing to participate in decisions about the program mattered.

These kinds of assumptions and considerations are central to the line of theorizing about the social/organizational contexts of human learning and development known as Cultural Historical Activity Theory, or CHAT (Engeström, 1987, 2001; Leont'ev, 1978). We are by no means the first researcher–practitioners to appreciate the value of CHAT as an orienting conceptual framework for analysis of the complex and layered work of teacher education (e.g., see Anderson & Stillman, 2013; Ellis, Edwards, & Smagorinsky, 2010). Like others, we found that CHAT directed our attention to the *systemic and collective* nature of organizational practice. This was particularly helpful in thinking about the ways that the individual motivations and actions of faculty and staff were situated in collective values and goals, and in noticing how these goals themselves shaped and were shaped by the kinds of data used to monitor and evaluate program outcomes. Perhaps most significantly, we found the focus within cultural–historical theory on the social organization of collective work activities, like a teacher education program, was consonant with the kinds of things teacher educators talked about regarding both their aspirations and the challenges they encountered in using data to inform and improve their practice.

While the theoretical assumptions in CHAT regarding individual and collective learning and organizational change provided a foundation for our work, in the present volume we adopt what we believe is a more accessible and practicable conceptual framework to present our research and development work related to data use. In this framework, proposed originally by McDiarmid and Peck (2012), we parse the dimensions of data use work into those related to the values, beliefs, and motivations of the *people* involved, those related to the *conceptual and material tools* used to carry out the work, and those related to the *organizational policies and practices* that shape the way the work is carried out (Peck & Davis, 2019). We define each of these constructs below and offer some examples of how we have used them to analyze data use practices in programs of teacher education.

People

Information systems in teacher education do not stand outside of the webs of meaning that program members construct about their work, both individually and collectively. We conceptualize this aspect of data use work to be about the *people* involved, including particularly the values, beliefs, and aspirations that motivate their engagement (or disengagement) with opportunities to learn that are afforded by program outcome data.

Tools

Clearly, the quality and accessibility of the various data tools, including measurement instruments, data warehouses, and "dashboards" for monitoring and analysis of program processes and outcomes matters tremendously. Our interests in *tools* extend also to questions about accessibility and flexibility, particularly with respect to their use by faculty, program staff, and even candidates themselves. At issue here is the extent to which data tools become internalized and used *within* the local culture of a program, or whether they remain essentially instruments used *on* the program by others.

Organizational Policy and Practice

A third dimension of the social ecology in which information systems and decision making in teacher education exist has to do with the "ways of doing things" that are negotiated in programs as *organizations*. Here we refer to program policies (compensation, tenure and promotion, job descriptions, and so on) and practices (meetings, data use gatherings, work routines, norms for collegiality) that affect participation in collective activities related to data use.

These three dimensions of data use work are, of course, highly interrelated and transactional. That is, the engagement of program members (people) with initiatives aimed at using data for program improvement will depend on how they interpret the validity and reliability of the available data sources (tools), as well as the extent to which program policies and practices (organizations) support opportunities for them to work individually and collectively to analyze and interpret the data relative to decisions about actions. Figure 1.1 depicts these dimensions of data use practice and some of the questions we have found useful to understanding the relationships among them.

Figure 1.1. The Interdependence of Measurement Tools, Organizational Practice, and Faculty Engagement with Data

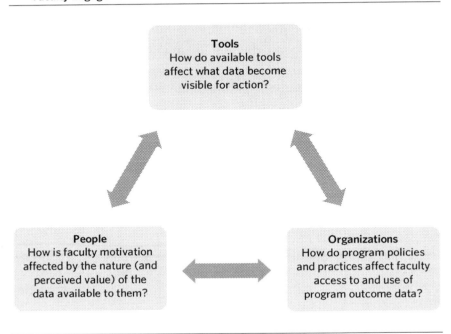

THE STRUCTURE OF THE BOOK

Part I: Conceptual and Empirical Foundations

One of our goals for the present volume is to represent the findings of our work in multiple "voices." Specifically, we hope to contribute to the formal knowledge base of the field by presenting a rigorous and theoretically grounded analysis of the data we have collected from the 10 programs we visited and studied over the course of the multiyear research project supported by the Spencer Foundation. To that end, in Chapter 2 we present the findings of a formal cross-case analysis of the 10 programs based on our analysis of individual interviews, focus groups, field observations, and relevant artifacts of practice we have collected over the 3 years of the study. As noted above, our formal data analysis has been guided largely by the theoretical and methodological assumptions of cultural–historical activity theory. We more thoroughly explain this theoretical perspective and how we used it in Chapter 2. Based on cross-case findings, we offer a number of general assertions about the kinds of organizational practices that can help make data both useful and used in program improvement efforts. Our general conclusion is that developing the capacity and commitment to systematic use of data for program improvement involves a complex orchestration of social, material, and conceptual resources—a far more challenging endeavor than one might guess on the basis of the kinds of facile mandates to "use data for program improvement" that emanate so often from policymakers and accreditation agencies.

Part II: Case Studies of High Data Use Programs

One of the most important things we learned in this study was that successful data use practices were often about "local intelligence"—by which we refer to the inventions and adaptations program faculty, staff members, and administrators make in response to the very specific organizational contexts in which their programs operate. In fact, local variation and related practitioner creativity appear to us to be just as important to understand as the kinds of more general principles that have emerged through our cross-case data analysis. With this interest in mind, colleagues from each of our three extended case study sites present "program portraits" of their own work, focusing specifically on the organizational policies and practices they developed in their own settings to support their efforts to use data for program improvement purposes. While each program team relied in part on the data we had collected in the larger research project as a resource for their writing, each program team was encouraged to write in its own voice about what they had experienced as most valuable and important in their data use work. The program portraits are presented in Chapters 3–5.

Part III: Promising Practices

Over the course of our program visits we were struck by the thematic nature of several "problems of practice" that emerged as programs expanded their engagement with the complex work of using data for program decision making and improvement. These included very specific challenges such as developing electronic data platforms that are actually used by faculty, making time and space for data use work, and building a common language of practice. Of course, we also observed broader challenges related to leadership and systemic change. Drawing on the practical examples we observed in the programs we studied, we devote Chapters 6–9 of the book to describing strategies for engaging common and recurring "problems of practice" related to data use. These chapters are focused on specific practical challenges related to motivating faculty engagement, selecting and adapting online platforms for data archival and analysis, creating focused time and space for data use work, and developing leadership strategy. It is worth noting that the practices we describe in these chapters should be understood as "promising" in the sense that they appear to have been effective in one or more programs, but are by no means "evidence-based" in the sense of having been subjected to rigorous evaluation and replication.

Part IV: New Directions

Both the case studies and the broader cross-case analyses in this volume carry substantial implications for next developmental steps in research, policy, and practice. In the final section of the book we include chapters on these topics, attempting in each to offer recommendations that appear warranted from our research, as well as those based on our collective experience in building and supporting programs that proactively engage the challenges and possibilities around using data for program improvement.

NOTE

*The authors gratefully acknowledge support of this work from The Spencer Foundation (Grant #201200045).

REFERENCES

Achenbach, T. M. (2005). Advancing assessment of children and adolescents: Commentary on evidence-based assessment of child and adolescent disorders. *Journal of Clinical Child and Adolescent Psychology, 34*(3), 541–547.

Alexander, J. (2000). The changing face of accountability: Monitoring and assessing institutional performance in higher education. *Journal of Higher Education, 71*(4), 411–431.

Anderson, L., & Stillman, J. (2013). Making learning the object: Using cultural–historical activity theory to analyze and organize student teaching in urban high-needs schools. *Teachers College Record, 115*(3), 1–36.

Brown, J., & Duguid, P. (2002). *The social life of information.* Harvard Business School Press.

Cochran-Smith, M. (2003). Assessing assessment in teacher education (Editorial). *Journal of Teacher Education, 54*(3), 187.

Conant, J. (1963). *The education of American teachers.* McGraw-Hill.

Council for the Accreditation of Educator Preparation (CAEP). (2013). *Introduction to the standards.* http://caepnet.org/standards/introduction

CAEP. (2015). *CAEP evidence guide.* http://www.caepnet.org/~/media/Files/caep/knowledge-center/caep-evidence-guide.pdf?la=en

Crowe, E. (2010). *Measuring what matters: A stronger accountability model for teacher education.* Center for American Progress.

Davis, S. C., & Peck, C. A. (2020). Using data for program improvement in teacher education: A study of promising practices. *Teachers College Record, 122*(3), 1–48. https://www.tcrecord.org/Content.asp?ContentId=23231

Ellis, V., Edwards, A., & Smagorinsky, P. (Eds.). (2010). *Cultural–historical perspectives on teacher education and development*. Routledge.

Engeström, Y. (1987). *Learning by expanding: An activity-theoretical approach to developmental research*. Orienta-Konsultit Oy.

Engeström, Y. (2001). Expansive learning at work: Toward an activity theoretical reconceptualization. *Journal of Education and Work, 14*(1), 133–156.

Estabrooks, C., Midodzi, W., Cummings, G., & Willin, L. (2007). Predicting research use in nursing organizations. *Nursing Research, 56*(4), 7–23.

Gaffikin, F., & Perry, D. (2009). Discourses and strategic visions: The U.S. research university as an institutional manifestation of neoliberalism. *American Educational Research Journal, 46*(1), 115–144.

Goodlad, J., Soder, R., & Sirotnik, K. (1990). *The places where teachers are taught*. Jossey-Bass.

Kornfeld, J., Grady, K., Marker, P., & Ruddell, M. (2007). Caught in the current: A self-study of state-mandated compliance in a teacher education program. *Teachers College Record, 109*(8), 1902–1920.

Leont'ev, A. N. (1978). *Activity, consciousness, and personality* (M. J. Hall, Trans.). Prentice Hall.

Levine, A. (2006). *Educating school teachers*. Education Schools Project.

Mandinach, E., & Gummer, E. (Eds.). (2019). *Data for continuous programmatic improvement: Steps colleges of education must take to become a data culture*. Routledge.

McDiarmid, B., & Peck, C. A. (2012, April). *Understanding change in teacher education programs* [Paper presentation]. American Educational Research Association Annual Meeting, April 14–19, Vancouver, BC, Canada.

Nicolini, D., Gherardi, S., & Yanow, D. (2003). *Knowing in organizations: A practice-based approach*. Sharpe.

Peck, C. A., & Davis, S. (2019). Building capacity and commitment for data use in teacher education programs. In E. Mandinach & E. Gummer (Eds.), *Data for continuous programmatic improvement: Steps colleges of education must take to become a data culture* (pp. 68–91). Routledge.

Peck, C. A., Gallucci, C., & Sloan, T. (2010). Negotiating implementation of high-stakes performance assessment policies in teacher education: From compliance to inquiry. *Journal of Teacher Education, 61*(5), 451–463.

Peck, C. A., & McDonald, M. A. (2013). Creating "cultures of evidence" in teacher education: Context, policy, and practice in three high data use programs. *The New Educator, 9*(1), 12–28.

Peck, C. A., & McDonald, M. A. (2014). What is a culture of evidence? How do you get one? And . . . should you want one? *Teachers College Record, 116*(3), 1–27.

Sackett, D. L., Rosenberg, W. M. C., Gray, J. A. M., Haynes, R. B., & Richardson, W. S. (1996). Evidence-based medicine: What it is, and what it isn't [Editorial]. *British Medical Journal, 312*(7023), 71–72.

Spillane, J. P., & Miele, D. B. (2007). Evidence in practice: A framing of the terrain. In P. A. Moss (Ed.), *Evidence and decision making* (pp. 46–73). Blackwell.

Sudsawad, P. (2007). *Knowledge translation: Introduction to models, strategies, and measures.* Southwest Educational Development Laboratory, National Center for Dissemination of Disability Research. https://ktdrr.org/ktlibrary/articles_pubs/ktmodels/

Thyer, B. A. (2002). Evidence-based practice and clinical social work. *Evidence-Based Mental Health, 5*(1), 6–7. http://dx.doi.org/10.1136/ebmh.5.1.6

U.S. Department of Education. (2006). *A test of leadership: Charting the future of U.S. higher education* (Spellings Report). https://www2.ed.gov/about/bdscomm/list/hiedfuture/reports/final-report.pdf

Weiss, C. H., Murphy-Graham, E., Petrosino, A., & Gandhi, A. G. (2008). The fairy godmother—and her warts: Making the dream of evidence-based policy come true. *American Journal of Evaluation, 29*(1), 29–47.

Wineburg, M. S. (2006). Evidence in teacher preparation: Establishing a framework for accountability. *Journal of Teacher Education, 57*(1), 51–64. https://doi.org/10.1177/0022487105284475

Young, K., Ashby, D., Boaz, A., & Grayson, L. (2002). Social science and the evidence-based policy movement. *Social Policy and Society, 1*(3), 215–224.

Zeichner, K. M. (2010). Competition, economic rationalization, increased surveillance, and attacks on diversity: Neo-liberalism and the transformation of teacher education in the U.S. *Teaching and Teacher Education, 26*(8), 1544–1552. https://doi.org/10.1016/j.tate.2010.06.004

Building Organizational Capacity and Commitment to Data Use in Teacher Education

Susannah C. Davis and Charles A. Peck

This chapter reflects a collaborative effort between researchers at the University of Washington (UW) and colleagues at the American Association of Colleges of Teacher Education (AACTE) to investigate the conditions under which programs of teacher education effectively use data for the purposes of program improvement.* We studied 10 high data use teacher education programs (TEPs) situated in varying state, local, and institutional contexts within the United States. The findings from the study provide the empirical foundation for the other chapters in this book.

In undertaking the study, we drew on prior research on data use from both the K–12 sector (Anderson et al., 2010; Hamilton et al., 2009), as well as previous studies undertaken in the field of teacher education (Peck & Davis, 2019). We sought to extend this knowledge base in ways that would be useful to practicing teacher educators. In this chapter we summarize some of the findings of the study; a more detailed report can be found in Davis and Peck (2020). Our primary research question was: What organizational tools, policies, and practices are associated with systematic use of data for program improvement in high data use teacher education programs?

THEORETICAL PERSPECTIVE

Questions about policy implementation, programmatic change, and learning can be engaged from a variety of theoretical perspectives, each with its accompanying affordances and limitations. Given our interests in the kinds of collective activity that are essential to program improvement work in teacher education, we found that sociocultural theories related to organizational learning and systemic change (Brown & Duguid, 2002; Engeström, 2001) offered a particularly useful set of orienting assumptions for this study. First, we assumed that institutional context and history would affect how program participants interpreted external policy initiatives related to data use and influence their motives for responding to these. Second, we assumed that the conceptual and material tools teacher educators used to monitor and evaluate program outcomes would affect what became visible and influential in the program improvement process. Third, we assumed that the social organization of the data use activities within the program—the way roles and responsibilities for data use were divided and supported by program policies and practices—would affect faculty and staff access and participation in data use work. Fourth, we assumed that the motives underlying data use activities, particularly tensions between inquiry and compliance orientations to the work that had been observed in previous studies (Peck et al., 2010; Peck & McDonald, 2014), would influence faculty engagement with the work. Finally, we assumed relationships between elements of data use practice (e.g., formal and informal roles and responsibilities, tools, norms and policies related to collaboration and decision making, and goals of data use) to be holistic and transactional in nature, thus shaping one another in a cumulative fashion over time (Engeström, 2001). In this chapter, we use the People-Tools-Organization framework described in Chapter 1 to represent this complex set of assumptions in as transparent and accessible a way as possible.

METHOD

Our study examined 10 individual cases of data use in TEPs situated in institutions that varied considerably in size, mission, and organizational structure. In using this comparative case study approach (Ragin, 2007), we hoped to identify a set of practices that were robust across variations in institutional setting, and which therefore might be useful to other teacher educators as they attempt to navigate the pressures of current accountability mandates in ways that are consonant with their aspirations for program improvement.

Program Selection

We began by identifying a set of TEPs around the country that were particularly engaged with the challenges of using data for program improvement. We purposefully included programs in states relying on value-added measures (VAM) of K–12 student achievement, as well as those relying on teacher performance assessments (e.g., the edTPA) as program outcome measures.

Using nominations from national teacher education associations and accreditation agencies, we identified 19 programs that represented substantial variation in institutional size and mission, state policy context, and regional location. We conducted telephone interviews with representatives of each of these programs (generally the dean or director of teacher education) to inquire more about the programs they operated, the kinds of data they routinely used for decision making, and the organizational policies and practices they had developed to support data use. Based on what we learned in these phone interviews, we invited 10 programs that had made particularly strong and strategic organizational commitments to the systematic use of data for program improvement to participate in the next phase of our study. Table 2.1 presents general descriptive data for these programs.

Each of the 10 programs[1] accepted our invitation and agreed to host a 1- to 2-day on-site visit, during which we interviewed relevant administrators, faculty, and program staff and collected program documents related to their data use work. Following our initial visits, we selected three programs for additional follow-up: Glenwood State University (GSU; a large regional teacher preparation institution), University of Longville (UL; a research-intensive public university), and Millville College (MC; a small liberal arts college). These programs were selected because they faced specific challenges around data use that were related to their institutional contexts: GSU faced challenges of scale related to the large number of candidates they served; UL was challenged to engage faculty attention and participation in the work of teacher education in the context of institutional pressures for individual research productivity; MC's data use was constrained by significant limitations in human, technical, and fiscal resources available to support the work. We made two to four on-site visits to each of these three programs in an effort to develop a richer understanding of data use policies and practices that had been developed in each institutional context.

Data Collection and Analysis

During each of our on-site visits we conducted individual and focus group interviews with a variety of program members. We gathered a wide variety of program documents, as well as state, university and program policies and practices affecting data use. The relatively brief and episodic nature of our site visits did not afford regular opportunities to observe program data use practices in action in most cases. However, when these opportunities did arise, we made field notes describing the activities and interactions of participants.

Our initial data analysis was based on the inductive logic described by A. Strauss and Corbin (1997) and Merriam (2009). We began with an open coding procedure wherein each member of our three-person research team independently read through transcripts, documents, and field notes,

Table 2.1. Characteristics of 10 Case Study Program

Program	Institution Size	Institution Type	Region	Annual Teacher Education Graduates	Outcome Measures
Franklin State University (FSU)	11,670	Master's colleges & universities: larger programs	South	201	Locally standardized TPA; graduate satisfaction, employer satisfaction
Glenwood State University (GSU)	27,511	Doctoral universities: higher research activity	Southeast	1,358	VAM; edTPA; graduate satisfaction; employer satisfaction
Kentwood Teaching and Learning Center (KTLC)	157	Private non-profit "Alternative route"	South	157	VAM; graduate satisfaction; employer satisfaction
Kirby State University (KSU)	40,131	Master's colleges & universities: larger programs	West	1,296	edTPA; graduate satisfaction; employer satisfaction
Millville College (MC)	5,000	Master's colleges & universities: medium programs	Midwest	90	edTPA; graduate satisfaction; employer satisfaction
Shorewood State University (SSU)	17,195	Public comprehensive doctoral granting	South	312	VAM; graduate satisfaction; employer satisfaction
University of Ashboro (UA)	43,685	Public doctoral universities: highest research activity	Midwest	253	Local TPA; graduate satisfaction; employer satisfaction
University of Baldwin (UB)	30,386	Public doctoral universities: highest research activity	South	423	VAM; edTPA; graduate satisfaction; employer satisfaction
University of Elwood (UE)	35,313	Public doctoral universities: highest research activity	Midwest	660	edTPA; graduate satisfaction; employer satisfaction
University of Longville (UL)	20,000	Public doctoral universities: highest research activity	West	120	edTPA; graduate satisfaction; employer satisfaction

identifying text segments of hypothesized relevance to our general research question. We then met to compare segments of text, and developed a coding system which we used to identify additional text segments in subsequent analyses. Themes in the coded data were investigated further through extensive use of written memos in which evidence related to specific patterns in the data were examined through an iterative process of presentation, discussion, and further query of the database.

Following our initial data analysis, individual members of our research team used the coded interview and focus group data, along with documents and field notes collected at each site, to create a case summary for each program. These case summaries, which ranged from 10 to 20 pages in length, included relevant data describing the program's institutional, state, and local policy contexts; programmatic goals related to data use; programmatic data use processes and practices; organizational factors supporting or constraining their use of data for program improvement; and program outcomes related to data use. We then used data matrices to identify thematic continuities and discontinuities across the 10 cases, drawing on case summaries and the corpus of coded data (Miles et al., 2020). The following section describes findings from our cross-case analysis; we identified a set of what we have termed "promising practices" related to using data for program improvement in teacher education.

PROMISING PRACTICES

People: Motivating Faculty Engagement in Data Use

The work of using data for program improvement requires organizational and leadership conditions that motivate and sustain faculty, supervisor, staff, and administrator engagement in individual and collective data use practices. In the programs we studied, creating such a motivational context involved supporting local agency and authorship at both individual and programmatic levels.

Support programmatic and individual autonomy and authorship. The programs we studied frequently articulated concerns and challenges related to motivating and sustaining faculty engagement. At Kirby State University (KSU), a dean explained, "having a commitment to [data use] obviously is one thing, but actually getting the faculty to participate and have that participation be meaningful has been an ongoing challenge."

While motivating faculty engagement was, in the words of another administrator at KSU, "an eternal struggle," academic leaders at the college expressed a strategic commitment to involving faculty and other program members in the process of data use, as one dean confirmed: "One of the things is that the faculty and the chairs and everybody—everybody's involved and it's a collaborative enterprise. It has to be collaborative; it can't be top down." In order to create a "collaborative enterprise," academic leaders tried to give faculty as much ownership over the process as possible (Davis, 2019). While there were often expectations around data use for "quality control" and program improvement, leaders tried to give both programs and individuals flexibility and independence in how they met those expectations. A faculty member who served as assessment coordinator explained their approach:

> If you don't like what you're using, make something better or come up with something—so the ownership is on the faculty really. . . . We're not saying this is a survey you have to use; there's very little of that. Most of it is from the ground up and it's supposed to be meaningful for them and their program, so (we say) develop it so it is.

Many faculty members reported that motivation to engage in data use, and a related sense of agency and autonomy, stemmed from a program inquiry orientation (rather than one motivated primarily by compliance to external pressures) and support for broad participation in data analysis and data-informed decision.

Value local contributions and expertise. As programs broadened engagement in collaborative data use practices, they often reported strategic reliance on expertise that existed within their own program as a resource for program improvement. Program leaders who explicitly respected, listened to, and valued the contributions of faculty and other program members facilitated the mobilization of distributed expertise (Davis, 2019).

The University of Ashboro (UA) program director articulated this approach in an interview:

> I try really hard to foster a community in which people recognize that their strengths are being acknowledged and valued. It's distributed expertise, right? There are different ones of us who have different strengths. I've tried really hard to have my work with the teacher educators with whom I work be one where we just take each other seriously and listen to one another. We don't always agree with one another for sure, but I think that we, for the most part, take each other very seriously and appreciate what one another brings to the table.

Teacher educators in the programs we studied spoke about the role of dissent and disagreement, which often functioned as an important resource in organizational change processes. What we heard from faculty and administrators suggested that the way dissent was treated, particularly by administrators, had a significant effect on the extent to which new data use practices involved collegial, inquiry-oriented dialogue about how to best reach desired programmatic outcomes. When leaders, faculty, and staff "take each other very seriously and appreciate what one another brings to the table," program members were able to contribute to the collective data use and program improvement activities and processes in a way that strengthened collective commitment to the work.

Tools: Using Multiple Data Sources for Program Improvement

The 10 cases we studied provided an opportunity to examine the functional affordances and constraints of different types of data relative to program improvement goals and efforts. Here we describe some of the ways in which the three most common types of data collected (VAM, satisfaction surveys, and TPAs) were (or were not) found to be useful to improvement work.

Value-added measures (VAM). In several of the programs we visited, large-scale comparisons between institutions using VAM related to the academic achievement of P–12 students in program graduates' classrooms generated a "sense of urgency" (Administrator, Shorewood State University [SSU]) and led to strong actions aimed at remediating identified programmatic deficiencies. A dean at GSU described VAM data as one example of "dynamite . . . a huge catalyst for change." At SSU, value-added data suggested that there were several specific areas in which program outcomes were not as positive as previously believed. In response, program members increased the selectivity of their alternative route program (which had weaker value-added scores than their other programs).

At other sites, program members described how VAM data, initially aggregated and reported by the state, were not readily interpretable at the program level. A faculty member at SSU articulated the problem: "I understand there's a fire alarm going off . . . and we don't even know which building . . . much less, which room." Other programs using state-level VAM data expressed similar reservations, noting that these data were only available for graduates representing particular grades, subjects, and schools. For example, an administrator at GSU noted that only 35% of recent program graduates within their state produce value-added data, and even among that subsection of teachers they cannot accurately trace which program those teachers came from. The time lag for analyzing and reporting VAM data also sometimes made it difficult to interpret those data in the context of program changes.

Despite these concerns, VAM data motivated several programs to make useful changes. For example, the 1st year their state produced and publicly reported value-added scores resulted in a crisis for the alternative route program Kentwood Teaching and Learning Center (KTLC), as they were identified as a "low-performing" program, particularly with respect to the reading achievement of students in their graduates' classrooms. In response, they hired a new reading instructor, made changes to the reading curriculum, and added an additional 35 hours of reading curriculum to their summer session program. According to their program director, in subsequent years their VAM scores in reading "started climbing." They "kept at it" over the course of the next 8 years, and then "finally . . . [KTLC] landed at the top in terms of reading outcomes."

Satisfaction surveys. All of the programs we visited had access to a variety of survey measures, including data from candidate and employer satisfaction surveys, various state or institution-mandated surveys, and locally created surveys. In general, these survey data were not reported to be particularly useful for inquiry-oriented program improvement efforts, and were used primarily for external reporting purposes. We did not observe much faculty engagement with these data sources. There were some exceptions to this general finding. For example, at KSU, an institution that is part of a network of state universities, survey data were reported to be helpful not only in seeing trends within their programs over time, but also across the network of state universities. While survey data sometimes were reported to help programs identify and prioritize particular concerns (e.g., preparing candidates to understand and respond to the needs of children with disabilities), the programs we studied typically relied on other data sources (e.g., VAM, TPA) to measure progress over time or to guide instructional improvement.

Teaching performance assessments (TPAs). In the programs we studied that had access to value-added data, survey data, and performance assessment data, faculty and administrators reported that the richer and more contextualized information produced by the performance assessment measures was most useful in guiding decisions about specific programmatic changes. For example, a program director and dean at GSU stated: "I would say the TPA data stream has affected our program far more than the value-added data stream." She also described TPA data as more valuable for program improvement than survey data: "The TPA is providing far more specificity and it is driven by student performance. [The surveys] tend to be a little more broad and more subjective, more opinion than performance-driven."

Faculty and administrators found the combination of quantitative and qualitative data from TPAs particularly useful. The TEP director at UL explained:

> [TPAs] provide different levels of data that we can access. We can look at the overall pass rates, then we can look at the scores by rubric

and get a sense of what's happening there. Then we can decide what documents we want to look at and what people might want to focus on.

The detail and specificity of the quantitative and qualitative data provided by TPAs helped facilitate inquiry-oriented program improvement efforts. The data coordinator at GSU explained:

The detail we get from the 15 [TPA] rubrics and the scoring of those has offered a lot of insight into where to look to offer more support for our students in particular areas, whether it's assessment or planning.

Program members from programs using standardized and/or local performance assessments found the qualitative data provided by these assessments particularly useful for facilitating faculty engagement and inquiry-oriented conversations about program improvement. A faculty member and the edTPA coordinator at MC explained:

I have found that even when the quantitative data [from the edTPA] do not necessarily cry out for the need for dramatic change, once you get the work samples in front of people, the actual portfolios where they are looking at what people are doing in very concrete ways and how they are explaining it and how they are making sense of their kids, even faculty who are getting really good quantitative feedback on their program will always find things to learn from those work samples. It is incredible how rich they are. I do not think I have ever read one where I have not learned something about teaching and learning.

At UL, where nearly all faculty and supervisors were involved in local scoring of edTPA and regular data retreats, the TEP director commented on the value of having the TPA as a common language across faculty and across university and K–12 partners:

The power of having something like a programwide, authentic performance assessment of teaching has been one of the most critical factors in creating a more cohesive program, creating a more integrated university/K–12 piece and in creating stronger faculty across the board; course instructors who know K–12 work, K–12 supervisors who are understanding more about the course work. . . . These things wouldn't happen if it were not for the fact that we have this data that we are using all the time, every year, and everybody is using it.

Organizations: Program Policies and Practices That Supported Data Use

Simply adding data use work to the existing tasks and responsibilities of program faculty and staff appears to be a prescription for failure, frustration, and reduction of data use practices to requirements for external reporting. Each of the 10 programs we studied made strategic adjustments to formal and informal organizational structures, policies, and practices that facilitated the participation of faculty, staff, and administrators in meaningful data use work involving substantive program improvement decisions and innovations.

Strategic division of labor. Programs that were successful in increasing faculty and staff engagement in data use often allocated some aspects of data use work (often accreditation-focused, compliance-oriented quantitative analyses) to support staff, while sharing other, more collaborative data use activities (e.g., inquiry-oriented consideration of student work samples from TPAs) among a broader constituency of program members.

Many programs developed administrative or staff position(s) responsible for particular data-related tasks. These tasks often included organizing data and data access using a data platform; compiling data into digestible and usable reports for faculty, supervisors, and administrators; communicating with program members about the results of various program outcome data; and running requested data analyses for individual faculty, groups or committees, and programs. By concentrating certain types of data-related work within specific administrative positions, these program members helped make time, space, and access for other program members, including faculty, supervisors, and administrators, to collaboratively engage in other inquiry-oriented, data use work aimed at program improvement goals.

In other contexts, programs benefited from broad distribution of data use work. Examples of this included local policies for joint responsibility for local scoring of performance assessments.[2] Scoring activities were recognized in these programs to be important contexts for both individual and collective learning. Scoring TPAs helped inform collective program improvement efforts and also helped build a common language of practice among program members.

Making time and space for collaborative data use. In order to support broad participation in data use activities, programs must create time and space for data analysis and interpretation activities. Some programs incorporated data analysis and decision-making activities into existing faculty or program meetings. Others created new collaborative structures to support using data for program improvement.

At UA, for example, "scoring parties" were created with "food and materials and a big space" where a collection of program faculty, administrators, supervisors, and graduate students gathered to score performance assessments. A faculty member explained:

> We have scoring parties so that everybody comes together. I think that's actually super important because that's where the conversation happens. It's sort of a hassle because you have to black out this huge chunk of time and that makes people cranky, but I think it also relieves some of the "I have to go score this all on my own," and that's where the conversation happens and [a committee focused on program redesign efforts] has been a place where follow-up conversations can happen. I think it's part of the manageability—if you're going to collect this data, create the space where you can have conversations about it and learn from it and figure out how you're using it and why you're using it.

Full and part-day data retreats were common among the TEPs we visited. These provided important collaborative venues for program members to access and discuss program outcome data. These retreats also facilitated cross-role collaboration (e.g., between disciplinary areas; between faculty and supervisors), expanding common knowledge and shared language of practice. For example, at GSU "data summits" were planned periodically to report on and evaluate progress on college pilot studies, and to present and interpret various program comparison reports (some based on local data, others grounded in state or national databases). The agenda for each data summit was carefully planned and orchestrated to achieve specific goals, including making the history and trajectory of the work transparent for faculty involved in teacher preparation work across the university, supporting faculty and staff participation in data analysis and program decision making, and developing faculty data literacy skills. For each of these data summits, program administrative staff prepared data sets to make the faculty's task of interpreting the data more manageable, while continually positioning faculty to make programmatic decisions.

Making data use a regular part of individual and collective responsibilities. In order to support increased participation in collaborative, program-focused data use activities among faculty, staff, supervisors, and administrators with myriad other responsibilities, the programs we studied implemented specific policies to support participation. These included workload adjustments, changes to job descriptions, and changes to promotion and tenure guidelines. At UL, normal activities were suspended for the week that TPA scoring took place. Supervisors were not expected to go out to K–12 classrooms and faculty were not expected to hold classes. Scoring became a job expectation and was "written right in [their job descriptions] that they'll be scoring the TPA whether they are teaching one course or seven" (TEP Director, UL).

At GSU, the dean and other program leaders changed faculty workload expectations so that they taught fewer classes but were also expected to be involved in "college-level initiatives." This shift in faculty workload expectations was referred to as the addition of a "fourth box" to the annual review, and related expectations for promotion and tenure:

> There's also a shift in how we look at faculty workload and that expectation of this "fourth box." You are providing service back to the program, to the university. You can't just operate within your own specific research project. There's this greater contribution. (Faculty/Program Administrator, GSU)

Orchestrating the Data Use Process: The Role of Leadership

While policy contexts differed across states and institutions, all of the programs we studied experienced intensifying demands for external accountability. Program leaders in these TEPs played a key role in turning those pressures into catalysts for change. The dean at GSU argued that programs should "never waste a crisis":

> You're not going anywhere without dynamite, a huge catalyst for change. . . . Value-added achievement [scores]. . . . That's a catalyst. The political winds are catalysts. Budget cuts are a wonderful catalyst because it forces you to say, "We can't do things like we did before," . . . I think it was one of Obama's people that said, "Never waste a crisis." He was right.

In each of the programs we studied, program leaders strategically used the "political winds" that emphasized evaluating and ranking programs to motivate organizational changes aimed at program improvement. Program leaders often reframed accountability narratives in ways that resonated with faculty values and commitments:

> Any kind of data collection should be framed in terms of inquiry, program improvement, and moving our practice forward. Putting an emphasis on the fact that it is a mandate is really counterproductive. (Program Administrator, UE)

While dean- and director-level leaders played a key role in articulating organizational narratives that emphasized inquiry goals over compliance, creating comprehensive organizational motives focused on inquiry-oriented data use processes also required strong *distributed* leadership across program members (Sloan, 2013). As a program administrator at UE explained:

That [focus on inquiry] ~~cannot be all top down~~, but must also be with individual faculty members and individual programs, right down to the supervisors and incorporating the teaching level.

Establishing goals for data use that emphasized inquiry over compliance was not simply a matter of leadership rhetoric. It also required that academic leaders orchestrate changes to the people, tools, and organizational dimensions of a program as an "activity system" (Peck & McDonald, 2014). This meant implementing leadership actions that coordinated the creation or adaptation of new data tools that facilitated equitable and transparent access to information about program outcomes; changing the division of labor for data use work among program members; and changing organizational policies, procedures, and norms to support broadened engagement in data use (Davis, 2019). As changes occur throughout the system and more people participate in collective, collaborative conversations and activities around data use, ideas about program improvement become more concrete and more widely shared, understood, and supported.

ONWARD

Teacher educators often experience contemporary accountability policies as challenges to local program values and integrity (Cochran-Smith et al., 2018; Kornfeld et al., 2007). However, each of these 10 high data use TEPs offers an existence proof that it is possible to navigate the intensifying pressures of contemporary accountability policies, including mandates for "using data for program improvement," without abandoning local program values and integrity. Indeed, the evidence we have collected suggests that each program has found ways to use data as a resource for *strengthening* program integrity and effectiveness. Taken together, patterns of common practice across the programs provide some tentative answers to questions about *how* these programs have built local capacity and commitment to using data as an important resource for program improvement. We have used the term *promising* to characterize these common practices, acknowledging the correlational rather than experimental nature of the evidence regarding their effectiveness. And, while our data refer directly to a relatively small number of programs, the fact that findings we report here were consistent across programs that varied significantly in size, mission, and state policy context suggests their potential value to teacher educators working in diverse institutional and policy contexts.

NOTES

*The authors gratefully acknowledge support of this work from The Spencer Foundation (Grant #201200045). The research reported here was conducted through a partnership with the American Association of Colleges of Teacher Education. A more detailed description of methods and findings from this study is reported in Davis & Peck (2020).

1. All program names in this chapter are pseudonyms.

2. Some programs engaged in collaborative scoring of internal performance assessments (e.g., MC, UA, and UE) and some programs engaged in partial or complete local scoring of standardized performance assessments (e.g., GSU, MC, UE, and UL).

REFERENCES

Anderson, S., Leithwood, K., & Strauss, T. (2010). Leading data use in schools: Organizational conditions and practices at the school and district levels. *Leadership and Policy in Schools, 9*(3), 292–327.

Brown, J., & Duguid, P. (2002). *The social life of information.* Harvard Business School Press.

Cochran-Smith, M., Carney, M., Keefe, E., Burton, S., Chang, W., Fernandez, M., Miller, A., Sanchez, J., & Baker, M. (2018). *Reclaiming accountability in teacher education.* Teachers College Press.

Davis, S. C. (2019). *Engaging faculty in data use for program improvement in higher education: How leaders bridge individual and collective development.* Manuscript submitted for publication.

Davis, S. C., & Peck, C. A. (2020). Using data for program improvement in teacher education: A study of promising practices. *Teachers College Record, 122*(3), 1–48. https://www.tcrecord.org/Content.asp?ContentId=23231

Engeström, Y. (2001). Expansive learning at work: Toward an activity theoretical reconceptualization. *Journal of Education and Work, 14*(1), 133–156.

Hamilton, L., Halverson, R., Jackson, S., Mandinach, E. B., Supovitz, J., & Wayman, J. (2009). *Using student achievement data to support instructional decision making* (NCEE 2009-4067). National Center for Education Evaluation and Regional Assistance, Institute of Education Sciences, U.S. Department of Education. https://ies.ed.gov/ncee/wwc/Docs/PracticeGuide/dddm_pg_092909.pdf

Kornfeld, J., Grady, K., Marker, P., & Ruddell, M. (2007). Caught in the current: A self-study of state-mandated compliance in a teacher education program. *Teachers College Record, 109*(8), 1902–1920.

Merriam., S. B. (2009). *Qualitative research: A guide to design and implementation* (3rd ed.). John Wiley & Sons.

Miles, M., Huberman, A., & Saldaña, J. (2020). Qualitative data analysis: A methods sourcebook. Thousand Oaks, CA: Sage.

Peck, C. A., & Davis, S. (2019). Building capacity and commitment for data use in teacher education programs. In E. B. Mandinach & E. S. Gummer (Eds.), *Data for continuous programmatic improvement: Steps colleges of education must take to become a data culture* (pp. 68–92). Routledge.

Peck, C. A., Gallucci, C., & Sloan, T. (2010). Negotiating implementation of high-stakes performance assessment policies in teacher education: From compliance to inquiry. *Journal of Teacher Education, 61*(5), 451–463.

Peck, C. A., & McDonald, M. A. (2014). What is a culture of evidence? How do you get one? And . . . should you want one? *Teachers College Record, 116*(3), 1–27.

Ragin, C. (2007). Making comparative analysis count. *Revista de historia comparada, 1*(1), 1–519.

Sloan, T. (2013). Distributed leadership and organizational change: Implementation of a teaching performance measure. *The New Educator, 9*(1), 29–53.

Strauss, A., & Corbin, J. M. (1997). *Grounded theory in practice.* Sage.

Part II

CASE STUDIES OF HIGH DATA USE PROGRAMS

CHAPTER 3

East Carolina University

Using Data for Program Improvement in a
Large Regional Teaching University

Linda A. Patriarca, Kristen Cuthrell, and Diana B. Lys

The teacher education faculty filed into the auditorium to attend a collegewide meeting. The dean was about to share a new state report that compared "program effectiveness" of various teacher education programs using K–12 student achievement data. The dean acknowledged mounting accountability demands for higher education and noted that this newest piece of state-released "data" was one such indicator: "Before we discuss the results, I want to make sure you understand that 'our score' was calculated in comparison to all other state institutions. In essence, the charts that we will examine today identify where our teacher education graduates fall with respect to the graduates of all other public institutions in the state on the student achievement of their pupils. To facilitate review and analysis, the state has organized its findings by program (e.g., secondary science; elementary reading), by pathway (traditional undergraduate, alternative pathway, Teach for America), and by institution."

As teaching faculty perused the data, negative comments could be heard throughout the room: "Who are they to be ranking our programs? We are the experts in preparing teachers." "This methodology was completely flawed." "Effective teaching isn't only about student achievement. But that's all they are looking at . . . that's absurd!"

Then a senior faculty member—whose program was found to be significantly below par—stood up and publicly dismissed the report and the entire evaluation model: "These rankings aren't about us. We do our jobs well. Our candidates are well prepared. I think we all agree that, in most cases, it's the schools that won't allow our graduates to teach the way we prepared and socialized them."

Throughout the meeting, it became clear that some faculty criticized the data while others discounted or simply ignored it. A small group, however, viewed it as a "call to arms" and expressed interest in studying the report to better understand the model and the data it utilized. As one such faculty member emphasized, "If our programs are going to be rated on the basis of student achievement data, then I want to know more about the process and how these findings were derived."

This vignette exemplifies an increasingly common scenario in higher education broadly, and teacher preparation more specifically, around the United States of America. Data were being gathered *about educators* that reflected *on educators*, yet educators had little input. Not only were data being collected and analyzed, but these data were being shared publicly and, in many cases, were being used to make decisions that impacted teacher education programs. In such a context, the teacher education faculty and the dean in the vignette above felt the college had three options:

1. Ignore the new accountability policies and hope they disappear.
2. Criticize the policies and work to discredit the methodology and/or the outcomes.
3. Be proactive about how the policies were implemented and use the data for the college's own goals and purposes—thereby getting on top of the data rather than being buried by it.

This chapter describes how the College of Education (COE) at East Carolina University (ECU), including the authors of this chapter, engaged the third option and highlights the key elements of the change process undertaken to transform its teacher preparation program and reculture its institution. The educational change process described here includes and extends beyond the typical structures associated with faculty work (reassignment of time, paper presentations of individual projects, and so on) to include restructuring faculty use of time, introducing new collaborative structures (teacher performance assessment liaisons [TPALs], data summits, innovation teams, program outcome data retreats, and so on), extending opportunities to learn for all stakeholders (tenure/tenure-track faculty, fixed-term faculty, intern supervisors, mentor teachers, administrators, and so on), and developing "systems of individuation" that would be necessary to meet the diversity of academic and social needs of a wide range of professionals involved in the enterprise. Before you can fully understand this narrative, you must understand a little bit about our context.

UNIVERSITY CONTEXT

East Carolina University, a large state-supported public university, located in rural eastern North Carolina is part of the University of North Carolina

(UNC) system. The university, and the region it serves, sees the College of Education at ECU as the primary preparer of teachers and administrators for eastern North Carolina. Offering initial licensures at the undergraduate level and advanced licensure at the graduate level, we serve both women and men with an enrollment of 27,000. We offer licensure in 17 program areas and average 700–750 completers each year. The majority of our students come from the surrounding areas; approximately 50% of students qualify for financial aid.

In the fall of 2008 four noteworthy events occurred that, taken together, constituted both crisis and opportunity:

- The Department of Public Instruction (DPI) in North Carolina required all programs to revise their curriculum to meet new standards (which included 21st-century skills) and to assess teacher candidate outcomes using multiple sources of evidence. Moreover, they added the unprecedented requirement that three of the "evidences" selected had to be utilized by *all* teacher education programs at a given university.
- The state-level University of North Carolina General Administration initiated a measure of program effectiveness using P–12 student standardized achievement test data as the outcome measure. Student achievement data were used to compare the "quality" of graduates by institution, by "program type," and by "preparation pathway" (traditional undergraduate, licensure only, alternate route completers, and so on).
- The university fell victim to the significant nationwide economic recession, resulting in budget cuts, hiring moratoriums, and wage freezes.
- A new dean arrived. This individual was not only new to the institution, but also a newcomer to the state.

Faculty experienced these changes in different ways. Most were unhappy. Some felt demoralized, unappreciated, and undervalued. Many faculty members viewed the accountability policy changes as assaults on the institution, their programs, and themselves. The "water cooler" talk around the college reflected the prevailing mood of the faculty:

"We just went through an NCATE [National Council for Accreditation of Teacher Education] review successfully. Why is DPI now making us revise our programs and come up with a bunch of evidence? What kind of nonsense is this?"

"To add insult to injury, we are now being asked to 'do more with less!' They are putting a freeze on new hires and we are not getting a raise for, at minimum, the next 2 years. Yet they expect us to do all of this extra work."

"How can the student achievement scores of our graduates be linked back to us? We don't control what environments our graduates go into or what support they get as new teachers."

"All of this testing stuff is just an excuse to privatize teacher education. They want to do to us what they did to K–12 education—create charter schools of teacher education!"

But there were others who viewed the changes as inevitable and wanted to turn a potentially negative situation into a positive one:

"We sit on so much data. How can we use them?"

"When I talk to the clinical teachers and principals in the field, they were excited about our students. Will the revisions we were engaged in keep that going?"

"I know we do a lot with our candidates in the content areas, but I didn't see that reflected in the student achievement data. How can we dig into that data? What is it really telling us?"

The new dean welcomed junior faculty, senior faculty, and staff to join in regular informal and formal conversations in order to grapple with the changes. The expectation was that we deliver—the bar was set high, the conversation was stimulating, and we were buoyed by constant acknowledgment of the worker bee's contribution. The cycle of frank feedback indicated a genuine, shared interest among staff and faculty. The dean's unwavering support for COE improvement established trust among the group members. The focus was turned onto our *program*, rather than our individual courses within the program. For administrators and program leaders, it was this focus on the collective that allowed us to unite around program data and accept it as *our* data. As a result, this group came to three conclusions. First, if the conversations that faculty engage in revolve around the ills being done *to* us, then we do, indeed, become "victims"—a very dissatisfying and demoralizing place to be. Second, if we "blame" the data and disassociate from the process of systematic inquiry around it, then we lose the opportunity to become more knowledgeable about our teacher candidates' successes and struggles, as well as the program's achievements and failures. Finally, and perhaps most importantly, if we fail to see data as a "resource" instead of an "indictment" then we lose the ability to create a data system that works *for* us rather than *against* us and we lose the opportunity to become the architects of our own fate.

The story we have to share revolves around how we learned to respond to the new policy pressures around data in a way that, rather than demoralizing faculty and staff, brought us together and improved our programs in ways that morally obligated us to participate in the work.

WHAT WE DID

This story starts with data and ends with data. As a new college administrator, the dean knew that the K–12 student achievement data showed which institutions were producing graduates who struggled in the classroom, but the data did not help faculty identify nuances of the struggle, nor how we should respond. Simply put: The state data told us there were problems, but it did not tell us what to do.

It became apparent early, through separate program meetings with the dean, that improving the preparation of our teacher candidates was going to require a strong, collective commitment that spanned the entire teacher preparation experience. Program improvement situated inside individual courses or field experiences would no longer suffice. We concluded that isolated course-level improvements were not large enough in scope and consistency to evoke any significant change in teacher effectiveness. Improvements needed to be coherent, coordinated, and systemic to achieve results. More focused and strategic research on our own practice needed to be an integral part of the work. Thus, even though we were a "large production" regional university (and not a "Research I" institution), we embarked on a research-integrated approach to program improvement.

We all knew that to achieve such lofty goals required vision, commitment, and action in size and scope sufficient to transform the culture of the institution. The backbone of the College of Education vision was a set of curricular and clinical reforms that were designed thoughtfully and assessed both formatively and summatively. We wanted results that were both trustworthy and informative for our overarching goal of program improvement. In the sections below, we describe a set of principles we used to guide our change process, including the strategic process we used to institute and study these reforms.

Vision and Goals

We assumed the change process would have to be grounded in a clear vision and set of goals. As an experienced teacher educator, our new dean identified four very simple but powerful goals that resonated with the faculty.

Illustrating the need for these goals with anecdotes from her own experience, the dean set the tone by sharing lessons learned from her own mistakes. The goals were:

- Create a set of innovations where teaching, research, and service were inextricably linked and seamlessly integrated into the work of faculty.
- Create an infrastructure that facilitates the continuous improvement of teacher education and provides consistent and continuous outcome data.
- Create a culture of collaborative research and program development around the enterprise of educator preparation rather than the individual project.
- Create a set of changes sufficiently large in scope, yet particularized enough to be implemented at different stages of preparation, such that the impact of the entire set has a magnitude great enough to change the institutional structure of the organization.

The goal here was to institutionalize the change—not simply to innovate.

A Systematic Implementation Process

The best vision with the most compelling rationale statements will not move the system, unless the process of implementation requires and supports participants to engage in strategic initiatives, collect data in a systematic way, and then use that data to achieve multiple ends. We knew that one size would never fit all, so we had to let program faculty try things out in smaller doses. But the key was that, if the idea/innovation was going to grow, faculty had to be willing to engage. As a result, one important feature of this process was that it must allow experimentation to occur without getting bogged down by the traditional hierarchical structures within the university. Another important feature of the process was that it must be described concretely and simply enough so that participants could envision the stages of the work and how they could engage in the work. Finally, the process must also ensure that the work being done outside the structure (if promising) could be reintegrated into the traditional hierarchical structure of decision making in the university relatively easily. In our case, we created a model comprised of six phases. As a nod to our university mascot, we named the model Pirate Continuum of Developing Expertise (CODE) Implementation Process. Figure 3.1 illustrates our implementation phases, each of which typically lasted 1–2 semesters.

First phase. This was the "squishy pilot" phase. At this stage, an individual faculty member experimented with an innovation in their respective

Figure 3.1. ECU Pirate CODE Implementation Process

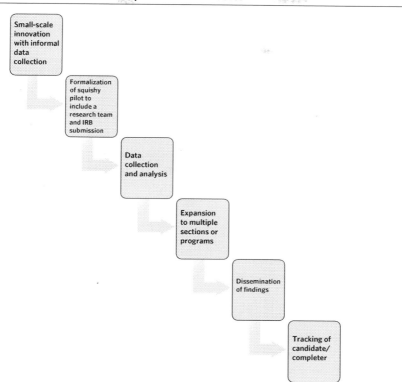

course section based on perceived needs as previously identified by a core group of faculty. The core group consisted of folks that taught the section or were interested in trying something out without the guarantee that all would go perfectly. These faculty would troubleshoot and smooth out the bumps in the implementation with stakeholders. They were supported with graduate assistant help and connected with other faculty to develop innovation components. During this phase, informal data such as anecdotal student feedback and samples of student work were gathered for the purposes of refining the ideas, processes, or assessments related to the innovation.

Second phase. If the innovation showed some promise through faculty and/or student recommendations, then a formal pilot study was initiated. Educational researchers, experienced faculty, methodologists, and so on were brought in to formalize both the implementation process and the data-gathering process for the pilot. A formal Institutional Review Board (IRB) application was created and submitted so that the data generated could be used for research and/or evaluation purposes. Additional early adopter faculty were contacted and asked if they would like to be a part of the innovation project.

Third phase. In this phase, data (e.g., student outcome data, survey results, student reflections) generated from the innovation were stored and catalogued within an integrated data system. First, candidate work was stored in an electronic portfolio system. Candidate participants were coded inside an information management system (at ECU, the Teacher Education Management System [TEMS]). This enabled queries to be run on just those teacher candidates involved in the innovation. Having an electronic portfolio system (Task Stream, Live Wire, and so on) was an essential feature of the process because it facilitated the use of data for multiple programmatic and research purposes.

Fourth phase. As a result of data analysis, the pilot was further refined and scaled up to two or more sections—in some cases all sections—of a given course. It was at this point that other faculty, those not yet involved by chance or choice, were contacted about participating or were drawn into the work if they teach an impacted course.

Fifth phase. As each innovative project matured and produced knowledge, faculty teams engaged in preparing findings for dissemination through publications and conference presentations. Team members on the individual innovation projects examined innovation outcome data across projects. Team members presented findings to college-level policy committees.

Sixth phase. In order to determine the impact of innovation, we relied on a candidate coding system to track individual candidate performance into the field. Coding candidates according to which innovations they received allowed evaluators to subcategorize candidates (according to the number of "innovations" they received) and linked this later to K–12 student achievement outcomes. During this phase of the process, faculty teams discussed designing and implementing extensions and adaptations of the current innovations or creating and initiating new innovation projects.

Over multiple cycles of data collection, this 2–5 year process—which began with a "squishy" pilot and culminated with an assessment of outcomes within and across projects—was institutionalized and adopted as the change/innovation implementation process in the College of Education. Importantly, the process of innovation was one where data collection, analysis, write-up, and action were central to the enterprise. This process and the scale-up that emanated from it created an expanded *culture of collaboration* around program development and research focused on the data and how it informed current and future work. Individual projects became part of an overall enterprise dedicated to continuous improvement. The individual project was viewed from the perspective of its contribution to the whole as well as its contribution to a particular facet of teacher education preparation. Since conducting research around implemented innovations was an integral part of the work, the systematic collection and analysis of "valid and reliable data" was a required component. Consequently, the "process" and the "content" of our efforts necessitated that we engaged in practices that yielded data, have a common electronic system for capturing/storing data, and actualized a commitment to analyze and write up the findings.

Over the course of 5 years, a core set of innovations went through the Pirate CODE innovation process. Table 3.1 provides a snapshot of the innovations. When looked at holistically, each of ECU's selected innovations highlighted a particular aspect/need in our teacher education programs. Although each one of them developed and expanded differently, all but one matured and scaled-up. This, in turn, has facilitated the development of large-scale communities of practice where faculty convened to deliberate and discuss candidate performance and needs (Lys et al., 2014).

WHAT WE LEARNED

In this section, we describe some of what we have learned about the process of strategically and systematically using data to improve our programs.

A Vision and Articulation of Change Process

Creating and presenting a vision for the change was an essential catalyst to instigate change. An example of an ultimate vision and mission was to change the focus of the organization from one where teaching was the central focus to one where learning was the central focus. This learning organization dedicated itself to using data to drive knowledge generation and innovative action around two key goals: continuous production of outcome knowledge and continuous improvement in the processes and procedures employed to prepare educator personnel.

At East Carolina University, having and articulating a clear vision for teacher education required focused conversations and a concrete heuristic of how the vision would be realized.

Leadership

Leadership is critically important in any sort of change process. The leader of the organization provides the vision—a target—for the change they want to see while providing time and space for faculty to hone and shape that vision. Leaders who foster such change cannot be dictators in the process.

Table 3.1. ECU Pirate CODE Innovations

Innovation	Description	Targeted Need	Pirate CODE Phase	Findings
Video Grand Rounds	Structured observation model utilizing video clips	Early experience observations	Phase 5: 6 programs	Increased abilities to identify important aspects of teaching; transferred observation skills to culminating field observations
ISLES: Instructional Strategies Module	Online modules modeling key instructional strategies at the declarative (what?), procedural (how?), and conditional (when? why?) levels	Core instructional strategies	Phase 6: 3 programs	CLASS observations show ISLES candidates have higher student engagement and use of high-leverage practices than non-ISLES candidates.
Co-Teaching	Two interns per classroom with one master teacher as well as the more common one-to-one model (one intern and one master teacher in a single classroom)	New models of internship	Phase 5: 6 programs	Co-teaching interns outperformed non-co-teaching interns in edTPA.
edTPA (Teacher Performance Assessment) Project	Assessment consists of three tasks related to the central focus of the learning segment: planning for instruction and assessment, instructing and engaging students in learning, and assessing student learning.	Valid performance assessment	Phase 6: 17 programs	edTPA overall scores and certain rubrics were predictive of later teacher performance once in the classroom (Bastian et al., 2016).

In a way, they have to be willing to allow the vision to evolve a little bit so others can buy into it. The change must be compelling, yet clear and specific enough to be easily understood. Individuals within the organization must be able to envision themselves as a part of the change and recognize how their roles and responsibilities in the organization might alter as a result of the change. The leader must engage the members of the organization and identify key allies in order to realize the proposed vision.

Getting faculty to sign on to such a high-risk venture was often predicated upon convincing them that the change was hugely important, desperately needed, and timely. The recruitment message needed to be powerful but sensible, and had to satisfy three important principles—moral imperative, responsiveness to changing environments, and sense of urgency. In addition to providing a compelling "rationale" for change, the leader also had to outline a concrete strategy or process that could be used to get the organization from Point A to Point B. A concrete strategy or implementation process was a crucial beginning step because it allowed people to imagine what they would need to do in order to realize the vision and achieve the goals.

Motivating and Recruiting Faculty Leaders

As the leader ignites transformational change in higher education (or teacher preparation), it is critical that they build a team to carry out various aspects of the work. Ginsberg and Bernstein (2011) provided a framework for conceptualizing how leaders can engage faculty in cultural change efforts. Leaders, like a dean or provost, have the institutional power and influence to lay out the vision, but it is critically important that they also assemble a team of change agent faculty and facilitators to lead efforts to realize the vision. Each member of the change team has an important role to play in driving change in the institution. This concept is explored more deeply in Chapter 9.

This conceptual framework provided a place for all persons engaged in the change to see a role for themselves as activities unfold. The leader for the vision—which happened to be the dean in this case—remained active and committed throughout the implementation of the Pirate CODE. Change agent faculty supported the dean's vision, gave it the fuel it needed to develop, and the substantive support it needed to flourish. The facilitators in the Office of Assessment and Accreditation and those in the Office of Teacher Education supported change agent faculty by using their knowledge of the programs and data systems to provide resources and structure.

As the innovations matured and increased in number, the dean could no longer be a "hands-on" leader of the change process. Instead, a model of distributed leadership emerged where key change agent faculty—those closely aligned with the dean's vision and possessing critical, substantive knowledge and passion for the innovations—took on the leadership role for individual innovations. These new "innovation leaders" recruited new faculty to the innovations, persuading them to join the change effort. Equally as important as the change agent faculty were the facilitators who worked to smooth the Pirate CODE Implementation Process. Their access to data and resources to support the vision and research allowed the dean and the change agent faculty to focus on sustaining the vision and passion for the change. Together, the dean, change agent faculty, and facilitators formed a powerful partnership leading the innovations from idea to implementation.

Engaging a critical mass of faculty in the effort is vital to its success, not only because the numbers of engaged faculty create a force powerful enough to shake off the criticisms and negativity that any change initiative faces, but also because the link between institutional culture and the change process becomes clearer as individuals within the institution emerge and are identified as key players in transformative change. When appropriately nurtured and supported, change agent faculty, oftentimes the pioneer implementers, recruit others early on to the cause. These recruitees are often called "early adopter faculty."

Identifying Outcomes, Metrics, and Measures

Crafting a vision/mission statement, identifying a process for change, and engaging a core team of motivated faculty, although critically important, are insufficient to guarantee success. The leader, change agent faculty, and facilitators also must identify measurable outcomes by which the success of the venture will be judged. For example, one outcome might pertain to job performance: First-year teachers will perform more like second-year teachers—on average—with respect to student achievement gains, principal evaluations, and scores on classroom observations. Another outcome might pertain to teacher retention: Graduates must be retained in teaching at a higher rate than the state average. This level of specificity is needed not only to evaluate the success of the work but also to underscore the need for data collection, analysis, and action. If an institution is to become data-driven, then the centrality of working with data both to achieve and assess the goal must be an integral part of the entire enterprise.

Structures to House, Access, and Analyze Data

Initially, the data system at ECU was one-dimensional and focused principally on gathering and reporting data to demonstrate compliance with those standards imposed by external state- and national-level accreditation and approval agencies. Course-related assessments were housed throughout the college on individual faculty computers. Other evaluation materials, such as student teaching observations, were completed on paper and pencil forms and submitted to the Office of Teacher Education at the close of the semester. Although lots of data were being collected, it was difficult to locate and impossible to analyze because there were virtually no common assessments, consistent formats, or centralized storage facility.

A vital feature of this transformative change was an integrated electronic system for storing and retrieving data, a system where all evidences, both formative and summative, were housed and where all individuals who work with the student (faculty, supervisors, adjuncts, and so on) had access. Thus one of the early goals in our change process was to identify and adopt such an electronic system and then to steadfastly and consistently drive all data collection to that system. We wanted a system that could support a way to code individual teacher candidates on a given set of dimensions (e.g., received a particular innovation; required an edTPA retake; enrolled in an experimental version of a given course) so as to allow for future analyses of particular teacher candidate subgroups. We adopted a system, the Teacher Education Management System (TEMS), and used it to house all of the data gathered on our candidates and code them in various ways. This system supported multiple needs and was much better situated to meet the increasingly complex research questions posed by faculty as a result of the innovations and "culture of evidence" emerging at the institution (Peck & McDonald, 2014).

Data available from TEMS and other institutional databases were more openly available to faculty and administrators for research, continuous improvements efforts, and the development of new innovations. In particular, faculty interest in the data for research began to drive development of the integrated data platform. The Office of Assessment and Accreditation provided supports to faculty data collection through e-portfolios and online surveys. In collaboration with the Office of Teacher Education, these tools created a dashboard for monitoring submissions to ensure data completeness and reliability. The Assessment Office continued to invest considerable time coding candidates, developing SQL data queries, and compiling and disaggregating large data sets in a way that facilitates faculty access and use of a variety of data sources.

Common Language and Places

Common Language

The development of a common language and cultivation of collaborative data analysis became central activities in our process of transformation. In our case, the field-testing of the Teacher Performance Assessment (edTPA) became an important turning point because it provided the conceptual framework and vocabulary that resulted in a common language. The edTPA field-testing led to authentic opportunities for collaboration around a clearly specified set of assessment metrics. The common language was viewed by many faculty members as pivotal to new levels of collaboration. Having access to this language of practice empowered program members who were latecomers to the work to fully engage in program conversations and decision making. For example, university supervisors became much more involved in program discussions during monthly internship meetings. The edTPA data were routinely prepared, shared, and analyzed, and these collaborative examinations by diverse faculty (tenured, tenure-track, fixed-term, adjunct, university supervisors, and so on) paved the way for action. The data-focused discussions also allowed new problems to come into focus and raised new questions about practices.

Common Places

In addition to having a common language and set of metrics for analyzing data, we identified and designated places to convene. Traditional venues, such as college assemblies, department meetings, and program get-togethers, that were typically utilized to dispense information, were repurposed, in part, to discuss innovation implementation, engage faculty in conversations of student performance, and obtain feedback on implementation changes and needs. One of the most powerful signals that a new culture was emerging resided in the creation of new "places and spaces" for convening that were designed specifically for data analysis tasks and policy discussions. In the case of our university, we cited two powerful examples: (1) data summits and (2) teacher performance assessment liaison (TPAL) meetings.

Data summits: These were annual meetings that included faculty representatives from every teacher education program. The major purpose of the data summit was to bring together faculty and administrators to discuss results of edTPA portfolio assessments through unit-level and program-levels lenses. The summits began with connections to prior summits, group think time, and an explicit framework for approaching the day's tasks. As part of these sessions, participants analyzed edTPA portfolio assessments and determined next steps in program improvements and innovations.

A gathering of this kind underscored the important connection between data analysis and programmatic decision making. The discussions that took place at these summits illustrated to faculty that their responsibilities as "curriculum-makers" were supported, not supplanted, by the data analysis process. This was quite important, as one of the common concerns of faculty in the context of new accountability policies and data was that their power and authority in curriculum matters would be eroded as larger data systems come into play.

Teacher performance assessment liaison (TPAL) meetings: Faculty liaisons representing every university teacher education program with respect to edTPA meet monthly in TPAL meetings in order to become versed in the assessment processes. Formative data such as lesson planning, video snippets of teaching, and critical reflections on instruction were collected and analyzed regularly, allowing the programs the opportunity to highlight their work and learn from others. Data-driven program improvements as well as policy discussions (e.g., number of retakes allowed, cut-off scores when local scoring was used, level[s] of support allowed) were regular features of the conversation at these monthly meetings. Faculty came to appreciate the camaraderie of the group and the educative nature of the collaboration, and viewed the data-driven actions they took as meaningful and important. These realizations motivated faculty to stay engaged in the work and recruit others. TPALs promoted faculty engagement by providing faculty with opportunities for leadership. Additionally, TPALs demonstrated the importance of continuous use of authentic performance assessment data to truly improve programs.

WHERE WE ARE NOW

As we sat and reflected on this case study of change and considered "where we were now," we saw that this journey has touched every aspect of the teacher education enterprise and every teacher education program in the institution whether they be housed in the College of Education or elsewhere on campus. We use the following to illustrate the significant shifts in thought and action that occurred.

Spread and Comprehensiveness of Innovations

Innovations that were initiated, pilot-tested, and refined in one program have been adopted by many other programs. For example, one of the innovations entitled "Video Grand Rounds," which was piloted in an early experience course in the elementary program, eventually became adopted by five other teacher education programs: Middle Grades, Special Education, Birth-Kindergarten, Health Education, and Business Information and Technology Education. Co-Teaching, another innovation piloted in the final clinical experience in the elementary program—namely, the student teaching course—became piloted by seven other teacher education programs: Middle Grades, Special Education, Birth–Kindergarten, Secondary Mathematics, Secondary English, Secondary Social Studies, and Foreign Languages Education. Ultimately, all 17 teacher education programs on campus adopted the edTPA, which was initially piloted in the Middle Grades program. Although the edTPA was an assessment and not an innovation, the data derived from administering the assessment have been used to pilot new program innovations.

Multiple and Varied Opportunities for Diverse Faculty Involvement

These widespread innovation adoptions and their accompanying research and data collection activities created multiple and varied opportunities for diverse faculty in many different programs to engage in the work. As the innovations became more varied and impacted more programs, we witnessed faculty who taught in different segments of a given program (foundations, methods, and field) as well as different types of faculty (tenured, tenure-track, fixed-term, and semester-by-semester hires) getting involved in some facet of the work. Although designing and implementing multiple pilots simultaneously placed greater demands on program leaders, it did facilitate widespread faculty involvement, which was a critically important factor in achieving institutional change.

Data Collection, Analysis, and Sharing Became an Integral Part of the Work

The way we think about and use data also has changed. We no longer view data collection and analysis activities as something we "needed" to do to stay in business or to satisfy external overseers (CAEP, Department of Public Instruction, university system, and so on). It was something we viewed as critically important and something we "wanted" to have. Our attention was much more focused on obtaining "quality" data that provide valid and reliable information about the strengths and needs of our candidates. Thus we were not only using data but also trying to find or create appropriate and informative data measures. Our facilitators were seeking to identify, craft, or refine a set of formative data collection measures so that we could use data not only to intercede with candidates who were struggling but also have data that was more predictive of who was likely to struggle so that we could intervene early in the teacher candidate's preparation.

Through this process of transformation, conversations shifted from talking chiefly about data *needs* to talking about data *use* within and among programs. Faculty who once used assessment data simply for grading or for some annual report were now analyzing teacher candidate data more deeply for trends and impacts associated with the innovations being implemented. Change agent faculty who took up the challenge to be more data-driven came to recognize the importance of having valid and reliable data and the value of data for informing them and their work.

To summarize, we were no longer using data to convince others that we were doing a good job: We were using data to help us assess our programmatic strengths and weaknesses; to provide us with insights as to what we might try in order to remedy deficiencies and/or enhance strengths; and to support faculty practice-based research to ensure that we were continual contributors to the knowledge base of research.

New Collaborations for Program Implementation and Scholarly Productivity

This active engagement of faculty across various components of a given program as well as among programs created a commonality of purpose, implementation goals, and research interests. The fact that a diverse set of faculty members were engaged in implementing and studying the same innovations across multiple programs created many opportunities for collaboration on national presentation proposals and manuscript productions among programs and faculty that heretofore would not have collaborated or worked together on such projects or products. This coming together of faculty with diverse sets of expertise from different teacher education programs led to the development of a fully functioning and meaningful "community of practice" among faculty, all of whom were dedicated to a similar set of goals, all of whom spoke a common language, and all of whom were using a common set of metrics to ascertain outcomes. A few of these faculty members share their experiences in Chapter 11.

Change in Traditional Curriculum and Policy Councils

Since the programmatic changes were so widespread and the assessment data so comprehensive, the traditional curriculum (department and college curriculum committees) and policy (Council of Teacher Education, Provost's Council) structures also have been impacted. One example is that the pilot process, described earlier in this chapter, became formalized and recognized as a legitimate step in the experimentation process through discussion and vote at the campus-level Council of Teacher Education. Moreover, there has been a shift in the conversations that take place in these traditional committees and councils. These venues were no longer places where administration and faculty largely disperse information and approve processes and protocols, but were now also being used as forums for discussion of philosophical and substantive issues associated with the work. Disagreements, challenges, and deliberations have emerged as being more characteristic of the conversations. Faculty were engaged in more spirited and meaningful dialogue around such topics as whether one can adapt rather than adopt an innovation, what data points should be collected in common, and whether all sections of a given course must participate in an innovation inside a particular program. These interactions, although difficult at times, signaled that the members of the institution were actively engaged and thinking purposefully about the programmatic decisions being made.

Faculty Originators, Participants, and Resisters

Those leading the change have garnered enough participants and supporters across the institution to render the force a formidable one in the change process. Those who see the change as negative realize that they no longer have sufficient influence to stop or reverse the forward progress of the group. Thus they have generally adopted one of three positions: (1) become more vocally negative, (2) maintain a low profile, or (3) get involved in the change and see where it leads. In the meantime, everyone involved in the change (leader faculty, participants, supportive department chairs, dean, and so on) continued to offer "naysayer" faculty opportunities for engagement—whether it be field-testing a new assessment tool, scoring research protocols, attending discussion forums, or something else. The ultimate goal was 100% faculty support of and involvement with the overarching goal: to become a learning organization committed to an agenda of continuous improvement using data-driven decision making.

Mind Shift Inside the Organization

Although a group of faculty members still do not support the changes, the majority have engaged over time and are able to articulate that they have witnessed a significant "mind shift" with respect to the way that they think about and do their work. There was a definite futuristic thinking and planning momentum that was not being fueled by administrators or faculty leaders. All across the college, faculty were thinking and talking about what the next innovation or "squishy pilot" should be. Faculty work groups were forming spontaneously to have these conversations and it was now typical to see such groups forming "across" as well as "within" programmatic lines. Work groups now were comprised customarily of tenure and tenure-track faculty as well as those who have been historically "marginalized" (part-time, fixed-term faculty), and all were now finding a voice at the table as innovations were developed, piloted, refined, and assessed.

Outside Recognition Increases Morale, Participation, and Scholarly Achievement

There is a famous line from the movie *Field of Dreams* (1989) that goes something like this: "If you build it, they will come." In point of fact, this was exactly what happened in our case. As the work gained momentum and increasing numbers of faculty gave presentations at national meetings, various external constituencies and policymakers wanted to know more about the transformative changes taking place in our institution. Consequently, administrators and faculty leaders were asked to: (1) present the work to state-level officials (Governor's Education Advisor, Board of Governor

Members); (2) serve on various task forces and committees (edTPA standard-setting and benchmarking activities with SCALE, Signature Assessment Design Studios); (3) give invited presentations at national meetings (e.g., AACTE, AERA, edTPA conferences); and (4) establish national organizations related to the innovation (National Association for Co-Teaching). These varied recognitions not only served to validate the work of the faculty leaders but also signaled to "fence-sitters" and "naysayers" that policymakers and the professional community at-large viewed the activities as positive and noteworthy. This external recognition as the well as the scholarly achievements of faculty (i.e., national presentations, article acceptances, and awards) served as catalysts for getting uninvolved faculty (especially frightened nontenured faculty) to come on board and be a part of the efforts.

Increased Interdependence Across Teacher Preparation

One of the most significant shifts that occurred in the college was a shift in the locus of control. As the projects unfolded, matured, and expanded, and as more and more faculty have become engaged, the rhetoric shifted away from talking about "my" course to talking about "our" program. More importantly, faculty started to recognize that the course they teach was only one element of a larger program and, as such, must fit into a developmental and coherent set of coursework and field experiences if we wanted teacher education candidates to leave the program with a core set of integrated dispositions, knowledge, and skills to be successful 1st-year teachers. Finally, faculty began to understand that their responsibility did not begin and end with the course they taught, but rather with the competence of the teacher they produced as a result of the entire program. These shifts in perspective signaled fundamental shifts in thought and action that converted faculty from operating as individual entrepreneurs to operating as collective activists and as members of a community of practice.

WHAT WE WISH WE HAD KNOWN AT THE START

In this section we share some of the lessons we learned from the experience. We have organized them into the following "categories of knowing": (1) communication and recruitment; (2) innovation design and implementation; (3) research design and implementation; (4) data system—purpose and usage; and (5) organization and support structures.

Communication and Recruitment

Identify compelling and motivational catalysts for change. In order to make changes, people need reasons and requirements. The reasons for change must be compelling and motivational. However, before people will actually act, there must also be some sort of catalyst or requirement to ignite the change. Although the catalyst may be positive—such as the infusion of new resources—typically it is some threat or negative event (loss of faculty lines, budget cuts, negative publicity about program graduates, and so on). The role of administrative and faculty leaders is to embrace the catalyst—whether it be positive or negative—and treat it as an opportunity. The first step is to develop a draft plan of action and then circulate it widely among all groups in the college setting. Once distributed, multiple and varied opportunities to discuss, criticize, and suggest revisions are scheduled.

Create attractive and inclusive heuristics to help stakeholders capture both the vision and the proposed change process. Communicating complex ideas is a difficult undertaking even in a small group; it becomes extraordinarily challenging when the group involves hundreds of individuals. We found that face-to-face dialogues were necessary, but having good heuristics, like Figure 3.1, helped people to intellectually capture both the vision and the proposed process. In essence, heuristics allow faculty to visualize the goals, the implementation approach, and the substance of the work.

Acknowledge that faculty resistance is both a typical and understandable reaction from a subset of individuals who find themselves on the margins of the change process, either by choice or by chance. It would have been very reassuring if we had fully comprehended that faculty resistance is both a typical and understandable reaction from that subset of individuals who find themselves in a change process they may not understand or support. Although the naysayers seem powerful and threatening, especially at the very beginning of the change process, it is essential for those who are involved to recognize that negative comments and passive aggressive behaviors are not emanating from a position of strength but rather may come from fear—fear that the change is going to impact them against their will. Recognizing resistance as a predictable consequence of any substantive change process allows leaders to engage naysayer faculty in activities that reduce fear while still staying the course. Abandoning the course of action is not the answer. Compromising the course of action is not the answer. Communicating and giving voice to the criticisms while staying confident and committed to the direction is the path to follow.

Communicate the vision and engage faculty in its design, implementation, and dissemination. It would have been so helpful if we had known that communicating the vision and engaging faculty in conversations about the draft plan were as important to the successful transformation process as designing, implementing, and studying the innovations. There is no substitute for taking the time and making the effort to conduct many large- and small-group discussions about the vision and process early on so that faculty and staff have multiple opportunities and venues to express their views and concerns, ask questions, and give suggestions. Conversations such as these can be contentious, but they are vital to understanding the pressure points of change. In essence, the work requires learning to embrace conflict as a normal and natural element of change rather than to fear it as was so often the case. It is also critically important to develop a dissemination plan that supports the vision. A plan to highlight initial successes, disseminate preliminary research, and share success stories with partners both within and across institutions makes the work visible and furthers its impact.

Innovation Design and Implementation

Create and implement a finite set of aligned innovations or assessments. It is important to create and implement more than one innovation or assessment project simultaneously so that faculty have choice and increased opportunities to participate. Having said this, the set must be finite, focused, and manageable, but constructed in ways that span multiple sets of coursework (e.g., early field, methods, student teaching). The set of innovations must inextricably link teaching, research, and service. The set must also allow for horizontal alignment and coherence across various components of the program.

Pace the implementation purposefully and strategically to avoid "change" fatigue. When engaging in designing innovations, be mindful about the pace of implementation. Time spent before launch—designing the innovation, defining desired outcomes, and identifying data collection measures that will be used to demonstrate success—is crucial to maintain momentum.

Create a well-articulated implementation plan that outlines goals, timelines, expectations, and guidelines to ensure fidelity of implementation. It is important to have a well-articulated implementation plan and timeline for each innovation so that you avoid the need to make numerous changes and adjustments during the piloting and scale-up phases or do "damage control" when things go awry. Implementation guidelines, developed alongside a diverse set of faculty, go a long way toward increasing faculty buy-in.

Engage P-12 partners in transformative efforts from design and development to implementation and assessment of the innovations. Although P-12 partners were engaged in the transformation process, they should have been included earlier, more systematically, and sustained throughout. Several (or most) of the innovations developed were in response to a P–12 need or concern. Thus

P–12 partners should be engaged from design and development to implementation and assessment of the innovations. We fully understand that this is easier said than done, but it is an important collaboration that should be forged from the very inception of the work.

Pair senior faculty with junior faculty to build community around the change and offset political rank and tenure tensions. Make certain that senior faculty are paired with junior faculty as the innovations get underway. This will eliminate a lot of the concerns that junior faculty often feel when they embark on a new project and believe that senior faculty (those who vote on their tenure and promotion) are opposed to it. All too often junior faculty find it difficult to engage in or stick with a project if they feel that to do so might jeopardize their own career goals.

Research Design and Implementation

Integrate opportunities for practice-based research—quantitative, qualitative, and mixed method—throughout the change process. Research is an essential part of the work. It cannot be compromised, put off, or engaged in as an afterthought. Planning research studies as an integral part of the piloting and implementation process ensures that the innovation is well thought out, the goals are clearly defined, and the outcomes are measurable. Since research design is a part of the innovative process with which teacher education faculty often have limited experience, it is important to seek the time and support of methodologists (both inside and outside the college) who understand teacher education and thus can serve as external "critical friends" or as members of the innovation team.

Support faculty through labor-intensive and time-consuming work by allocating resources in support of research efforts and the dissemination of findings through multiple venues. Innovation work of this kind is labor-intensive and time-consuming. Thus it is essential that faculty engaged in this work, especially junior faculty, have the support they need to conduct the research, give the presentations, and do the writing necessary to be eligible for tenure or promotion. This is another reason why engaging the services of methodologists at the front end is so important. Most of us have learned (the hard way, unfortunately) that it takes just as much time and energy to conduct research that is seriously flawed in its design as it does to implement methodologically sound studies. Thus one sure way to support junior faculty is to make sure that the work they do is credible, publishable, and presentable.

Invest in the successful development of career-long faculty scholarship. Finally, research of this kind is not only critical to support faculty productivity for tenure and promotion, but it is also important to the successful development of career-long faculty scholarship. Creating and implementing a research agenda is a crucial ingredient in the continued development of faculty expertise and their continued scholarly productivity. Yet it is all too often lacking among junior faculty. This is one way that the institution can support faculty development—development that will pay big dividends not only for the individual faculty member, but also for the teacher candidates, the program, and the institution.

Data System, Purpose, and Usage

Develop or adopt a centralized and integrated data system for data collection, storage, and retrieval. In order to engage in change at a level or scale that is transformative, the importance of having or adopting a centralized system for data collection, storage, and retrieval cannot be underestimated. Whether one uses a commercial program or has an in-house system, it must be flexible, expandable, and user-friendly. In order for it to have the scope and power needed for the work, it must be capable of handling all of the different types of formative and summative assessments gathered on all teacher education candidates in the college (e.g., video snippets, student teaching evaluations, and teacher performance assessment data). It must contain all of the evidences required by state or national accreditors. Everyone who works with the student (full-time and part-time faculty, student teaching supervisors, and public-school clinical teachers) as well as the teacher candidates themselves must be taught to use the system.

Assign the data system to a director or assistant dean who understands and participates in the work. The data must be overseen and managed by a director or assistant dean who not only understands the work but is a participant in it. This is vitally important because it is in the director or assistant dean's office, or one like it, that data will be made available to faculty for review and discussion. It is in this office that data will be stored, retrieved, and analyzed for annual reports, accreditation exhibit rooms, and national presentations. This office is "data central," and the person who runs it must be savvy, both with respect to data and the substance of the work. This office will not only share but also mine the data at multiple levels often. Since it is very difficult for faculty leaders, tasked with spearheading innovation design and implementation, to ensure that the data mining and analysis opportunities are provided in a timely manner, it's important to think about identifying project leaders who coordinate different sets of responsibilities. One might take on the responsibility for implementation while the other oversees data collection and analysis.

CONCLUSION

As we have argued in this chapter, it was important to articulate a mission-driven moral imperative—why the change was necessary and why we, as teacher educators, were morally obligated to participate in the work. Equally important, though, was having a straightforward and simple change process to implement and adapt as well as a heuristic that would help faculty and staff visually capture the "big ideas" undergirding the change process. Creating and implementing powerful, needed, and appealing substantive innovations was at the very core of the work. In order for faculty to get excited and stay excited, they must see the content of the change (the innovations themselves) as being needed and potentially important improvement actions that will move them toward their own desired professional goals as well as the institution's desired goals (i.e., transforming the college into a learning organization dedicated to the continuous production of outcome knowledge and continuous improvement in the processes and procedures employed to prepare educators.)

Data was another central feature of the change process. Having "common data" and multiple kinds of data to review and analyze was a fundamental component of the transformative process because it was through this activity that people would come together to examine the outcomes of the work, ask hard questions about the findings, and make adjustments in the plan. This activity not only affords opportunities to collaborate and have deeper conversations about the work, but it was community building.

To recruit faculty—particularly during the initial stages of change—it was important to identify, secure, and commit resources. These don't have to be massive. What was important was that they be viewed as strategic investments. Therefore, any reassigned time, graduate assistantship assignment, or research consultation provided needs to have a written memo of understanding attached to it so that each party knows what they can expect to receive from the investment.

Although the last to be mentioned, the value of leadership cannot be overestimated. There is no substitute for having visionary, courageous, committed, and resilient leadership inside the organization. In order to mobilize individuals, there must be leaders who are able to articulate the change(s) they wish to see. The vision must be compelling enough—both morally and pragmatically—to recruit early adopter faculty. The leaders must be courageous because there will be negative reactions, push-backs, and criticisms to contend with, especially at the beginning when the change process is most vulnerable. The leaders must be committed because there will be times when it seems easier to abandon or compromise one's goals rather than stand firm for the change. Finally, the leaders must be resilient because there will be setbacks, dead-ends, and disappointments along the way. The leaders can't afford to become discouraged because so many people were either using the leaders' demeanors to gauge the strength/status of the transformation or were looking to the leaders to lead the way and stay the course.

While we have learned a lot over the course of the last several years, there is so much we still need to learn. For example, we don't know whether, and to what extent, all of the components we describe are necessary and in what order they might be needed. We don't know the size of the transformation needed to effect positive and measurable changes in the preparedness of program graduates. We don't know whether the transformation that we now believe to be institutionalized in the culture will withstand changes in leadership or faculty departures.

We hope that, after reading this chapter, you will decide to take part in a transformative change process in your own institution because it was only through case studies of change—like the ones in this book—that we will learn how to: (1) build a capacity for engaging in educational change, (2) create a collaborative infrastructure that supports the needs of a learning organization, (3) meet the unique professional development and professional autonomy needs of individual faculty, and (4) transform the culture of a college, including the norms, roles, beliefs, responsibilities, ways of thinking, and professional dispositions.

REFERENCES

Bastian, K. C., Henry, G. T., Pan, Y., & Lys, D. (2016). Teacher candidate performance assessments: Local scoring and implications for teacher preparation program improvement. *Teaching and Teacher Education, 59,* 1–12.

Ginsberg, S. M., & Bernstein, J. L. (2011). Growing the scholarship of teaching and learning through institutional culture change. *Journal of the Scholarship of Teaching and Learning, 11*(1), 1–12.

Lys, D. B., L'Esperance, M., Dobson, E., & Bullock, A. A. (2014). Large-scale implementation of the edTPA: Reflections upon institutional change in action. *Current Issues in Education, 17*(3), 1–11. https://cie.asu.edu/ojs/index.php/cieatasu/article/view/1256/588

Peck, C. A., & McDonald, M. A. (2014). What is a culture of evidence? How do you get one? And . . . should you want one? *Teachers College Record, 116*(3), 1–27.

CHAPTER 4

Alverno College

Using Data for Program Improvement in a Small Liberal Arts College

Désirée H. Pointer Mace and Patricia Luebke

Ashley, a Secondary English candidate, sat with her mother in the office of the dean of the Alverno College School of Professional Studies. The dean and the director of Graduate Education Programs sat in the other two chairs at a round table, a laptop positioned in the middle. Mother and daughter sat with rigid spines and rigid faces. Ashley's mother began, "She just doesn't understand why, if she was successful in the first education practicum, and she was successful in the second education practicum, why she isn't successful now!"

Ashley shifted in her chair.

The director opened Ashley's electronic diagnostic portfolio, turned the laptop so that everyone could look at it together, and said, "You're right. Ashley, you did meet outcomes in your first course. You were able to design lesson plans with standards, objectives, and some assessment procedures. I see in your video here that you spoke clearly and made some initial attempts to get to know your learners. You were rated proficient in all areas. In your second field course, I see that you had some areas of your practice that were evaluated as strong, including content area strategies, but others that were evaluated as emerging, particularly around learner-centeredness in your teaching. In this, your most recent field course, I see here that in your plans, your reflections, and your observed lessons and videos, you haven't developed in this area, and so you have received an 'Unsuccessful' in this course. Tell me about that. What do you see here?"

Ashley glanced at her mother and said, "It's really hard to get to know 180 students in a high school setting!" The director responded, "Yes, it really is. But it's still important. So tell me generally: Who are the artists? Who are the socially powerful kids? Who are the loners? Who are the teacher-pleasers? Who's showing you during your lessons that they're really with you, and who is staring out the window? Who shows oppositional behaviors?" Ashley said she didn't know.

Changing tactics, the director said, "Okay, how about your content. I see here that your feedback says you had challenges developing lesson plans to engage your learners with the texts in the course." Ashley responded, "Well, I don't think kids can connect with that book." The director responded, "Let's think about something that you would really want to teach. You're a Secondary English candidate. I bet you love to read. What's something you would love, love to teach to high school students?"

. . . Silence.

Ten, twenty, thirty seconds elapsed. Finally, Ashley's mother exclaimed, "But you *love* to read!" Ashley shot her mom a glance and retorted, "Not things that I would want to teach!"

The director said, "That's really important what you just said there. And it echoes what I see here in your portfolio of work. Teaching *is* hard. It is difficult to learn interesting and memorable characteristics of 180 young people. It is hard to find points of connection for yourself and your learners to the texts you're expected to teach. And I have to tell you, our level of expectation gets higher from here. This road ahead gets steeper, not easier. And teacher preparation is not as rigorous as everyday teaching. This has to be a kind of hard that you embrace, a challenge that you love. If you don't, you need to listen really hard to your gut. Do you really want to be a teacher? If you do, then our policy for people who have been unsuccessful in a field course is that you write a memo to the Division of Education leadership setting forth a self-assessment of your evidence of practice in your portfolio, and how you plan to be successful in a subsequent attempt. You have to show that you have what it takes: the knowledge, skills, and dispositions to be a teacher. If you decide that this path is not for you, that's okay too. Kids need teachers who are going to love the challenges of everyday practice. At Alverno, you have to earn your way through our program through evidence of your teaching competence."

At Alverno College, data use is not solely for external stakeholders. In an outcome- and evidence-based program, data use is for everyone. Data include various kinds of measures of candidates' competence: artifacts of teaching, self-assessments, video, standardized test results, portfolios, interview assessments, and the edTPA. All of those inform conversations that multiple stakeholders are able to have about our common work. Collegewide and in the Division of Education, faculty have a strong sense of community, explicit and shared rules of engagement, and a clear orientation about the object of our work: to create the teachers our students and schools need.

CONTEXT

Alverno College is a small Catholic liberal arts college in Milwaukee, Wisconsin, founded in 1887 by the School Sisters of Saint Francis. A tuition-driven women's institution at the undergraduate level, Alverno serves both women and men students at the postbaccalaureate and graduate level. Alverno mirrors the diversity of Milwaukee County, from which most of the college's students come. Half of our students come from underrepresented ethnic groups, approximately 75% are the first in their families to attend college, and a similar percentage are eligible for federal Pell grants, an indicator of the low socioeconomic status of many of Alverno's students. The college has a deep commitment to educating a diverse group of students, students for whom K–12 education has not typically provided opportunities that higher socioeconomic contexts might have. Alverno recommends between 60–100 candidates for Wisconsin initial teacher licensure each year at both the undergraduate and graduate levels.

Historical Context for Authentic Assessment

In the early 1970s, changes in society, the city of Milwaukee, and the Catholic Church posed significant enrollment challenges. The faculty of Alverno and their leadership responded through a rigorous and intensive process of re-conceptualizing the purpose of the institution. They asked themselves: Why should someone attend our college? What are the common habits of mind we should develop within majors and across disciplines? They asked members of the community: What do local organizations, districts, and hospitals need from a well-educated college graduate? Over a span of several years they distilled the responses to these questions and began to create a framework for ability-based education. They also saw significant enrollment expansion in response to the reforms.

While it has changed and developed over time, the Alverno assessment and curricular framework now consists of eight abilities that are taught, assessed, and self-assessed in all undergraduate majors: Communication, Analysis, Social Interaction, Problem Solving, Effective Citizenship, Developing a Global Perspective, Valuing in Decision Making, and Aesthetic Engagement (Alverno College Faculty, 1994). All courses taught to undergraduates are aligned with this framework, such that each undergraduate major's required courses chart a pathway through all eight abilities and "validate" for four levels of increasing sophistication in each.

When graduate programs began at Alverno in the mid-1990s, the faculty designers created corresponding ability frameworks anchored in the particular habits of mind of the disciplines, that is to say, the MBA program abilities for businesspeople are distinct from the MAE ones for educators. Across the college, student self-assessment using explicit criteria is required of every major assessment in every program (Loacker & Rogers, 2005).

Because those working in a system are most familiar with the intricacies of its functioning, the Alverno College faculty have published various projects intended to develop our own faculty, as well as those interested in applying or replicating this model in other contexts (for a list of publications, see https://www.alverno.edu/ecommerce/ieo/publications/publications.php?c=32&p=70). For example, a document affectionately called the "Four-Pager" (https://lampout1.alverno.edu/archives/alphistory/pdf/ability%20statements%202016%20v17.pdf) provides one-sentence descriptions of each of the four levels of the eight undergraduate abilities. A 71-page volume, *Ability-based Learning Outcomes: Teaching and Assessment at Alverno College*, unpacks the eight abilities in chapter-length descriptive accounts, providing examples of students' development in various disciplines. Other program-based publications (*Self-Assessment at Alverno College, Feedback is Teaching, Student Assessment-as-Learning at Alverno College, Assessment at Alverno College: Student, Program, Institutional*) expand on specific features and challenges of implementing authentic assessment in higher education. Higher education professional learning institutes held at Alverno, and consulting provided by faculty and leaders of Alverno, have developed other institutional settings in their efforts around the globe.

Sister Joel Read, president of Alverno College from 1968 to 2003, led many of the change initiatives that the college still benefits from today. She frequently commented that requiring members of the college community to meet regularly was one of the best decisions she and her colleagues in leadership made. Other organization practices, such as the development and use of a data system, flow out of this collaborative stance. The collaborative dynamic, development of relational practices, and mutual orientation toward student outcomes inform the use of tools to drive program improvement, not the reverse.

At Alverno, each full-time faculty member has an identity not only as a member of a discipline department, but also as a member of one of the eight ability departments. There are multiple levels in which the institution prioritizes time and space for use of data to inform program work.

Every member of the Alverno College community engages in regular self-assessment: students, faculty, administrators, and staff. Students do so connected to individual assignments, courses, and benchmark portfolios. Faculty engage in self-assessment as part of an annual review process linked to promotion and continuous appointment. Staff have a similar process for self-assessment related to their retention.

As a teaching institution, no full-time faculty would be hired if they viewed teaching as secondary to research. In review and promotion, faculty self-assess and are evaluated according to criteria related to Effective Teaching, Responsible Work in the College Community, and Developing Scholarship. All of those criteria at Alverno would be challenging to do well while simultaneously ignoring or marginalizing use of program data to improve teaching, support the college, and engage in inquiry. It is not an institutional norm for faculty to engage in pretenure hermitage; rather, when faculty are preparing for promotion review, it is more common for them to be thinking expansively, collaboratively, and deeply about pedagogy and curriculum design, both individually and at the institutional level.

Common Course and Meeting Scheduling

Alverno's institution leadership prioritizes time for collegewide collaboration; no classes are held on Friday afternoons, so that they may be used for discipline meetings, cross-disciplinary ability meetings, or all-faculty workshops (e.g., exploring the role of emotion in analysis and its implications for assessment and self-assessment). At the level of the department or unit, the Alverno Division of Education has arranged courses so that no education courses are offered on Tuesdays between 12 and 2 p.m. This allows for weekly meetings of the Committee of the Whole, or smaller subgroup gatherings to work on specific licensure program tasks.

Faculty–Staff Collaboration Around Outcomes and Data

Alverno offers multiday "institutes" for collaboration and learning three times a year (in August, January, and May), many sessions of which are attended by faculty as well as staff. During whole-college sessions and breakout meetings, members of the Alverno community present and advance their understanding of the Alverno curriculum and envision responses to emerging issues and challenges. Many of these sessions focus on what all can learn from students' evidence of outcomes.

Another strong practice at the college level is an Assessment Center, staffed by experienced Alverno staff colleagues who coordinate collegewide assessments. Many of these draw heavily on hundreds of community colleagues (alumnae as well as organizational partners and agency and corporate leaders) to serve as assessors for students. This is a critical way in which the scope of the assessment community at Alverno far surpasses those who are employed by the college. As one example, every single undergraduate at Alverno participates in a social interaction assessment as part of a required course on Small-Group Behavior, and is managed by the leaders and staff of the Assessment Center. The description shown in Figure 4.1 evokes the focus of the assessment and the outcomes for our students.

Figure 4.1. Assessing Social Interaction: Small-Group Behavior Decision-Making Task

To generate evidence of Social Interaction Level 1, in their first semester of study at Alverno, all 1st-year students engage in a small-group-interaction assessment. In this Social Interaction Level 1 assessment, students first learn about various frameworks for effective group interactions. In professional and organizational contexts, they consider and evaluate real-world scenarios: If a group is seeking consensus in order to make a collective decision that all members can accept, what must each of the members of the group do (and *not* do) to accomplish this goal? They should likely seek information from others, for example, or provide information that only they may have. They should offer their own opinions, but also seek out and consider the opinions of others. They might need to pause and summarize the group decision-making process thus far. They might be alert for group members who are silent or minimally participating, and find ways to invite those voices into the conversation. All of these positive behaviors can be observed, and feedback can be sought regarding an individual's demonstration of those behaviors. One person might advocate for a particular stance or decision. Another might respectfully challenge that person's stance. As they do, another group member might mediate this disagreement and help the two recognize the value of each other's view, or recognize an error in their thinking. As they near a decision, they might analyze the effectiveness of the group's process, or deliberately seek closure and set goals or following actions.

This assessment, like others that touch on validating each level of each ability, gives students and faculty alike access to a common vocabulary to describe learning and growth. A professor teaching a course for 2nd-year students can refer to the criteria in the Social Interaction 1st-year assessment as a touchstone, providing shorthand and concise criteria for expectations, for example, "How will we avoid engaging in 'blocking' behaviors in this discussion?" Building an academic language for teaching, learning, and assessing is a real strength provided by the ability-based model.

On the day of the assessment, students work in groups of four, and each of the four is given partial and distinct materials related to the nomination of a candidate for a governmental council on environmental regulation. One of the four might have an opinion piece from a newspaper and a resume of one candidate, while another student might have two resumes and a job description. A third student might have information about the other environmental council members, and the fourth might have some information that could prove troubling about one or more candidates. Together the students enter a room with their materials, understanding that they have approximately 20 minutes to engage in a conversation and attempt to come to a consensus decision. Meanwhile, also in the room are four assessors who are trained in this assessment, social interaction behaviors, and giving feedback to students. Because this assessment requires a 1:1 assessor:student ratio, Alverno College has created a cadre of hundreds of volunteer assessors, many of them graduates of the college itself or community friends of the college, and then has trained all of them in this assessment process. It is labor intensive, and requires significant investment by the college, but because it provides such a significant learning experience for the students and substantive assessment of their social interaction ability, it is seen as worthwhile.

As the students enter the room, they are seated at a table in the middle of the room. Each assessor sits in one corner of the room, and is oriented solely on watching one of the four students, making comprehensive notes and tagging the notes with particular behaviors noted. After approximately 20 minutes of conversation, whether the group has come to a consensus decision or not, the assessment is drawn to a close. Each student then provides peer feedback to each of the other three students about the behaviors they demonstrated, and she self-assesses her own behaviors as best she can. These peer feedback forms and self-assessments are then routed to the assessor, who then engages in a conversation, literally sitting down beside the student, in which they look together at the self-assessment, peer feedback, and the assessor's own noticings. The purpose of this conversation is *not* to confirm that the student has a high level of ability at that point in social interaction (though she may), but rather, to give her an experience in self-assessing and receiving feedback about her own ability.

Thus the assessment becomes a threshold and a mirror, the student being given feedback, perhaps for the first time, about her effectiveness in a social interaction situation. The assessor and the student might note in her self-assessment and her peer feedback that she too often fell silent while others conversed. Or they might identify that she effectively sought the opinions of others, but didn't offer her own. Or in some cases the feedback might show that she engaged in blocking behaviors that negatively affected the group's process. The purpose is not to be perfect in all elements, but to understand that social interaction *is* behaviors and their results, and that we can set appropriate goals based on feedback about our effectiveness or lack thereof.

This experience changes a student. She recognizes that she can transform her effectiveness with others based on things that are within her ability to control. She becomes open to peer feedback and that of her assessor. She connects this feedback to her own self-assessment as well as to her goals for further development.

Community Connections

Alverno engages outside stakeholders in analysis of program data through program advisory councils, which meet several times per year. In a 2015 advisory meeting of the Initial Licensure in Special Education program, for example, advisory committee members reviewed student performance data on the edTPA and Wisconsin Foundations of Reading test for students who had taken these assessments in the past year. Since 2014 was the 1st year that special education candidates completed the edTPA with external scoring by Pearson and also the 1st year that the Foundations of Reading Test was required for special education teachers, the 1st year of data provided a baseline for student performance that led to review of our courses and overall program effectiveness. Advisory committee members participated in reviewing the data, generating questions leading to further inquiry, and setting direction for further data analysis.

Program Expectations and Gathering of Candidate Data

Within each major, Alverno also aligns courses to advanced disciplinary abilities; within the Division of Education, they are Conceptualization, Communication, Coordination, Diagnosis, and Inclusive Interaction (Advocacy for Learners and the Profession). These advanced abilities are also used with our postbaccalaureate licensure pathways. Teacher candidates are assessed via internally designed performance assessments as well as external ones (e.g., PRAXIS, the edTPA). For example, early in their programs the candidates engage in a zero-credit interview assessment, which requires them to have a professional conversation with a member of the education faculty. The teacher candidate must arrange the time and day of the assessment and come prepared with two pieces of evidence demonstrating her early development in Alverno's education abilities as well as the national InTASC standards. In the conversation, the faculty probes the student about her claims, and together they derive one or two goals for the student to work toward in coming semesters. This early assessment demonstrates several things—professional dispositions (can she take responsibility for arranging the meeting, show up on time, and come prepared?), conceptual framework clarity, and the ability to connect evidence from her teaching practice to these frameworks. Then, a few semesters later, each teacher candidate builds on this early process by developing a portfolio establishing her readiness to advance to student teaching. In that assessment, the candidate must address each one of the advanced education abilities, as well as all of the InTASC standards, and the portfolio is assessed by a two-person team of an education faculty and a practicing teacher.

Selectivity

The Alverno Division of Education takes a unique approach to admissions. Instead of being highly selective on the way *in* to the education major as measured by test scores or high school GPA, Alverno's education programs are selective on the way *out*. In order to receive a diploma or professional license, Alverno teaching candidates (like Ashley, introduced earlier) are required to demonstrate at each step of their program that they "have what it takes" to be a teacher, linked explicitly to evidence from their practice and self-assessment in relationship to criteria. Faculty in the Division of Education and colleagues in the disciplines regularly access student learning data, analyze them, and mine them for questions (National Research Council, 2001). The college does not require a very high GPA or high standardized test scores for entry into licensure programs, because there is a strong emphasis on value added within the programs themselves. While candidates may start their programs with differing strengths, they all are required to attain the same high outcomes by the end of the program in order to be recommended for licensure.

Institution-wide Commitment to Performance Assessment

For every student at Alverno College, demonstrating performance outcomes begins the same week she begins her program of study, through a requirement to video-record and self-assess a speech about her prior learning. Students continue this "show what you know" approach throughout their college program, so much so that undergraduate commencement student speakers regularly get a big laugh from the graduates and their families with comments regarding self-assessment, evidence, and the abilities. The language of learning is made explicit to students, who are required to show evidence of their learning and growth, and this creates diverse and interesting sources of data that faculty can interrogate.

The same values hold true for graduate teacher licensure students; they spend less time at the college than undergraduates, but in each education practicum, methods, and content course, candidates are required to demonstrate multiple measures of their attainment of course outcomes. This means that when faculty have to have hard conversations with candidates, there's lots of evidence and minimal reliance on opinion and anecdote. Data supports everyone's work—the candidate's ability to self-assess progress, individual faculty's ability to look at where learners have been prior to their course, faculty cohorts' ability to look across candidates and courses to discern patterns in performance, and for Division of Education leadership to recommend needed changes to ensure that the college is preparing teachers worthy of the students that they will serve. Through careful and descriptive rubric design, for example, even in an ungraded system Alverno faculty are able to leverage our portfolio system to engage in continuous improvement, test assumptions about candidate development, and make needed changes.

The Alverno College community is centered on performance and emphasizes the importance of outcome-oriented teaching. Faculty dispositions to teach and assess authentically are embedded in the hiring process, supported in new faculty's 1st years at the college, and expected collegewide. Alverno has a robust internal language of practice to describe student performance related to ability levels and criteria. This is developed through a careful and developmental mentoring process among faculty, including professional development for new faculty in their 1st years at the college. Some examples of such offerings might include the challenges inherent in writing quality criteria for assessment and self-assessment, how to write feedback that can guide students to apply it to their future learning, and detailed interrogations of abilities and levels. This supports faculty in writing feedback in the assessment system that can then be used to write end-point narratives of student performance upon graduation or program completion. The publications authored by Alverno faculty mentioned earlier are in use by new faculty, who then also contribute to their revision and author new and needed guides.

The college found in the early 2000s that no external portfolio tool was yet able to align performance criteria with student and faculty assessment-for-learning (Stiggins, 2005), so they built their own, the Diagnostic Digital Portfolio (DDP). All faculty had access to all data within this system. In 2015, after noting challenges inherent in a homegrown system and the financial burden of updating and revising the system, the college transitioned to using LiveText as a portfolio system (see Figure 4.2 for comparison of DDP and LiveText Assignment Faculty View). Because the prior system was

Figure 4.2. DDP Assignment Faculty View and LiveText Assignment Faculty View

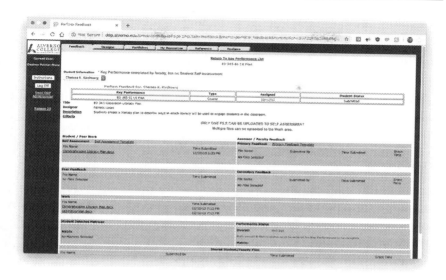

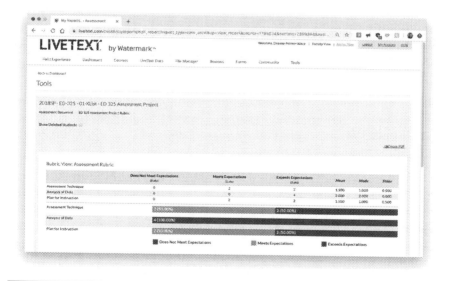

outcome-based and standards-aligned, the transition was a smooth one, more of translation than of revolution.

Motivating faculty to use data has not been challenging at Alverno; supporting faculty in efficiently providing feedback to students that is intelligible to colleagues has been. Because the college does not offer grades, the feedback to students throughout the portfolio becomes the basis of graduation narrative transcripts as well as, when needed, the conversion of those feedback documents to grades for graduate school applications. There is a careful and connected process to engage faculty in writing clear, timely, and criterion-based feedback to students so that the student can make sense of it as well as colleagues who may be tasked with understanding trends, addressing concerning gaps, or reinforcing program strengths. Without faculty accountability for creating feedback that is useful to candidates and to other colleagues, the opening interaction would not be possible. Having access to developmental, complex data throughout a candidate's program means that conversations about unsuccessful performance are never "She said, she said" disputes between faculty and student. They are centered on the evidence generated in the normal course of teaching and learning.

What We Have Done: Pervasive and Frequent Demonstrations of Candidate Competence

Opportunities for teacher candidates to demonstrate competence live within as well as outside of courses at Alverno. While faculty may teach the same course over multiple semesters, there is not a sense that any one professor "owns" a course. The ability-based context requires that any changes to a course maintain the outcomes and the ability "validations" or holistic demonstration of outcomes in order for the course pathways to remain developmental and coherent. The opening vignette of this chapter describes multiple data sources drawn from within the first courses in a program, showing candidates' performance in their field settings.

The Role of External Assessments

In addition to their course-based evidence of learning, candidates are regularly expected to draw together their reflections on their advancement in the program across multiple courses and engage in "external assessments" that may be faculty interview assessments (mentioned earlier), small-group simulations (e.g., the social interaction assessment), or portfolio presentations. These "externals" have multiple features of externality—they reside outside of courses, and often involve external practitioners and community partners as evaluators (for example, practicing teachers who are alumni of the college, or area principals). The externals do not carry credits, so they don't require additional financial burden for candidates, but do have course names and numbers, so that they can be required at particular points in a student's program.

A midprogram assessment, ED 399 (for undergraduate students)/AC 636 (for graduate students): "Vision of Teaching," requires candidates to look across more courses and write an evidence-based narrative with specific prompts that were drawn from language used in the edTPA: How does the candidate come to know what their students already know with respect to the content they will teach? How do they come to know their students as individuals and as members of multiple communities and contexts? How do they use what they know to design for instruction, create methods of assessing student understanding, and make sense of assessment data? After writing an initial reflection, this assessment also requires faculty or small-group engagement in which the reflections are shared. Candidates then are introduced to the rubrics for the edTPA for their content area and developmental level, self-assess in relationship to the rubrics, and set goals for the next two semesters of field practicums.

Prior to advancement to student teaching, candidates create a reflective longitudinal evidence portfolio aligned with all ten Wisconsin Teaching Standards and all five Alverno Advanced Education Abilities, as well as the Council for Exceptional Children Standards for special education licensure candidates. These portfolios demonstrate candidates' readiness to assume the professional expectations of clinical practice. These portfolios are assessed in small groups of candidates by a team of assessors that includes one Alverno faculty and one practicing teacher who holds the same certification as the candidate's program. The candidates are then able to see each other's portfolios as well as engage in a professional goal-setting conversation with their peers and assessors. Candidates who identify or are identified as having areas in need of remediation either revise their portfolios or are required to complete additional field experience prior to reattempting the portfolio and advancing to student teaching.

The ultimate experience through which candidates demonstrate that they have what it takes to teach occurs, of course, in their clinical practice semester. All initial licensure candidates complete the edTPA within their first 9-week placement of the 18-week state-required student teaching experience. Alverno was one of three Wisconsin institutions to pilot the edTPA, having been selected in part because of the institutional commitment to performance assessment, and the first institution in the state to implement the assessment with all candidates for official scoring. This transition was much easier to negotiate at Alverno because the edTPA had a high degree of similarity to a prior performance assessment required during candidates' student teaching semester. Like the edTPA, that assessment required that candidates design a sequence of lessons, describe and justify their rationale for their plans, be observed by their supervisor teaching at least one lesson, and analyze and interpret the student learning data generated during the sequence.

Unlike the edTPA, the prompts for candidate commentary, justification, and analysis were more broadly based, as were the rubrics for evaluating candidate practice. As a result, when the edTPA was presented to Alverno faculty, they immediately saw points of connection between a prior source of data and the new state-proposed requirement. In fact, faculty embraced the higher degree of specificity afforded by the prompts and rubrics in the edTPA. The edTPA adoption process has not gone entirely without controversy—faculty have raised concerns about the high testing costs required of elementary candidates, which approach $1,000 for all state-mandated tests. But the content, the expectation, and the data generated by the summative performance assessment of teaching was uncontroversial. Faculty have added categories of inquiry around the edTPA scores and student work, things that the assessment cannot show: What, if any, impact does the licensure pathway have on candidate scores? Or poverty level of the placement school? Or whether the candidate is a first-generation college student? (Answers so far: Some, None, and None).

WHAT WE HAVE LEARNED: BUILDING CAPACITY TO SCALE MOUNTAINS OF DATA

The above examples only describe a few select experiences where candidates create complex sources of data that stakeholders can then interrogate, but the same is true for each course experience. Institutional values of holistic, authentic, engaging performance assessment hold throughout. This means that opportunities to investigate and problematize individual candidate data, program data, and course data are regular, strategic, and tightly linked to continuous program improvement, for example, used as supporting evidence in annual Continuous Review Process visits with the Wisconsin Department of Public Instruction. In considering candidate admission to student teaching, for example, students enrolled in the advancement to student teaching portfolio course post their work to the portfolio system, which enables the faculty to directly examine each student's work to determine her readiness for the challenges of clinical placement, rather than rely on personal experiences and "anecdata."

Within the Division of Education, data retreats and meetings among the education faculty often involve bringing up the data from candidates' portfolios to test assumptions and provide evidence for claims. In the fall of 2014, for example, Alverno began official scoring for the edTPA after several years of internally scoring the assessment. In analyses of the official scores, faculty were able to trace and test scores on the edTPA back through the portfolio system, examining candidates' evidence of prior learning, to see how, as one example, a candidate's ability to engage in evidence-based writing developed over time, or how video of candidates' development might show an increasing ability to ask generative questions of students while teaching. When confirming readiness to progress to student teaching, or when counseling out, these rich data sources inform evidence-based decision making. Alverno faculty have been motivated to use program data because the data are interesting, comprehensible, and useful. Because of the variety of data gathered on (and by) each candidate, the assessment system also supports a case-methods orientation (Shulman, 1992). This ability to look back at a single candidate's work also supports difficult conversations when candidates are not attaining expected outcomes, as with Ashley's case. When counseling out, a compassionate approach that keeps the needs of all of her potential future students in mind means that we use the data to help reach a consensus about the candidate's fit for the demands of the profession.

Data as Renewable Resource

Alverno students' work itself is the most generative source of data—an infinitely renewable resource for engagement, interrogation, and program improvement. As required by the state of Wisconsin, Alverno teacher candidates all take required standardized assessments (which may include the ACT, PRAXIS Core, PRAXIS II, Foundations of Reading Test, and the edTPA), and so those scores are available and shared. Other data sources emerge from courses; each candidate compiles evidence drawn from each preclinical field practicum course, for example: lesson plans taught, video of the candidate's work with children, evaluation forms from supervising and cooperating teachers, and self-assessments related to all of those data completed by the candidate.

In addition, the Alverno Division of Education works regularly with colleagues in Alverno's Office of Educational Research and Evaluation. These staff members coordinate, deploy, gather, and analyze completer surveys and employer follow-up studies to help discern patterns of strength and growth in the unit. Those data suggest that Alverno teachers in their 1st year of practice are considered to be very strong as compared to graduates from other local institutions; perhaps because of the institution-wide emphasis on self-assessment, completers rate themselves slightly lower than their hiring principals (Zeichner et al., 2000).

This institutional orientation toward authentic data gathering, interrogation, and use also means that when new expectations or mandates arise there is a strong internal language to talk about what these changes mean for candidate learning and program revisions. The recently mandated Foundations of Reading Test meant that literacy faculty looked back at candidate work and course documents in their courses to identify strengths as well as areas where they would need to make changes in order to ensure that candidates had opportunities to attain outcomes measured by the test.

With the edTPA, because of its significant similarity to a previously existing performance assessment in student teaching, faculty were also able to recognize those points of consonance and make smaller tweaks necessary to incorporate the new instrument into the program.

Identifying Opportunities for (and Within) Change

With a strong community, change is not a threat as much as an opportunity to be resilient and inquiring. Moving from a decade of experience with a bespoke portfolio system to a third-party partner has brought up differing levels of fluency among faculty in their ability to translate what they did before to document candidate performance within and across courses to a new system. Rubrics might be identical, or they might require that faculty mine their creativity to find where a criterion fits, how it connects with standards, and how it will result in reports that will be useful.

Alverno is also in a state where public dialogue about the teaching profession and national economic trends have resulted in a significant decline in the number of candidates statewide (as much as 30% in a 5-year period at some institutions.) At the same time, being in a large high-poverty urban context and facing impending retirements of large numbers of Baby Boomer veteran teachers, there is a demand for excellent teachers in all P–12 settings, particularly those of greatest need and highest faculty turnover. Alverno has seen increasing numbers of our candidates in high-demand pathways (for example, Special Education) become hired as practitioners of record while they pursue licensure. The college partners with Teach for America (TFA)–Milwaukee, another population of provisionally licensed teacher candidates. Both of those candidate groups have unique needs related to their roles as teachers of record. They may also have less time available to reflect on their teaching, or prepare long-form lesson plans for observations, or gain perspective from multiple and varied preclinical placements. But they have extensive and deep opportunities to practice, chart a course, and create relationships in school communities. In the case of the TFA partnership, the earn-your-way-to-licensure approach may be in tension with the external partners' vested interest in ensuring that candidates persevere through their entire 2-year commitment. The college faculty plan to adapt key course assessments and benchmark externals to ensure that each pathway maintains high standards and yields practitioners worthy of the children they will serve.

WHAT WE WISH WE HAD KNOWN

The work in Alverno College's Division of Education to interrogate and use candidate performance data rests on 40 years of institution-wide collaborative work. But it's not necessary to have an institutional revolution and multiple decades of revision processes in order to generate a dynamic in which data are used as a resource, not a requirement.

The essential question undergirding Alverno's education faculty work is: What is a well-prepared teacher ready to do on day one? What are her habits of mind, hand, and heart? Once that vision of a well-prepared candidate is clearly and explicitly described, then faculty can engage in setting forth the experiences, reflections, and artifacts that will demonstrate with confidence, clarity, and reliability to all interested stakeholders (including, most importantly, the candidate herself!) whether the candidate has what it takes to do the work of teaching. Then faculty and leadership can ensure that time and space are organized so that invested stakeholders can engage in evidence-based conversations about data, including asynchronous collaboration and virtual spaces. The work is hard, but if done well, it's the kind of challenge that educators love.

If we return to Ashley's story, after our intervention conversation, she was offered the option to complete additional fieldwork in which she could receive observation and feedback centered on her areas of growth. She ultimately decided not to pursue teaching as a career, and shared that she'd enrolled in the licensure program more because of her mother's desire for her to become a teacher than her own sense of a professional vocation. The expectations and feedback reviewed in the conversation allowed her to realize she really didn't want to teach, something she had been afraid to tell her mother. The majority of our students do in fact persevere through our program and become reflective practitioners, using the same evidence that Ashley used to self-assess their progress and improve over time. The evidence we gather proves useful for many different kinds of conversations about professional preparation.

People, Tools, Organization

At Alverno, the institution emphasizes the interconnections between teaching, learning, and assessment collegewide. In fact, publications authored by Alverno faculty often connect these as inextricable concepts (e.g., assessment-as-learning, feedback-as-teaching). In the case of teacher preparation faculty and their work, this context supports collective effort toward a shared vision of what an Alverno-prepared teacher should know, believe, and be able to do. Subject differences are less salient; visiting a meeting of the Alverno Division of Education Committee of the Whole, it would not be immediately apparent which faculty are full-time, which are part-time, which are doctorally prepared, which are from content areas outside the Division of Education, which are staff. Tools may be internally designed or externally mandated, and the strong assessment culture and emphasis on evidence of outcomes inform and govern their adoption and use. As a college that for the majority of its history functioned with a faculty composed primarily of women religious and now consists of a majority lay faculty, negotiating nuances related to people and their tools within an organization can be a challenge. What is fair to expect of faculty? How much time should they spend on the extensive narrative feedback necessary for the functioning of the institution and data analysis? What is a reasonable expectation for timeliness of feedback and responsiveness to student concerns? The strong engagement with data and inquiry orientation at Alverno necessitates a commitment on everyone's part to their share, but what a fair share is in an intensive system can be contentious.

Why This Approach Supports, Nourishes, and Inspires the People Who Work With It

Alverno College's founders were a community of women religious, the School Sisters of St. Francis. Though the faculty now are almost entirely laypeople, that sense of mutual ownership of, commitment to, and responsibility for the integrity of the teaching, learning, and assessing model is paramount. Even more importantly, the value of evidence of outcomes is so effectively transmitted to Alverno students that they are positioned powerfully to advocate for the model and to serve as mentors for new and adjunct faculty.

The people matter. Faculty are evaluated and promoted based on explicit criteria and evidence, consistent with the teaching–learning–assessing model. Faculty come to Alverno because they know it positions them to teach, to engage in scholarship, and to have an influence in a different way than almost anywhere else.

The tools matter. A teaching stance that requires generation of evidence aligned with outcomes and evaluated by descriptive rubrics means that the mechanisms for faculty feedback and student self-assessment must mirror the coherence of the pedagogical mission. For the faculty at Alverno, the use of a data system is inextricable from the commitment to learner-centered and ability-based teaching.

And the organization matters. Faculty come to Alverno not via job talks, but through a deep commitment to deeper learning at the higher education level. The value of this work doesn't show up on faculty compensation packages. The interconnected structures of collaboration, faculty generosity with each other in sharing assessment tools and criteria, and a context that is fundamentally optimistic about the human ability to learn and grow is what truly makes the Alverno context one in which learning lasts, for everyone.

The strong teaching–learning–assessing–self-assessing culture at Alverno has its own gravitational pull that enables our small institution to navigate change smoothly. When there is a new instructional or divisional leader, or even a new adjunct faculty member, all members of the community, including the students, have clear and shared expectations of what it means to "do Alverno." Explicit assessments enable faculty to share courses without letting go of the commitment to generate evidence of outcomes. No complex human endeavor, which a college or university program of teacher preparation certainly is, can be perfect. But by focusing on careful selection of faculty and support thereafter, intentional use of tools to gather and make sense of evidence of outcomes, and an organization that continues to grow and improve, we can gradually improve over time. This commitment will drive us forward as we continue to prepare the teachers our city, region, state, and nation's children need and deserve.

REFERENCES

Alverno College Faculty. (1994). *Student assessment-as-learning at Alverno College* (3rd ed.) Alverno College Institute.

Alverno College Faculty. (2015). *Feedback is teaching.* Alverno College Institute.

Loacker, G., & Rogers, G. (2005). *Assessment at Alverno College: Student, program, institutional.* Alverno College Institute.

National Research Council. (2001). *Testing teacher candidates: The role of licensure tests in improving teacher quality.* National Academies Press. https://doi.org/10.17226/10090

Shulman, J. H. (Ed.). (1992). *Case Methods in Teacher Education.* Teachers College Press.

Stiggins, R. J. (2005, September 1). *Assessment for learning defined* [Paper presentation]. ETS/Assessment Training Institute's International Conference: Promoting Sound Assessment in Every Classroom, Portland, OR, United States. http://downloads.pearsonassessments.com/ati/downloads/afldefined.pdf

Zeichner, K., Miller, L., & Silvernail, D. (2000). *Studies of excellence in teacher education: Preparation in the undergraduate years.* AACTE. https://www.researchgate.net/publication/245146165_Ability-based_teacher_education_Elementary_teacher_education_at_Alverno_College

CHAPTER 5

University of California, Santa Barbara

Using Data for Program Improvement in a Research-Intensive University

Tine Sloan and Jennifer Scalzo

> Well, I see them engaging with problems that they've not been willing to engage with before. ELL and Special Education are two obvious examples where our faculty—like every other faculty in every other program I've seen—have floated along engaging in, at a certain level, commitment to rethinking their practice with respect to the inclusion of kids that don't speak English or kids who have learning disabilities. But they haven't really tackled it in many cases and that's true of me too. I've floated along for the last 15 years with a kind of rhetorical response to the need to rethink classroom practice around the inclusion of kids who don't speak English, but I've never learned, gone through the practical rethinking of my practice in a way that gets past the rhetorical level of commitment. I think that people are required to figure that out now. (Program Director, 2002)

In 1998 California introduced legislation (Senate Bill 2042) establishing a comprehensive Learning to Teach System intended to align teacher preparation efforts across undergraduate subject matter coursework, professional education, and induction phases of teacher education. It also included a high-stakes accountability system for evaluating preservice candidates' readiness to teach. The sweeping policy required significant changes to the way preservice programs operated. It proposed new standards for practice—the Teaching Performance Expectations (TPE)—that were to be measured with a state-approved teaching performance assessment (TPA). Though the policy was responsive to a range of professional and political pressures for improving outcome measures in programs (Cochran-Smith, 2001), it was also criticized for narrowing the scope and vision of the previous standards (Whittaker et al., 2001). In addition, the implementation of the TPA imposed serious fiscal and procedural responsibilities on programs without the benefit of new resources. All in all, these highly prescriptive state policies carried many of the dilemmas of high-stakes testing, increased state control, and loss of teacher agency, which had characterized P–12 reform at that time (Mcneil, 2000). It also ushered in a new era for teacher preparation, one that was grounded in accountability and public mistrust, in a complex field that lacked an agreed-upon set of preparation practices.

The field continues to grapple with these issues. We have learned much from working with policy levers aimed at accountability and improvement (McDiarmid & Caprino, 2018; Piety, 2013). In California, post SB2042 has been a time for programs to implement and inform critical processes in accreditation, program improvement efforts, and candidate assessment. That said, what programs did, how their efforts were effective, and how efforts informed change, varied widely. So then does our understanding of how these policy levers affect outcomes for programs. As a result, this chapter offers an account of how one teacher preparation program navigated this new era of outcomes-based accountability. It is a detailed case study that may inform programs that are engaging in similar data use activity. It is also a story that analyzes why the program emerged stronger, more cohesive—and contrary to tendencies of prescriptive policy—more autonomous in the end.

THE CONTEXT OF OUR WORK

The teacher preparation program is housed within the Gevirtz Graduate School of Education at the University of California, Santa Barbara (UCSB), one of 10 campuses in California's public research university system. The campus itself is of moderate size, with approximately twenty thousand students and a thousand faculty. The Teacher Education Program (TEP) serves 80–100 teacher candidates per year—roughly a third of the students in the graduate school (the remaining two-thirds are MA or PhD students). Most of the program's 35–40 faculty have only part-time commitments in the TEP and are comprised of approximately 40% tenure-line, 20% doctoral students, and 40% instructional and supervisory adjuncts (though these percentages have varied over time). Note that the term *faculty* is used by members of the TEP to refer to all people with academic appointments in the program (though this is a departure from its use in the rest of the school which is to solely denote tenure-line faculty). Sometimes we (authors) use *instructor* or *supervisor* to clarify a particular role a person plays.

The preparation program is designed to take one cohort of candidates at a time through a 12-13 month developmental sequence of learning-to-teach experiences (13 months to complete the optional master's degree).

Fieldwork spans the academic year and runs concurrent with coursework; candidates are in school sites during the day and at the university in the afternoon and evening. The program partners with schools that serve a diverse population of students from different socioeconomic, cultural, linguistic, and ability backgrounds. Candidates are placed in cohorts of 5–10 per school site, and each school has a dedicated university supervisor and site-based in-house coordinator. Both supervisors and in-house coordinators support candidates and serve as a liaison to administrators, cooperating teachers, and UCSB faculty. Overall, the postbaccalaureate program is known to be rigorous and selective, and prepares teacher candidates for a California teaching credential plus an optional master's degree in education.

Prior to implementing the new policies, program leadership included a program director and coordinators for each of the credential areas: elementary, special education, and secondary (in the content areas of math, science, history/social science, English, and, at one time, art and world languages). Over time, leadership grew to include a TPA coordinator, a faculty director of the master's program, a credential analyst, and an assessment and accreditation coordinator. All leadership roles were part-time appointments, though the faculty in these positions served other instructional roles in the program.

In the early days of TPA work,[1] program leaders framed an approach that would support faculty in adopting an "inquiry" stance to the policy mandate (Reason, 1988). The approach included a general process for data collection, analysis, and planning—part of an "inquiry–action" process that was to be guided by a self-study of the process. In taking such an approach we (authors and program leaders)[2] understood ourselves to be simultaneously engaged in theory-building, decision making, and evaluation—essentially a process of "praxis" (Freire, 1970) enacted at a programmatic level. We viewed this strategy for responding to state mandates as an appropriate blend of two perspectives on the TPA policies. The first involved the need for critical resistance to those aspects of the policy we saw as reflecting a regressive view of education and teacher education. The second perspective reflected the value and importance of developing better program-level approaches to evaluating the outcomes of our program. The tension between these perspectives was one of the most significant and enduring contexts of the implementation problem.

In the self-study, the research team (a program leader, a researcher, and a faculty member) utilized methods of qualitative case-study research as described by Yin (2003), Merriam (1998), and others to construct descriptive accounts of the events and outcomes of the program change process (Peck et al., 2009; Peck et al., 2010). These accounts were based on several triangulated sources of data, including participant observations, repeated interviews with key participants/informants, written artifacts of faculty and student work, and open-ended questionnaires aimed at assessing faculty and candidate perceptions of their experience with the change process.

We begin our case describing work in the early years of implementing the new policies. We label this "key foundational work" because it proved necessary to later programwide data use practiced at UCSB that continues to this day.

KEY FOUNDATIONAL WORK

In the early 2000s the state was in the process of building and piloting a teaching performance assessment (the CalTPA), while a consortium of universities was building and piloting a separate TPA (the Performance Assessment for California Teachers, or PACT). The state would eventually adopt both as options for programs to use. Several UCSB candidates piloted an early version of the CalTPA in spring 2002. When they completed it, the program director organized a meeting with select faculty and K–12 administrators for the purpose of examining candidates' performance on the tasks. This was a strictly qualitative exercise, as scoring rubrics were not yet available. In later interviews all confessed to entering the meeting with the expectation that candidates would perform quite well. During the meeting participants expressed surprise and dissatisfaction with several areas of candidates' performance. Faculty participants talked of immediate changes to their own practice, and both faculty and administrators raised suggestions about programmatic changes. Given the state's rapid timeline for implementation, change was needed as early as fall. Hence the director recruited several faculty members to serve on a summer task force.

The goals for this task force were to outline plans for embedding TPA tasks into program curriculum and to suggest specific experiences for fall courses. Members studied the tasks, revisited candidate responses, examined program curriculum, and came up with a plan. This was all well and good until presented to faculty. Given the significance of the task force's request (add/change/drop assignments as determined by someone outside your course) and short time frame (courses were to begin in 2–3 weeks), suffice it to say people's reactions were a mix of anger, angst, and ambiguity about what they were supposed to do. Further, many did not see value in changing what they were already doing. It became clear that all faculty needed opportunities to learn in the same way task force members had. Most were in the dark about *how* to support candidates in new ways and *why*. It was one of the program's first lessons in the limitations of top-down directives that require complex change to an individual's practice. Implementation carried on that year with a subset of willing participants, most of whom had been part of the task force.

Alongside that process, program leaders launched a series of bimonthly faculty retreats—full-day and half-day opportunities to learn—that occurred throughout the academic year (and continue on a quarterly basis to this day). Early retreats were opportunities for faculty to conduct careful, collaborative examinations of TPA tasks. They also served to articulate state policy, frame our approach to the work, and provide data for program leaders to guide the implementation process. At the first retreat the director described an approach to the work that combined the implementation of policy mandates with a self-study of this implementation. He framed this approach as an opportunity to make the program visible and accountable to the public while we (faculty and leaders) learned more about program features that supported candidates' developing practice. What ensued was an action–inquiry process that used faculty learning as guidance for leadership's action. The self-study revealed three key *areas of inquiry* that supported implementation work. The first rose from making sense of state policy.

First Area of Inquiry: Making Sense of the Policy

Data from early retreats and faculty meetings revealed that many faculty felt threatened and overwhelmed by the policy mandates. As one instructor expressed, "The amount of information required in order to bring the classes/programs/students together seems overwhelming and politically driven." Several faculty expressed anger and questioned what was "left out" of the state policies. For example, a relatively new instructor–supervisor, a program graduate herself, said, "I feel like it's so linear and we're really taking away from the core of what makes this teacher ed program very strong." And a longtime instructor–supervisor put it this way:

> I looked at it as a process that was very similar to the processes that I had faced as a teacher in terms of policy changes. And to me the writing was on the wall very visibly. So I entered [this process] with a very strong concern for maintaining and extending a particular vision of the profession within the program.

Leaders planned two retreat activities to address these faculty concerns. First, they asked the faculty to write about and discuss the question, "What would you want a graduate to report that they took away from this program?" From this, the group created a list of values and goals. Second, the faculty worked in small groups to study the text of four documents: the program's current mission statement, two sets of state standards for candidate performance—the Teaching Performance Expectations (TPE) for preservice and the California Standards for the Teaching Profession (CSTP) for inservice—and the TPA tasks. They were then asked to consider the following questions:

1. What values and images of teachers and teaching are reflected in each of these four documents?
2. What policy changes are evident as one moves from the CSTP to the TPE, and to the TPAs?
3. Considering our stated values and goals, what is missing from the new policy frameworks?
4. What are the implications for our policy implementation work this year?

The faculty's reaction to this work was captured in free-writes at the end of the retreat:

> Reformulating our mission statement is important, as is the notion that we do not merely tailor our program to meet the TPEs and TPAs, but we embed them within our own larger mission.

> I was really impressed with the responses that we gave, as a group, to what we considered were the main components and priorities for teachers in the classroom. It was nice to realize we are all on the "same page."

> I think it's pushing people to think about: What is this program supposed to be doing to prepare these teachers to go out into the field, and what does it really mean if we say that this is a program that is preparing teachers to work with diverse learners, English Language Learners, and to focus on equity and access?

At the next retreat the program director brought a synthesized list of Valued [candidate] Outcomes for the groups' consideration. Discussion centered on what to do with them and how we would know if candidates achieved them. One person pushed for some type of assessment process of the Valued Outcomes. Another person added that they might collect examples of student work over time. Several faculty members pushed the idea that if we assessed the constructs we valued, it would raise their level of importance on par with the high-stakes TPA. Taking shape was a concrete response to concerns about what was perceived as left out of the policies.

Thus began a process of *productive dissent* that program leaders found important to developing a *culture of inquiry*. They came to understand this process as ensuring that dissenting voices had space, not just to push back on what they did not like, but to shape a productive response to external pressure to change. In fact, the threats to faculty's work served to mobilize important learning and improvement of the program's work. It meant that faculty had to collectively come to an understanding of what they valued and what they expected candidates to leave the program with. They also needed to create change in their own practice.

A Second Area of Inquiry: Faculty Learning About Practice (Their Own and Others')

While all faculty were making sense of the policy in relation to their values, several were implementing formative work designed to increase candidate success on this high-stakes assessment. Our self-study focused on understanding what all faculty were learning through these processes, and used this lens to examine program and course artifacts, field notes, and interview responses. With respect to implementation work, we found faculty engaged in both collaborative and individual learning processes. Both processes supported programmatic learning.

The collaborative learning process. One type of collaboration that had pre-existed the implementation efforts were a number of *communities of practice* (CoP) in which a group of faculty coalesced around the practice of supervision or around instructional content (e.g., literacy or English language development). We have several examples of CoPs in our data, and through the self-study came to understand their importance to programmatic change. We illustrate with one CoP which involved a group of three instructors who worked together across the year teaching the CLAD courses (Cross-cultural Language and Academic Development). One member was a long-term program leader and instructor, another a new faculty member who was both an instructor and a supervisor, and the third, a doctoral student who was teaching in the program. They called themselves the "A-team," a pun based on the fact that their names all started with "A." Together these instructors struggled to make sense of the TPAs in the context of their joint engagement in the work of teaching. One of the members described the process this way:

> I think what really helped me this year was being able to make sense out of this in the company of others. The fact that I co-taught that fall class with them mattered. I was sharing it with someone who I could problem-solve with. Here was a puzzle we were all trying to make sense out of and by sharing the resources and the perspective, it actually becomes fun.

She relied on the camaraderie of the "A-team" and the insights and perspectives that came from the fact that each of them had a different set of experiences to bring to the work. In the following vignette, Adriene refers to an incident that took place with their students one night in which the students began to critique one of the TPA requirements, chastising the detailed data that the task was asking them to collect as unnecessary busywork. She reports, "We had that conversation in the parking lot that Tuesday night, where April says, 'Oh my god, that was not my idea of a good time.'" She continues:

> And there were three of us to make sense of it. And so, what might have felt really bad to April, we could help her realize it wasn't all that bad because from where I was standing in the room it wasn't. . . . Or, if I was reading the lesson plans in the fall and they were just horrible, the fact that we were reading them together, we were able to provide a benchmark for each other. It was stabilizing and plus it was creative, and it was collegial, and it just . . . mattered. It really mattered.

These comments reveal the supportive structure these communities held for faculty. And in fact, we came to understand the importance of collaborative supports for faculty engaged in this new, high-stakes, programmatic work. Further, we have many examples in our data of additional CoPs that existed before the TPA and shifted to a more programmatic focus after TPA. For instance, the elementary supervisors saw a need to convey a unified message to candidates about how the TPA was embedded in student teaching. This effort grew into creating a performance record of year-long student teaching benchmarks for use with all elementary candidates and cooperating teachers. They also created a common agenda for their individual weekly seminars in order to ensure more consistency across them. Prior to this, seminar content varied by supervisor and benchmarks for student teaching were quite broad.

Our data also revealed new CoPs emerging out of new necessities. For example, one retreat discussion about lesson planning (one of the TPA tasks) revealed the assorted ways faculty required candidates to design lessons for different purposes (ELL faculty wanted a focus on SDAIE,[3] subject area faculty on subject-specific pedagogy, special education faculty on accommodations, and so on). Candidates had to make sense of the when, what, and for whom (for a class? student teaching? real life as a teacher?) to write a lesson. Faculty agreed it was time for faculty to make sense of this for candidates, and in response, there was a shared effort to determine programwide expectations in lesson design that would better support the Valued Outcomes for candidates. A group volunteered to work on a common lesson-design frame, guided by TPA expectations and Valued Outcomes. After multiple revisions and feedback from the rest of the faculty, the frame was adopted for use in all classes and student teaching across the program. This frame has undergone revisions over time, but it is still a programmatic practice to this day.

The individual learning process. As with the collective learning opportunities, individual sense making also had a place in programwide change. For example, one instructor reflected on her experiences embedding the Teaching Performance Expectations (TPEs) in her course syllabus. She worked through both documents, via color-codes to uncover their relationships:

> And so I realized, for example, that one assignment might address four different TPEs but not all of any one of those TPEs. So again, I highlighted and color-coded all of it so that I could be articulate about it. And that was where I really got it. It was in that process that it started gelling and making sense.

For another instructor and program leader, the process involved actually doing the TPA tasks himself. He elaborates:

> I realized that reading them is one thing, but actually doing them was another. And that's when I actually began to learn. I realized in doing them that this was not an impossible thing at all.

Another instructor described a research stance that led her to approach the TPAs in a particular manner.

> So, I was looking at the TPAs ethnographically and analyzing what was there and what wasn't there, what could be seen. Because that's what I do; I look at student work and I look at language and what's inscribed and I looked at the TPAs that way. I needed to think about that because we were beginning to divide these things up so that we could see how they were going to look within the courses.

The programmatic learning process. Having some knowledge of *what* faculty were learning and *how* they were approaching it was helpful to leadership in several ways. Retreats became the forum for bringing both collaborative and individual learning efforts to a collective level. Sometimes it was as simple as asking faculty to share their processes; other times it was having them organize an activity for the whole faculty based on a process an individual designed. This was the start of a distributed leadership process that became foundational to organizational change. We discuss this further later in the chapter (see also Peck et al., 2014; Sloan, 2013; Sloan, 2015).

A Third Area of Inquiry: Faculty Learning About Candidate Outcomes

This area of learning became one of the most fundamental processes for program development. In May 2003 faculty members were granted access to candidate performance on the TPA for the first time. Faculty were issued common samples of candidate documents to examine. Rubrics were available, but faculty had not been trained to score with them and none of the documents had been scored. So the faculty's analysis was qualitative, guided by rubrics, and facilitated by questions about what they were seeing in the data. They worked on this in small groups.

Data from the small- and whole-group discussions revealed the ways faculty were making sense of what they were seeing—and not seeing—as related to a range of issues. These included acknowledgment of what the program did not cover, a wariness about the validity of the exam, and a realization that candidates might not have been learning what we thought they were learning. As one faculty member expressed in a later interview,

> One of the big areas Rob identified, I had identified, and people in
> that session had identified, was the issue of assessment and how there
> were misconceptions about what assessment should be. There was this
> sort of misconception that tests were contests that you win or lose.
> The idea of really analyzing what a student knows and using that to
> guide your instruction was sort of a nebulous idea that wasn't really
> concrete in the [candidates'] understandings.

In additional to gaining insights into candidates' teaching performances, perhaps one of the most important and frequent comments raised was in regard to the value and potential in collaborative examination of candidate work. A longtime instructor in the program describes this well:

> The most recent meeting [May 2003 retreat], where we brought
> the TPA three student work samples to the table. That was the first
> time there really was an acknowledgment, for me there was a real
> acknowledgment, that we were all doing this together. This feels
> different because those were *our* candidates. And that's why that
> day was so important. It was because we had real candidate work
> and we didn't go off and one read social studies, one read math, one
> read language arts, and then come together and talk. That's how we
> had been doing it. I thought that was just a profound day for me, in
> terms of professional development personally, as well as professional
> development as a program. I just thought it was the best in 20 years
> that I've been here in terms of what the potential can be.

Collaborative examination of this type of work—candidates' work outside one's own course or supervision group—was not a common practice in our program at the time, nor was it likely to be in most programs. Over the next few years we saw the ways in which this collaborative analysis of a program-level artifact became crucial to program change.

Summary of Key Foundational Work

Within this key foundational work, we came to appreciate the value of our collective efforts to make sense of the policy in ways that harnessed productive dissent, helped us understand collective and individual faculty learning, and pushed us to begin collaborative examination of candidate data. This work laid the foundation for a more purposeful data use practice that drove programmatic change. Looking back now, we cannot underestimate the importance of each of these areas for inquiry, and we further elaborate on them in the section "What We Learned." The next section describes our developing practice in programmatic use of data.

MOVING TOWARD PROGRAMWIDE DATA USE

In addition to the foundational work, we identify two areas of continued work that were integral to developing programwide data use. One was the continued use of a complex performance assessment of teaching, in particular the process of scoring that assessment. The second was the self-study process of implementing this performance assessment. The following took place over the course of a decade.

Scoring the Performance Assessment of Teaching

For well over a decade the program used the Performance Assessment for California Teachers (PACT), which was the assessment that grew into the national edTPA (which the program began using in 2014). PACT, like edTPA, had similar requirements in that candidates created a portfolio of teaching artifacts taken from a 3–5-hour slice-in-time of classroom teaching. The portfolio was organized around three basic tasks of teaching: planning, instruction, and assessment. Artifacts included lesson plans, instructional materials, video of their teaching, and student work. Candidates also responded in writing to prompts about their rationale for decisions, reflections on teaching, and analyses of student learning. Each task area (planning, instruction, assessment) required candidates to demonstrate the ways that English learners and students with special needs were supported in learning content. Thus candidates' pedagogy required particular adaptations that were both general and content-specific, which meant candidates needed to integrate what they learned about supporting English learners and students with special needs with what they learned about teaching content. Hence, they had to be in a student teaching placement long enough to understand each of their students' particular needs in order to design instruction and assessment around that knowledge. The UCSB candidates had approximately a month in their semester-long placement before starting

PACT, which they completed by the end of winter quarter (approximately 9 months into their 13-month program).

For the 1st decade of our work, TPA scoring was conducted within the program rather than via a centralized mechanism run by test developers. PACT developers trained lead faculty scorers who then trained other program faculty, who then scored candidates' portfolios within their program. Scoring was based on a 4-point scale using 12 different rubrics covering multiple dimensions of teaching and learning. Each point on the rubric scale included descriptors of practice that characterized different levels of sophistication in the dimension being measured. Scorers engaged in extensive training to learn how evidence in a portfolio constituted a particular level of performance.

At UCSB, scoring occurred in early spring each year. All faculty (including program leaders) were expected to participate. What began as an effort to promote equity ended up a powerful variable in organizational learning and change. We found that when all members of the program were part of the scoring process they had to confront both their own knowledge and skills related to the assessed areas, as well as the effectiveness of their practice on candidate learning. We also found they became more intrinsically involved in TPA implementation and other program-level efforts (more on this below).

We organized the scoring process roughly as follows: New scorers would have a half- to full-day training the week before "scoring week." During scoring week, we arranged the program calendar as much as possible to suspend normal activity so that supervisors would not have observations and course instructors would not be teaching. This signaled the importance of the program-level work and created time and space for people to engage. The Monday or Tuesday of scoring week included a full day for all faculty, who met in one room for updates on the calibration process (and lunch) and then dispersed into small, predetermined groups according to content. Because rubrics were content-specific, faculty calibrated in content groups according to expertise. We made every effort to ensure both supervisors and course instructors were part of each content group. At the end of these 2 days, people had "homework," where groups of three scored another benchmark document and a common candidate's portfolio. Everyone would meet again for a half-day on Thursday or Friday to calibrate the homework documents. They left scoring week with two to three portfolios assigned to them (a very manageable workload), and had another 2 weeks to independently complete their scoring.

When scoring was complete, the director and TPA coordinator organized scores and artifacts for faculty interrogation at the final retreat for the year, generally a month to 6 weeks after scoring. This retreat typically included a collaborative analysis of scores, followed by examination of select artifacts of the portfolio. A faculty member/coauthor of this chapter offers her perspective on this activity in the box below.

FACULTY PERSPECTIVE

As the retreat work begins, the data are presented to us in various forms: raw scores, and aggregated comparative analyses across time and content areas. Additionally, we have the common samples of actual candidate work (PACT documents) in front of us. The intent for today's look at data is different than the scoring/calibration day. Today we are given agency to embark on a journey of inquiry into the data. We are encouraged to see if and how candidates integrated what they learned from coursework and fieldwork. In order to do this, it is necessary to bring multiple perspectives from the TEP program to the work.

In the early days, the artifact was either part of a TPA task with three samples at differing levels of proficiency, or a longer portfolio in each content area—something that was accessible for a 2-hour activity. In later years, artifacts might include other assessments within the program. Leadership chose which artifacts to focus on, generally because it was an area where PACT/edTPA scores were lower, or it was an area we were trying to grow more innovatively. The actual activity would vary from year to year, but the goals were fairly consistent: to allow faculty to share what they were seeing and suggest implications for our work.

Program-level scoring was important because it was the mechanism by which UCSB faculty could *see* how candidates applied their learning in the enactment of their teaching. Because all or most program faculty scored, access was programwide and workload was reasonable (two to three portfolios at 2–4 hours each). All faculty had an opportunity to view scores in the last retreat of the year, but scores only told us where there might be a problem. Candidates' TPA artifacts told us what that problem was. Some artifacts were new opportunities to see candidate practice not normally accessed, for example course instructors' access to video of candidates' teaching and supervisors access to their commentaries on how theory guided decisions. Scoring week included collaborative interrogation of the artifacts as evidence for rubric distinctions—distinctions that depicted different levels of sophistication of practice. These collaborative interrogations, particularly of artifacts faculty may not normally use in their practice, benefited from the diversity of colleagues' expertise. This added to faculty's understandings of each other's and the programs' practice. In addition, discussing evidence vis-à-vis rubric language created a shared language of practice that facilitated communication about candidates' practice.

Unfortunately, at the time of this writing, most California programs, including UCSB's, no longer engage in program-level scoring. In part this was due to a changing accountability landscape that relied more on outcomes, which created a need for stronger warrants on the reliability of scores across programs (Piety, 2013). In part this was driven by the significant resource burden the unfunded mandate posed to programs. Programs managed the burden of scoring in different ways, including paying scorers (some outside the program) or having a subset of scorers (often supervisors) do all scoring. Often scoring practice did not bring value to the overall program's work. And though it brought tremendous value to UCSB, after a decade of PACT scoring the faculty and leaders considered the idea of centralized scoring attractive. The hope was this would open new data practice options with different artifacts outside TPA. To some extent this has been true, but it has been a struggle to engage in the deep data practice that existed when scoring was required. We offer further thoughts on this toward the end of our chapter.

Working with the Self-Study on Implementation

The second area of work integral to developing programwide data use was our self-study process of policy implementation. The program director and researchers used an inquiry–action, self-study process for this purpose. Figure 5.1 illustrates this inquiry–action cycle of program development:

Figure 5.1. Inquiry–Action Study Process

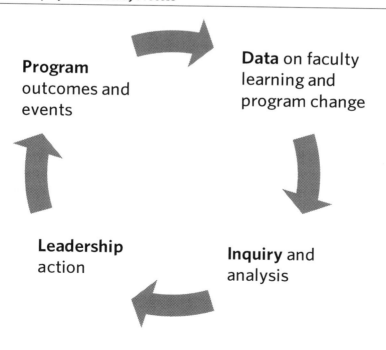

This repeating cycle included four phases. The "Program outcomes and events" phase captured program-level activity (as opposed to individual practice activity), such as faculty retreats, and the TPA scoring week (for local calibration and scoring that included all faculty). It included smaller groups of faculty coordinating across courses or creating programwide artifacts (such as a lesson-design frame, or a student teaching record). It also included policy and practice activity such as modifications to workload, development of a research program, or changes to a curriculum sequence. In the next phase, "data on faculty learning and program change" were gathered directly from these events (observation notes, faculty free-writes, workshop materials), as well as gathered outside of them (faculty interviews, course syllabi, other curriculum artifacts). These data were regularly fed into an "Inquiry and analysis" phase where researchers and program leaders worked jointly to make sense of it (note some data were first processed by researchers to ensure confidentiality). These analyses focused on what faculty were learning, how they were learning, and how the program was changing. Sometimes the analysis was short and informal (a few hours), other times prolonged and systematic (with an actual retreat from campus for 2 days). These inquiries would frequently reveal pockets of faculty work that leaders saw as strategic to programmatic growth. These faculty were often asked to join the "Leadership action" phase, during which leaders used data from the inquiry to plan and execute next steps in the program change process. Leaders often shared what they were finding in their inquiries—what they saw faculty learning and where the program was changing. As programmatic work grew, faculty created offshoots of this inquiry–action cycle to lead other areas of programmatic work.

In each program event, leaders tried to organize data to make faculty learning and program change more visible. For instance, leaders organized comments from free-writes and interviews and presented these to the group so people could see how they were collectively thinking about the work. At other times, leader–researchers inquired into course artifacts or assignments and asked individual faculty to share their work in the public space in order to facilitate programmatic learning. At still other times, leaders created time and space for small groups who decided to take on a programmatic task (like the lesson-design frame), and then organized the opportunity for the larger faculty to engage with it. The point being, each of the research questions on how and what faculty were learning and how the program was changing was both explicitly revealed to faculty and used by leaders to guide program activity.

The self-study revealed some key findings that were integral to pay attention to when designing actions to promote faculty learning and program change. These findings were as follows:

Who sits at the table matters. Findings revealed the importance of not only having everyone participate in collaborative analysis of TPA data, but having people strategically seated for that activity. When this activity included diverse perspectives and expertise, it opened a host of opportunities for understanding the evidence, the program, and others' practice. In addition, because PACT tasks were carried out in K–12 classrooms, those closest to that practice (supervisors) had important expertise to contribute. The following is a recollection of one faculty member (and coauthor) involved with the work.

FACULTY PERSPECTIVE

The work around the performance assessments is particularly significant in that every faculty member has a "way in" to the work, as the supervisors, course instructors, and administrators hold a stake in various parts of the assessment. Each faculty member's expertise is not only valued, but necessary to have a comprehensive understanding of how our work in courses and in the field influences what we see in the data and how we can use it to inform our individual practices. As another faculty member remarked, "PACT [edTPA] work has always been great because of the nature that requires the candidates to integrate from across the program." This integration is a cornerstone to our program.

I recall working in small groups with a set of candidate scores and written work. Sitting with me were a content field placement supervisor, a literacy instructor, and a doctoral student. The engagement with this common text from multiple perspectives ignited critical conversations about what we were seeing. We each tuned in to the parts relevant to the contexts in which we work with candidates. For example, the content instructor noticed that the candidate's lessons were similar to ones she had taught in her methods course. The literacy instructor homed in on the use of questioning and discussion strategies as a means of assessing student understandings. I was focused on the integration of academic language, supports for English learners, as well as the alignment between assessments and evaluative criteria.

It was through the sharing with and listening to my colleagues that I was able to get a more thorough picture of what the edTPA was telling us about the level of integration that was being taken up or not by teacher candidates. Our collective analysis provided us with a way to imagine how we could hone, modify, and adapt our individual practices to strengthen program integration.

Ensuring a supervisor was present in seating arrangements expanded programmatic learning and improvement. From supervisors, people learned when classroom contexts might constrain candidates' abilities to use certain arrangements in teaching (e.g., cooperative group work) or when strategies taught in courses were absent or evident in candidates' everyday practice. Data retreats strengthened the integration of supervisors' work with overall program work, and made the supervisor voice stronger in program discourse. We saw evidence of more cross-practice collaborations between courses and fieldwork, so that course assignments were either coconstructed with supervisors or received feedback from them prior to instructors using them. A regular practice in the elementary program meetings was to have two to three course instructors share their course. These "Windows on our Work" opportunities started as loosely defined presentations of a class that grew into more focused discussions to develop assignments and supervisors' supports for candidates with those assignments.

More voices entered public conversation during scoring and calibration, retreats, and program meetings. What was once a power differential, represented by a small group of experienced faculty who shared a language for their practice, became more broadly distributed as a new shared language that emerged around PACT. Throughout the self-study, course instructors reported their practice was more responsive to elements of K–12 classroom instruction, and supervisors reported their mentoring was more focused on strategies taught by course instructors.

The power of a shared language of practice. Prior to PACT, we were working with the new standards for practice (the TPEs) and trying to articulate how we prepared candidates for each area of practice described in the standards. K–12 classroom assessment was one such area. Discussion and syllabi revealed that people had varied understandings related to terminology, purposes, and foci for preservice candidates. The wide range of people's meanings was not really evident until we each had to evaluate candidate evidence of their assessment practice, using PACT rubrics and calibrating these evaluations with each other. The rubric descriptors, combined with evidence of what candidates were doing, helped faculty develop a common language to discuss practice. The shared language facilitated shared understandings. This became essential to programmatic work. Conversations were becoming grounded in commonly understood evidence of the kinds of teaching practice we strived to have candidates learn and do.

When there is a need to know. Calibration conversations, scoring, and follow-up retreats revealed people's discomfort with some areas assessed by PACT. People admitted that their ability to score reliably required that they learn about dimensions of practice that were not predominant in their work (e.g., supporting students with disabilities). This was the initial impetus for learning outside one's area of expertise. Throughout the implementation years faculty took on this learning in several ways, from creating workshops for colleagues to creating new alignments of practice. The following describes one of many workshop processes over the years.

FACULTY PERSPECTIVE

Our full-day retreats typically have multiple topics, tasks, and leaders. I have had the opportunity to present my ongoing work to my colleagues at these retreats. Faculty are given the opportunity to educate each other and engage in topics with which we have expertise. We are all seen as and valued as having expertise by not only our director, but by our colleagues.

Some of these opportunities to educate each other grew out of a need to understand the language of the performance assessment (PACT or edTPA) prompts, requirements, rubrics, and our candidate work. Throughout the years of scoring PACT and the first years of transitioning to edTPA, several faculty members voiced that academic language was something that was unfamiliar, at least in the way that it was framed in the rubrics for PACT and edTPA. Looking at the performance assessment data together gave us a programmatic reason for *all* to care about academic language and understand the way the concept of academic language was framed in PACT/edTPA. The confusion around academic language prompted my colleagues and me to take on a leadership role to help other faculty members better understand academic language, as well as to enrich our developing understandings.

My colleagues and I began by presenting what we teach our teacher candidates about academic language. This allowed us to have a common text and a common language between teacher educators and our candidates. With this as a foundation, we then used candidate work and the PACT and edTPA rubrics to distinguish between levels of performance and "what counts" in our candidates' work as a comprehensive level of understanding of academic language.

The need for this particular professional development grew out of a need to deepen our understandings about academic language for edTPA, but the outcomes of those conversations had greater implications programwide. One outcome was that we as a faculty now have a deeper understanding and appreciation of discourse and the explicit attention to academic language as an integral part of teaching and learning, not just something for TPA.

Other faculty-led groups emerged to work on issues identified in data retreats. For example, when TPA artifacts revealed a cursory response by secondary candidates to address their students' literacy needs, a group of faculty from across disciplines worked over several years to develop strategies to improve candidates' literacy teaching in all content areas. These new communities of practice offered ways for faculty to learn from each other, as evidenced in program conversations, new co-teaching arrangements, and guest teaching in each others' courses. In one guest teaching activity, the ELL instructor went into several different content methods courses and taught a session on subject-specific SDAIE methods with the content instructor. We also saw faculty choose to co-teach courses rather than teach their course sections separately (even though they received workload credit for one course only). They also suggested different course sequencing in the program curriculum.

People were taking the lead on programmatic change and had some autonomy to do so. There was no additional compensation for the hours spent on this programmatic articulation work, though leadership paid constant attention to supports they could provide (again, data from these efforts revealed where a teaching assistant (TA) or graduate student research assistant (GSR) might be money well spent, or where a simple lunch provided for a working group went far in signaling appreciation and support). Leadership also provided retreat forums to bring faculty's new work into the public space. This allowed people to share what they were learning, what candidates were learning, and how TPA results were reflecting these efforts. The "need to know more" was an impetus for processes that grew throughout the program. The synergy and reciprocity evident in new alignments were integral to improving program practice. They also energized faculty. To reiterate the earlier quote from the "A-team," working in collaboration and having influence on changing the program meant "it really mattered." And with TPA data they had evidence of their efforts to change candidates' practice. This visible, public evidence was a very powerful motivator.

Creating shared responsibility requires practice to go public. When all faculty scored, candidate outcomes became visible to all. When engaged in collaborative sense making about what they saw, faculty became more knowledgeable about each other's practice. We believe this public visibility created some important opportunities. First, we saw many instances in self-study data where people felt more accountable to how their practice shaped candidate outcomes. Second, we saw a collective responsibility emerge for these outcomes. One instructor reports:

> And we looked at the PACT data [during a faculty retreat] and
> realized that academic language sucks. It was so bad. I stood up and
> apologized to everybody. And Chris said, "Why should it be your

responsibility? It should be all of our responsibility." So the next year our professional development focused on academic language.

People were more attuned to the program's effectiveness as a whole (and their part in that) as well as how their practice was supported by that effectiveness (in other words, how other instructors and supervisors built on or reinforced what they were teaching candidates).

Creating a Culture of Inquiry

The self-study informed our response to policy pressures in ways that preserved people's willingness and excitement and sense of purpose. The inquiry–action process was a powerful tool for leaders to grow programmatic data practice, which in turn created program cohesion. Our engagement with data created a culture of inquiry and evidence that has improved the preparation we provide our candidates. It has also been responsive to the many policy mandates that come our way (and there have been many). Figure 5.2 illustrates key program changes uncovered in the self-study data of our early work that we believe contributed to this culture of inquiry.

WHAT WE LEARNED

Chapter 1 of this volume describes the theoretical framework each of us use in our case study chapters to analyze and present what we have learned about our data practice. It is also a framework the director of UCSB program used to guide her work in leading the program. The framework (see Figure 5.3) parses the dimensions of data use work into those related to the conceptual and material tools used to carry out the work, those related to the organizational policies and practices that shape the way the work is carried out, and those related to the values, beliefs, and motivations of the people involved (McDiarmid & Peck, 2007). Each construct is used below to describe the interrelated processes surrounding data use practice that changed the UC Santa Barbara program.

Tools: Working with Assessments That Facilitate Programmatic Data Practice

Several features of the teaching performance assessment tool contributed to our ability to develop programmatic data practice. One feature was that it measured multiple dimensions of teaching (e.g., supporting students with special needs, teaching English learners, using content-specific pedagogy, applying classroom assessment principles), which candidates learned in multiple places across the program. In order to score all dimensions faculty

Figure 5.2. Early Programmatic Changes That Led to a Culture of Inquiry

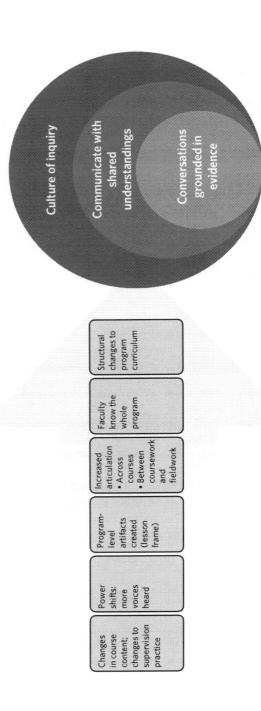

Figure 5.3. The Interdependence of Measurement Tools, Organizational Practice, and Faculty Engagement

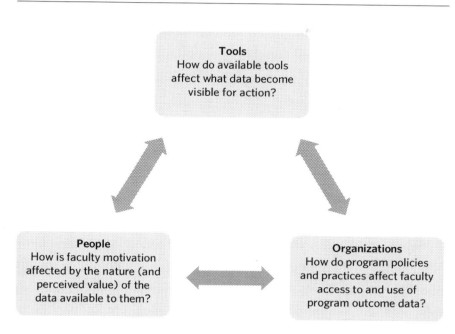

required learning opportunities to expand their expertise, which also served to further their understandings of the whole program. The fact that the TPA was not owned by any one course or field experience further enabled whole-program learning in ways we had not previously experienced. As one instructor describes it:

> I think the nature of our conversation has changed because we now have student work on the table. It is now not just "oh that came from Adele's class or Evan's class," now it is a common set of work that all of us are needing to support. Each of us is supporting it in different ways, but all of us are supporting it together. That has been more the focus of our conversations—how can we in concert be playing the same tune and speaking the same language so that we are not playing a different tune? I think it has really helped with program articulation in ways that were—I will speak for myself—unexpected.

The TPA also attempted to measure the holistic outcome of these dimensions or constructs of teaching practice. Candidates needed to demonstrate, in a slice-in-time of teaching, that they had considered and integrated multiple constructs to enact teaching. This integrated application of a candidate's preparation was perhaps one of the most important contributions of this tool. It revealed shortfalls that we believe are endemic to most preparation programs. Our program, like most, disassembled constructs of teaching into specific course- and fieldwork experiences in order to build proficiency of each construct. And people had thought very carefully over the years about how to design our program to do this. Where we fell short was in providing candidates with clear and consistent programwide supports to reintegrate constructs when enacting teaching. It was fairly common when first working with TPA data to hear faculty express dismay over the fact that what they taught was not what they saw in candidates' teaching.

A final feature to note was that TPA artifacts were varied and provided different windows into practice (e.g., video, analysis of student learning, lesson plans). This helped faculty build a more complete understanding of what candidates were doing. It provided windows previously unavailable to them. And rubrics facilitated their understandings by providing language for evaluating practice revealed in these windows.

In summary, each of these TPA's features afforded faculty opportunities for deeper learning about candidates' capabilities. It also expanded their learning about the program (when facilitated by organizational practices explained below). That said, the tool also created constraints to program work. It was a very big assessment that took up a great deal of everyone's time—candidates', faculty's, and leaders'. These requirements were often at odds with workload conventions and the research culture of the school. Its size threatened to monopolize the curriculum. Working with the tool required attention to organizational practice that would maximize affordances and minimize effects of these constraints.

Organizations: Structural Changes That Facilitated Improvement

Faculty retreats were one organizational practice created to maximize the TPA's affordances. One of the first things faculty did in retreats, and between retreats, was interrogate the validity and value of the tool for any kind of use. Without this opportunity there was little chance PACT would get used for more than compliance of a mandate. It is why we describe faculty learning processes in such detail in the "Foundational Work" section above. It was vital to understanding the complex assessment and what it might offer. Once data hit the table on a regular basis, we moved far beyond a compliance stance. That move was carefully structured in the beginning, informed by the self-study. Over time these structures have become program norms for what people can expect. For example, in a retreat one can expect to learn something new, engage with data, work with colleagues in diverse roles, contribute expertise and have it heard, take on a leadership role at any time to conduct next steps, and bring private work to the program-level space.

Creating time and space for the work was one of the most important structural supports our self-study pointed us to. Faculty retreats were one space–time mechanism. They were only meant to be used during the 2-year policy transition timeline designated by the state. Nearly two decades later we still engage in quarterly faculty retreats. They are an event faculty look forward to and many are loath to miss.[4]

As much as possible we held retreats in venues outside the university (including the director's home), to create a space for engaging in TEP that differed from daily demands. We provided good food and built in time to simply catch up with each other. We celebrated new babies (who were always welcome to attend) and life events. There was a great deal of laughter that punctuated these days.

Another practice to create time and space included repurposing monthly program meetings to serve as follow-ups to retreats. Information issues were relegated to print/email so shoulder-to-shoulder time could be used for program work (such as the "Windows on our Work" process described above). Another practice was rearranging the program calendar for scoring week, freeing faculty from observations and class sessions. And another was the support leaders provided when groups of faculty took the lead on developing programmatic work. Such supports included TAs, GSRs, room space, food, and, most importantly, time in retreats and meetings to bring their work to bear on programmatic change.

Workload was another organizational structure that required attention. In the research-intensive culture of the school, PACT scoring and collaborative data analysis were not part of the tenure process for research faculty, nor a part of doctoral preparation, nor were they part of workload for adjunct faculty. Regardless, within this institutional culture many were able to change the nature of their work. For example, leaders encouraged researchers to take up programmatic research opportunities and provided graduate student resources and other funds as able. These researchers had access to candidate data and most faculty were willing to participate and

---

A RETREAT DAY

It is another retreat day, and the room is filled with lively conversation over food and coffee. Before we settle into the content of the retreat, we introduce ourselves and our roles within the teacher education program. While this may not seem to be a particularly remarkable practice, as I hear the multiple roles of my colleagues, I am always astonished by the expertise we have in this room. These introductions signal the inclusive nature of our program, whereby everyone has specific knowledge and skills to contribute to the work. We need each other to do this work well.

learn alongside them. For doctoral students, one faculty member taught a course on assessments of teaching that engaged students in the PACT scoring and data collaboration work alongside TEP faculty. For adjunct faculty, work shifted from more isolated to more collaborative practice, facilitated by the time and space considerations discussed above.

Institutional workload definitions changed more slowly than the nature of the work and, in our opinion, still need significant changes (e.g., the engagement in programmatic scholarship should count for more than "service" in the promotion process; and this type of engagement should be added to adjunct workload definitions). Despite the lag in institutional policy, faculty were committed to change their work. Many were energized by the shift to more collaborative workspaces even though it meant less flexibility with their time. And the time commitment was (is) not inconsequential (program meetings and retreats across the year, small-group meetings to articulate across class- and fieldwork, and other programmatic work like admissions interviews). Competing demands on people's time and the significant learning curve for new faculty continues to pose challenges in the absence of broader institutional policy change. And now, teacher candidates are quick to condemn a faculty's practice that does not make deliberate connections to other parts of their program. Arguably the job got harder. So why do people engage in it so passionately?

People: Supporting Their Practice, Enabling Programmatic Practice

One of the greatest advantages to working in teacher education is that our colleagues are teachers, most of whom bring a high level of integrity, passion, and sense of greater purpose toward their work. For them, teaching can feel intensely personal. We have seen course evaluations bring more than one colleague to tears. Nias proposes that "teachers' personal and professional identities are often so inseparable that classrooms and schools become sites for their self-esteem, fulfillment, and vulnerability" (Nias, 1996, as cited in Uitto et al., 2015, p. 124). We think this important to consider when structuring reform efforts. We learned to pay attention to policy levers that prescribed people's practice and could be seen as threatening to autonomy.

We ask the reader to recall people's initial reactions to the TPA in general and to the recommendations of the summer task force to change people's course assignments (not good). We saw how "productive dissent" was important to maintaining people's passion and motivation for the work. This dissent process was not just about an opportunity to be heard, it was about channeling appropriate criticism in ways that increased opportunities for people to engage in work that they cared about.

Understanding the ways emotion, integrity, and identity contribute to what motivates people in their individual practice was an important foundation upon which to understand how people developed a *collective motivation* to do program-level practice. It makes sense that the motivation to hold one's own practice to a high standard was precisely what supported a collective motivation to create new programmatic practice. So rather than top-down recommendations for changing practice, our work revealed that when TPA evidence made visible the ways in which an individual's practice was not being taken up by candidates, these individuals sought answers. Because the TPA also uncovered the interdependence of effective preparation practice, people were motivated to learn the ways different roles and expertise came into play. When provided with opportunities to learn and collaborate, there was no stopping the momentum. We believe that a shared responsibility for the work emerged when everyone's voice, practice, and innovations were seen as necessary sources in the improvement of program practice. As one supervisor recently noted:

> As individuals, I feel like I can go to anybody—and I do it—to be able to ask questions that for me are related to what I think they have to share with me. Each of us has our own strengths, and I think we use each other very wisely. That goes beyond the supervisors' network. That is continually moving.

This environment also required a democratic discourse and trust among its members. We saw that as cross-practice collaborations grew, power differentials lessened (e.g., supervisors' voices were more present). We saw that within communities of practice people provided emotional as well as structural supports for the work (and created work that "mattered"). People developed a shared responsibility for candidate outcomes, which created safe spaces to discuss each other's practice.

These safe spaces also required the director to pay attention to and act on cases where an individual's participation undermined trust and commitment and equity among colleagues. Sometimes faculty needed extra supports to learn the work of TEP, sometimes their contributions were repurposed, sometimes faculty chose to leave, sometimes they were required to leave. Whatever the outcome, and no matter how daunting higher education processes might seem to a leader, the express and public attention to issues of equity, safety, and shared responsibility is a key responsibility to their colleagues. As the TEP director of many years recently stated:

> TEP faculty are what make this work so joyous and so good. I look around now and do not see one person I believe is not being effective, and this was not always the case. But we're here now. And it makes such a difference in the work. I can honestly walk into any meeting, any retreat, and hand things over to any number of people to lead. I trust them, I learn from them, and so does everyone else. It's also why

I can wholeheartedly and honestly commend them for their work, every time I see them.

WHAT WE KNOW NOW THAT WE WISH WE HAD KNOWN THEN

If we were starting this work again, there are a few things we would focus on differently. In particular we would conduct more research on program outcomes to contribute to the research-intensive mission of the school, to inform the field, and to inform our work. To date, programmatic research has been idiosyncratic, based more on researcher's interests than program needs. We think a better strategy would be to create a process that systematized opportunities for faculty and practitioners to come together to determine research problems worth investigating and support one another to do it.

A second improvement would be to find more ways to engage our K–12 partners in the TPA work. We scraped together financial supports to engage K–12 partners in our processes, but ultimately these efforts were not robust enough or widespread enough to make much of an impact on our mutual practice. Instead, we require a process for the mutual development of a collaborative data process that provides mutually beneficial growth in each of our practices as teachers, teacher educators, administrators, and the like. We think this is possible.

A third issue we wish we paid attention to was developing a data platform and process that utilized the plethora of data now required for accreditation. We need to determine how to make data available to faculty in ways that promote the deep inquiry we experienced with our TPA work. At the same time that local scoring of the TPA diminished, data reporting increased. Accreditation now requires multiple data sources. We have not kept pace with the requirements in ways that allowed for broad faculty engagement with data inquiry. We look to other efforts to inform our work here in future (e.g., Bastion, Henry, et al., 2016; Bastian et al., 2018).

A final issue would be monitoring our rate of change. We became so good at responding to what our data were showing, and so motivated to try new things, that we had been in a constant state of change for well over a decade. Not only were people feeling overwhelmed, we were not getting adequate feedback on the changes we made. We have to move forward carefully and thoughtfully.

CONCLUSION

As we reflect on this long chapter describing nearly two decades of work, we want to conclude with the importance of "stance" in responding to change.

We believe the success in our response to mandates were due to thoughtful and strategic management of essential tensions between resistance and inquiry, between autonomy and compliance, and between what Wenger (1998) refers to as "reification" and "participation." We see the importance of managing these tensions in ways that supported people's identity development within the larger community—an identity that is tied to the power to contribute to and negotiate changes in the work at any time. It is why we state in the beginning that contrary to what many experience with top-down policy mandates, the process at UCSB left people feeling autonomous yet connected, excited, and engaged. The challenge is always how to continue the work and how to bring new people in when such a collective wealth of learning is required to do the work now. We have found the way to do this is to continue to create opportunities for each member of the TEP community to participate meaningfully in the ongoing renewal of the program. One faculty member's comment illustrates this rich phenomenon:

> One of the things that, for me, animates all the work, keeps it moving, is the flexibility and purpose that is true of most of these conversations. . . . What I mean is, it's always possible that a conversation is going to break into a questioning of our purposes, like "What are we doing here in teacher ed?" It's always possible that the conversation becomes "What counts as good teaching?" That's a big deal. I'm always excited about that conversation. It keeps it moving. The possibility, the flexibility of the purposes of these conversations means that they're alive. The end goal isn't inert. "Animate" may be the right term. In the process of trying to figure out whether or not this one student is minimally competent, we might wind up having to talk about what we think it means to be a teacher educator. That's pretty cool. That keeps it alive.

When we have this, we want to come to work, even when the work is hard.

NOTES

1. Our account of the early years is based on the research and writings of Gallucci, Peck, and Sloan (Gallucci et al., 2005: Peck et al., 2006).
2. The authors use "we" throughout this chapter to represent the collective views of leadership, researchers, and faculty—in essence, the participants of the program. Together, the authors served in all of these roles.
3. Specially Designed Academic Instruction in English
4. One coauthor served 14 years as the program director and was the recipient of countless emails expressing dismay when someone fell ill or otherwise could not attend a retreat.

REFERENCES

Alverno College Educational Research and Evaluation. (2011). *Follow-up surveys of Alverno prepared teachers and their employers.* http://depts.alverno.edu/ere/pdffiles/intergratoin%20of%20NCATE%202011%20Reporting.pdf

Bastian, K. C., Henry, G. T., Pan, Y., & Lys, D. (2016). Teacher candidate performance assessments: Local scoring and implications for teacher preparation program improvement. *Teaching and Teacher Education, 59,* 1–12.

Bastian, K. C., Lys, D., & Pan, Y. (2018). A framework for improvement: Analyzing performance-assessment scores for evidence-based teacher preparation program reforms. *Journal of Teacher Education, 69*(5), 448–462.

Cochran-Smith, M. (2001). Higher standards for prospective teachers: What's missing from the discourse? *Journal of Teacher Education, 52*(2), 179–181.

Freire, P. (1970). *Pedagogy of the oppressed.* Herder and Herder.

Gallucci, C., Peck, C. A., & Sloan, T. (2005, April). *Leveraging state policy mandates for program improvement: A learning in practice perspective* [Paper presentation]. American Educational Research Association Annual Meeting, Montreal, Quebec, Canada.

McDiarmid, B., & Peck, C. A. (2007, March 16). *Theories of action and program renewal in teacher education* [Paper presentation]. Northwest Association for Teacher Education 2007 Conference, Seattle, WA, United States.

McDiarmid, G. W., & Caprino, K. (2018). *Lessons from the teachers for a new era project: Evidence and accountability in teacher education.* Routledge., https://doi.org/10.4324/9781315312057

Mcneil, L. M. (2000). Sameness, bureaucracy, and the myth of educational equity: The TAAS system of testing in Texas public schools. *Hispanic Journal of Behavioral Sciences, 22*(4), 508–523.

Merriam, S. B. (1998). *Qualitative Research and Case Study Applications in Education* (Rev. ed.). Jossey-Bass.

Peck, C. A., Gallucci, C., & Sloan, T. (2006, June). *Negotiating implementation of teacher education policy mandates through inquiry: A case study* [Paper presentation]. Self-Study of Teacher Education Practices 6th International Conference, East Sussex, England.

Peck, C. A., Gallucci, C., & Sloan, T. (2010). Negotiating implementation of high-stakes performance assessment policies in teacher education: From compliance to inquiry. *Journal of Teacher Education, 61*(5), 451–463.

Peck, C. A., Gallucci, C., Sloan, T., & Lippincott, A. (2009). Organizational learning and program renewal in teacher education: A socio-cultural perspective on learning, innovation and change. *Educational Research Review, 4*(1), 16–25.

Peck, C. A., Singer-Gabella, M., Sloan, T., & Lin, S. (2014). Driving blind: Why we need standardized performance assessment in teacher education. *Journal of Curriculum and Instruction, 8*(1), 8–30.

Piety, P. J. (2013). *Assessing the educational data movement.* Teachers College Press.

Reason, P. (Ed.). (1988). *Human inquiry in action: Developments in new paradigm research*. Sage.

Sloan, T. (2013). Distributed leadership and organizational change: Implementation of a teaching performance measure. *The New Educator, 9*(1), 29–53.

Sloan, T. (2015). Data and learning that affords program improvement: A response to the U.S. accountability movement in teacher education. *Educational Research on Policy and Practice, 14*, 259–271. doi:10.1007/s10671-015-9179-y

Uitto, M., Kaunisto, S.-L., Syrjälä, L., & Estola, E. (2015). Silenced truths: Relational and emotional dimensions of a beginning teacher's identity as part of the micropolitical context of school. *Scandinavian Journal of Educational Research, 59*(2), 162–176. doi:10.1080/00313831.2014.904414

Wenger, E. (1998). *Communities of practice: Learning, meaning, and identity*. Cambridge University Press.

Whittaker, A., Snyder, J., & Freeman, S. (2001). Restoring balance: A chronology of the development and uses of the California Standards for the Teaching Profession. *Teacher Education Quarterly, 28*(1), 85–107. https://www.jstor.org/stable/23478337

Yin, R. K. (2003). *Case study research: Design and methods* (3rd ed.). Sage Publications.

Part III

PROMISING PRACTICES

CHAPTER 6

Motivating Faculty Engagement With Data

Susannah C. Davis and Kristen Cuthrell

It's 9 a.m. on the day of the all-program data retreat, and the room is filling early with faculty, field supervisors, graduate students, and several cooperating teachers, many of whom are graduates of the program. There is a sense of an extended family reunion as people greet one another. The program director briefly welcomes the group saying, "I thought we'd start by welcoming new members of our community." Projected on the screen behind her are pictures of all the new babies born over the last several months, along with a set of photos of all the new mothers. "Okay . . . let's see how good you are at making connections. Who belongs to whom here?" The group erupts with laughter as they try to match babies and mothers.

The tone soon shifts as the group quickly engages in reviewing the carefully prepared agenda for the day. The new edTPA scores are in, and the director has created several handouts that allow program members to see the data in several different ways, including data for the students that they had taught themselves, as well as scores for all candidates. The group quiets as everyone becomes absorbed in examining the data. The program director asks the group to move into program-level teams (elementary, secondary, special education) and interpret the data through the lens of three questions: (1) What do these data suggest we are doing well? (2) What issues/areas appear problematic and need our attention? and (3) What kinds of evidence (e.g., candidate work samples, course assignments, field observations) would help us understand the problem better? The groups discuss these questions for some time, and then report their findings, sharing their ideas and identifying specific areas for deeper inquiry. Ad hoc teams are identified and charged with examining several sources of data related to these issues and returning with recommendations for collective action.

The program director then directs the group's attention to a slide she has prepared showing edTPA scores for rubrics related to "academic language." This has been an area of programwide concern for several years, and the group is eager to see how candidates have performed this year. They have taken significant collective action over the last year to provide technical assistance to each methods instructor, helping them infuse specific performance expectations around teaching English language learners (ELLs) into their methods courses. And the data this year suggest they are on the right track—candidate scores are up, and a sample of candidate work confirms that there is encouraging improvement in their integration of academic language concerns into their lesson planning and classroom assessment methods. In reviewing the gains, the faculty members who have historically held primary responsibility for teaching ELL content observe that it took all of them— methods course instructors, supervisors, and cooperating teachers—working together to achieve the observed improvements. There is a palpable sense that this is a team victory. Later, as the meeting ends, a field supervisor talking with one of the course instructors is overheard saying, "I love these meetings; it just feels like we are all on the same page."

Program leaders face the challenging task of motivating faculty, supervisors, cooperating teachers, administrators, and other program members to come together to collaboratively forge a vision for data use and engage in the demanding and time-consuming work of using data for program improvement. While studying educator preparation programs across the country and then diving deep into the inner workings of program improvement in 10 very different institutions, key strategies emerged for motivating faculty engagement. We open this chapter with a vignette from one of these case studies that illustrates some of the rewards of engaging faculty in the oftentimes challenging and arduous task of data use. Key practices for motivating and sustaining program members' engagement in collaborative data use aimed at inquiry and improvement were skillfully enacted within the meeting in the vignette. We discuss these practices further in the remainder of this chapter, grouping them into four overarching strategies. First, we discuss how to create agendas for collective research and program development. Next, we explore how to invest in program faculty as innovators. Third, we discuss ways to support faculty access to data and collaborative data use activities. Finally, we dive into the relatively unchartered territory of valuing collaborative program improvement work.

INQUIRY ORIENTATION TO DATA USE

It is fundamentally important that all data use work is organized around local program goals and values. This ensures that the work is understood to be about inquiry and learning rather than compliance. Research in teacher education has documented the importance of an inquiry (versus compliance) orientation to data use work (Cochran-Smith & Boston College Evidence Team, 2009; Peck et al., 2010; Peck & McDonald, 2013, 2014;

Sloan, 2013). Our larger 10-case study also found this to be true (Davis & Peck, 2020; see also Chapter 2 in this volume). Additional studies on data use in teacher education have highlighted the importance of an inclusive, inquiry-oriented approach to data analysis and decision making (Cochran-Smith & Boston College Evidence Team, 2009; Davis, 2019; Davis & Peck, 2020; Peck et al., 2010; Peck & McDonald, 2013, 2014; Reusser et al., 2007). Such an inquiry stance to data use should involve multiple stakeholders (e.g., faculty, supervisors, administrators) and often requires organizational supports and incentives. Chapters 7 and 8 explore several organizational supports such as data platforms and making time and space for data use work.

Strategy #1: Building Agendas for Collective Research and Program Development

Faculty are often concerned about the effects of new accountability policies, fearing that local program voice, values, and identity will be buried under new mandates and measures. In Davis and Peck's cross-case study of high data use programs (Davis, 2019; Davis & Peck, 2020), program leaders who were successful in garnering support and engagement for data use from program members often began by reframing accountability to focus on local goals, values, and agency related to inquiry and program improvement. Both these studies and previous evidence (e.g., Cochran-Smith & Boston College Evidence Team, 2009; Sloan, 2013) suggest that program leaders' articulated goals for data use impact how faculty interpret the purposes of data use, which in turn is key to their engagement with the work. In particular, aligning data use work with faculty values promotes engagement (Cochran-Smith & Boston College Evidence Team, 2009; Davis, 2019; Peck et al., 2010).

In the 10-case study, we investigated how program leaders worked to motivate faculty engagement within the changing accountability landscape. Some leaders used "crises"—which came in forms such as budget cuts, new accountability mandates, or the publication of negative outcome data—to create a compelling reason for engagement and collective action (Davis & Peck, 2020; see also Chapter 2 in this volume). Though these crises were generally external to the program, leaders did not approach them motivated by compliance, but instead reframed these external circumstances and mandates as opportunities to advance local goals and values. Failing to bring people together to face these challenges can lead to isolation and demoralization among faculty and staff as people retreat into the silos of their individual work. By focusing on how the program could benefit from changes to existing practice, these crises could provide the motivational context for collaborative program improvement as well as a sense of being "in this together."

In order to motivate faculty engagement in data use work in the face of accountability pressures, leaders worked to preserve a sense of local control. One leader described the function of data use work this way: "[Data use work] isn't just to satisfy an accrediting agency. It isn't just to do the minimum to get approved. It isn't just about satisfying a doubting public. It's really about taking control of your own institution and charting a course for doing what we do better as an integral part of the everyday work" (Dean, GSU). By motivating faculty and other program members to engage these challenges together, leaders created a sense of collective agency (Davis, 2019).

In a multiple case study of three of the high data use teacher education programs from the larger study, Davis (2019) described several relational *bridging practices* that program leaders (and others) engaged to support the coconstruction of a collective agenda for data-informed program improvement. These bridging practices motivated and sustained faculty engagement in data use work by aligning and supporting individual and collective motives, knowledge, responsibility, and agency. By clarifying the values and goals of collaborative data use activities, program leaders made the relevance and importance of collective action visible and compelling, thus creating an evolving sense of purpose around data use work. Key aspects of these practices included articulating and demonstrating both individual and collective benefits of data use, allowing variation in individual engagement, addressing dissent respectfully and productively, and developing shared responsibility for program outcomes (Davis, 2019). A faculty member from GSU described the importance of individuals and the collective mutually benefitting from collaborative data use work: "For us . . . it's not like it's a one way [process]. It's a shared [process]. We get back from it."

In the opening vignette, a program leader carefully orchestrated a data analysis meeting in ways that bridged individual and collective goals. For example, she provided several digestible representations of program outcome data, which were strategically chosen so that each program member would have access to data they found meaningful and relevant to their own practice. In this program and others that we observed, teaching performance assessments (TPAs) were particularly useful in helping faculty connect data

DEAN'S PERSPECTIVE

You're not going anywhere without dynamite, a huge catalyst for change, . . . Value-added achievement [scores], . . . That's a catalyst. The political winds are catalysts. Budget cuts are a wonderful catalyst because it forces you to say, "We can't do things like we did before." I think it was one of Obama's people who said: "Never waste a crisis." (Dean, GSU) to their own practice (see Chapter 2 for more discussion of the affordances and constraints of different data use tools). For example, faculty we spoke to appreciated how candidate work samples provided concrete illustrations of whether or not specific practices covered in coursework or fieldwork were being taken up in classroom practice. The program leader in our scenario strategically gave each group a sample of candidate data that included data from candidates each group member taught and/or supervised, which helped program members connect to program outcome data in a personally meaningful way. She later included activities that moved toward collective goals related to academic language, making sure that she approached the small- and large-group conversations about academic language data in ways that facilitated individual program members' sense of connection to the data and responsibility for candidate outcomes. The holistic nature of TPAs help facilitate this kind of connection by evaluating candidates' performance in ways that transcended individual course- or fieldwork experiences (Bunch et al., 2009; Davis & Peck, 2020; Peck et al., 2014).

Strategy #2: Investing in Program Faculty as Leaders and Innovators

In the 10-case study, program leaders who were able to broaden faculty engagement positioned faculty members as innovators and leaders in the process of forming a collective agenda and implementing data-informed program improvement efforts (Davis, 2019; Davis & Peck, 2020). These program leaders were keenly aware of nodes of energy and interest in both individual faculty and existing communities of practice. They cultivated engagement and commitment to the data use process by inviting individuals and groups to investigate specific issues of interest and to make recommendations for action for the larger program. As leadership responsibilities were taken up by both individual faculty and small ad hoc working groups, program leaders made sure to distribute airtime at program meetings across program members.

We saw successful program leaders provide clear expectations around engagement in data use while simultaneously giving faculty latitude to exercise their professional expertise and autonomy in decision making about programs, curricula, and assessments. High-level leaders had a big impact on whether and how leadership opportunities were distributed in programs. For example, at SSU, leadership by the dean played a role in the culture of collaboration and distributed expertise:

> We have a culture that has been developed by the dean, in my opinion, that allows us, each one of us in this room, to have our moment to shine in our own area of expertise. . . . He helps us to understand our own wonderful role and place in making this big thing work. If you go to him and you say, "I have an idea," he doesn't turn anybody away

about an idea. Then if the idea is really good, he says, "Go with it. Check back with me." If the idea's not too good he says, "Let's talk about it a little bit more," and he'll bring in somebody else to discuss the idea. (Administrator, SSU)

Similarly, a program chair at UA discussed how both she and their dean worked to "[foster] a community in which people recognize that their strengths are being acknowledged and valued." While their dean "got the conversation going" (TEP Director, UA), it was faculty discussing their own goals and concerns, such as better supporting high-needs school settings and English language learners, that drove continued attention to data-informed program redesign efforts.

Faculty, field supervisors, and other staff in many (perhaps most) teacher education programs function in relative isolation from one another, resulting in lost opportunities to learn from one another and a potential lack of programmatic coherence. Programs within the 10-case study often created ways of making individual practice, whether situated in courses or in fieldwork, more visible and accessible to all program members by making time at program meetings to present and discuss specific courses, assignments, evaluation tools, and other artifacts of practice. Program leaders fostered faculty agency and engagement by explicitly asking them for input on goals and program improvement efforts.

When individual and group ideas and experiences became public, they became resources for individual and collective learning and improvement. Think back to the Pirate CODE Implementation Process and the program innovations described in Chapter 3. Faculty were positioned to help determine areas of need in their teacher education program and then were empowered to lead the development and expansion of innovations. Organizational structures were adopted that provided faculty time and supports (i.e., access to data, research tools, travel support) to study different program improvement efforts. In upcoming Chapter 11, the Pirate CODE faculty innovators share their experiences with collaborative research and writing related to structured program improvement efforts. Across the programs in the larger study, we saw that the agency attributed to faculty to help determine the program improvement agenda and decide how they wanted to participate fueled their motivation, and organizational supports helped sustain this work. In the next section, we discuss further different ways programs valued and supported such program improvement work.

Strategy #3: Supporting Faculty Access to Data and Collaborative Data Use

Data cannot inform program improvement if they are not accessible and used. As a faculty member at SSU put it, "Access to different data sets brings about conversations. . . . You have to have conversations." In this program and others in the larger study, additional organizational supports fostered faculty engagement in collaborative data use and decision making conversations. In order to allow faculty and other program members time and space to participate in the time-consuming collective work of data-informed program improvement, program leaders would both integrate data use activities into existing meeting structures (e.g., departmental faculty meetings, program meetings) and create new collaborative structures, such as data retreats (see Chapter 8 for more on making time and space for data use). Providing time and space for routine data conversations strengthens the relationship between faculty identities, program culture, and engagement in data use activities. Involving multiple stakeholders, such as field supervisors, clinical teachers, and tenure-line faculty, is critical in this exercise (Cochran-Smith & Boston College Evidence Team, 2009; Davis, 2019; Davis & Peck, 2020; Peck et al., 2010, 2015; Peck & McDonald, 2014; Reusser et al., 2007).

Once collaborative structures have been created or repurposed for data use conversations, a combination of structural and relational supports help motivate faculty to participate in them (Davis, 2019; Davis & Peck, 2020). Ideally, adjustments should be made to program members' work responsibilities to accommodate new and recurring data use events. For example, one program from the cross-case study suspended all departmental activity (e.g., classes, supervision) for a "scoring week" for candidate performance assessments. Not only was this incorporated into the annual calendar for program faculty, but scoring expectations were written into faculty position descriptions. Organizational supports such as scoring meetings and other open avenues for collaboration are necessary to motivate and extend conversations that bridge data analysis, programmatic decision making, program improvement implementation, and data-informed reflection on program changes. Honoring faculty's agency and expertise in formal and informal data-oriented conversations is equally important.

Data use events are also important venues for faculty access to program outcome data, particularly in digestible forms that help program members make sense of the data. Often some staff members or administrators with explicit data use responsibilities (or, in some cases, working groups of faculty, supervisors, and clinical teachers) would do some initial analysis of program data and create digestible representations of findings to present in meetings. From there, faculty and staff from across the program could further interrogate and make sense of the data and come up with ideas for further inquiry and program improvement. Other times, as with scoring parties, faculty would have access to raw data. These were also opportunities for program members to make sense of program data individually and collaboratively. The TEP director at UL discussed the importance of collaboration during data analysis meetings like scoring parties: "I think the key is having somebody to talk to about it, doing it together. It's not that they're alone doing their scoring and then that's it, they turn it in. It's the opportunity to talk."

The importance of collaboration, communication, and transparency were themes that ran through many of the comments of the faculty and administrators in the cross-case study. In their view, the most important function of the data was to identify important issues for discussion and problem solving.

> If you can give any advice to groups in terms of taking data and then actually implementing it, I'd say the three things that helped us were transparency, accessibility, and then going back to that conversation. Transparency—and I want to thank the Dean for this—is that any time there's a set of data that comes from any of our gods, little g, he gives that to the department heads so we have access to this no matter what it is. Then from there we have the opportunity to share that with specific faculty or to the entire faculty. Then that data is accessible. At any time, at any point, an individual can come and actually look at this particular set of data and decide what they want to do with that particular set of data. Then the conversations, again, because of the transparency, and because you have that data, you are welcome at any point in time to come and talk to anyone sitting at this table and anyone within your smaller groups, and have conversations about what exactly we're going to do about implementing specific projects. (Program administrator, SSU)

In the above excerpt, we see both structural and relational supports at play: faculty are able to access data in a variety of ways, including at various program meetings, and are also given the agency to "decide what they want to do with . . . [the] data." It's important that program leaders allow faculty and other program members not only access to data (see Chapter 7 for more about building useful data systems), but also access to conversations where people make sense of data and make decisions about how to use data-informed insights to change aspects of the program.

This is not easy work—in an age where programs experience increasing pressure to use more and more forms of data, managing data use expectations among faculty's other work responsibilities is a major challenge. Below, a program chair at UA reveals the tension underlying expectations to collect and utilize data and to do it under tight time and budgetary constraints:

> We've really moved to the use of video a lot, and you'll hear instructors say, "I'm literally drowning in video. I have 7 hours for each student." . . . It's part of the sustainability issue, but it's also: we're so data rich now in a way, it's trying to help people think logically and reasonably about how they're going to [manage it]. . . .

I know there's one instructor who had students submit a video for every assignment. It's not surprising at the end of the semester to hear that this person is drowning and is way behind on grading and all of this other stuff. . . . My mantra to faculty is you have to make it so that you can actually teach this course in a reasonable manner. I can't give everybody credit for teaching two classes when it's really only one class. I can't do that. That's not financially responsible.

The ideas described in this strategy related to providing access to both raw and digestible representations of data, making time and space for data use conversations, and supporting collaboration through organizational policies and practices all help faculty incorporate new data use practices into their work. As the quote above highlights, program leaders and other program members need to work together to determine what is feasible and sustainable.

In the next strategy, we discuss how programs and their leaders can provide additional structural and cultural supports to help faculty not only manage new data use work among their other job responsibilities, but also receive unit- or institution-sanctioned recognition and reward for these activities. Such supports can motivate and sustain faculty engagement by explicitly valuing data-informed program improvement work in ways that matter to faculty.

Strategy #4: Valuing Collaborative Program Improvement Work

Existing policies and practices that privilege independent research (and, in some cases, teaching) over collaborative program improvement make it difficult to motivate faculty engagement in program improvement efforts. Many administrators and faculty worry that engagement in collaborative program improvements will take up valuable time and energy at the expense of getting research published. In programs in the cross-case study that successfully broadened engagement in data use among a variety of program members (faculty, supervisors, administrators, staff, and cooperating teachers), leaders found ways to amend unit policies and practices so that data use work could benefit both the individuals involved and the collective program (Davis, 2019).

We observed faculty become more engaged in the work of the program when they were given opportunities that (1) combined individuals' needs for research publication with programmatic needs for data-informed reflection and renewal by supporting the development and dissemination of faculty research related to program improvement; and (2) amended promotion and tenure policies to recognize the time and expertise needed to improve programs. For example, at GSU, the dean instituted new workload policies. The program added a "fourth box" to promotion and tenure policies aimed at expecting and rewarding data-informed program improvement work. Under this new policy, faculty taught fewer classes and were expected to contribute to program-focused research and development. Faculty were encouraged and supported in publishing research related to collective program improvement work and related program innovations, which also benefited them in promotion and tenure processes. Collaborative improvement efforts increased when engagement in data use work provided clear, officially reified benefits for individuals as well as the collective.

At another program, a strong value around collaborative continuous program improvement (informed by data) permeated the institution's culture. At MC, participation in collaborative structures that integrated data-informed program improvement work was an official, recognized aspect of all faculty members' jobs. This included participation in collaborative communities and structures at different levels of the institution (e.g., department, institution, various disciplinary and cross-disciplinary long-term working groups). These expectations were incorporated into promotion and tenure guidelines. As a dean explained,

> I think a big thing is that we are a teaching institution and our research is focused on our work to improve our teaching. That doesn't mean that a good number of us don't do other kinds of research or writing, but we don't get promoted for that. We get promoted for teaching well and for developing systems that support other faculty members.

This institution-wide commitment to continuous improvement resulted in a situation where "it's really easy to do this stuff here now because everybody has bought into these processes and the purpose behind using the assessments and using data" (Dean, MC).

Depending on the mission and emphasis of the institution, valuing data use efforts as part of promotion and tenure processes might look like a fourth-box model in which the work of course development, implementation, assessment, and improvement is supported or continuous improvement efforts are considered an aspect of service requirements. By aligning programmatic policies and practices with a clear cultural value of data-informed program improvement, this work becomes an expected and rewarded aspect of faculty's jobs and serves both individual and collective needs.

CONCLUDING THOUGHTS

Based on our research and experiences, the commitments identified in Figure 6.1 are key to (1) building a collective, inquiry-oriented agenda for data-informed program improvement, (2) investing in program faculty as

Figure 6.1. Motivating Faculty in Data Use

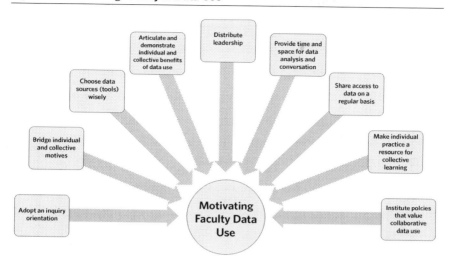

leaders and innovators, (3) supporting faculty access to data and collaborative data use activities, and (4) valuing program improvement—all of which motivate and sustain faculty engagement with data for program improvement.

As a program's data use journey continues, issues of sustainability will arise. One of the main challenges for sustaining new practices is faculty and administrator turnover. When data use policies and practices such as those described above are enacted and institutionalized, engaging, inquiry-based, and meaningful program improvement efforts are more likely to continue despite personnel shifts and other changes. Program leaders must work to motivate initial faculty engagement and sustain a commitment to data use that extends beyond one person or one semester. To stay viable, this commitment must be embedded within the program culture, policies, and practices. In the next few chapters within this "Promising Practices" section, you will find deeper dives into making time and space for data use work, building data systems, and leadership strategies.

REFERENCES

Bunch, G. C., Aguirre, J. M., & Téllez, K. (2009). Beyond the scores: Using candidate responses on high stakes performance assessment to inform teacher preparation for English learners. *Issues in Teacher Education, 18*(1), 103–128.

Cochran-Smith, M., & Boston College Evidence Team. (2009). "Re-culturing" teacher education: Inquiry, evidence and action. *Journal of Teacher Education, 60*(5), 458–468.

Davis, S. C. (2019). *Engaging faculty in data use for program improvement in higher education: How leaders bridge individual and collective development.* Manuscript submitted for publication.

Davis, S. C., & Peck, C. A. (2020). Using data for program improvement in teacher education: A study of promising practices. *Teachers College Record, 122*(3), 1–48. https://www.tcrecord.org/Content.asp?ContentId=23231

Peck, C. A., Gallucci, C., & Sloan, T. (2010). Negotiating implementation of high-stakes performance assessment policies in teacher education: From compliance to inquiry. *Journal of Teacher Education, 61*(5), 451–463.

Peck, C. A., & McDonald, M. A. (2013). Creating "cultures of evidence" in teacher education: Context, policy, and practice in three high data use programs. *The New Educator, 9*(1), 12–28.

Peck, C. A., & McDonald, M. A. (2014). What is a culture of evidence? How do you get one? And . . . should you want one? *Teachers College Record, 116*(3), 1–27.

Peck, C. A., McDonald, M. A., & Davis, S. C. (2015). *Using data for program improvement in teacher education: A study of promising practices.* American Association of Colleges of Teacher Education.

Peck, C. A., Singer-Gabella, M., Sloan, T., & Lin, S. (2014). Driving blind: Why we need standardized performance assessment in teacher education. *Journal of Curriculum and Instruction, 8*(1), 8–30.

Reusser, J., Butler, L., Symonds, M., Vetter, R., & Wall, T. J. (2007). An assessment system for teacher education program quality improvement. *International Journal of Educational Management, 21*(2), 105–113.

Sloan, T. (2013). Distributed leadership and organizational change: Implementation of a teaching performance measure. *The New Educator, 9*(1), 29–53.

CHAPTER 7

Building (Useful) Data Systems

Diana B. Lys and Désirée H. Pointer Mace

Our common work as teacher educators is to prepare educational professionals who are ready to meet the needs of their students, from day one of their professional careers. Our selection, structuring, use, and improvement of platforms for archiving, analyzing, and representing program data should be done with this outcome in mind. Just like educators in P–12 settings, teacher educators should ask: What are our expectations for teacher candidates? How do we know if we are effectively meeting their needs? How do they show us what they know, are able to do, and believe? What does our data tell us, individually, in groups, and in aggregates?

In this chapter we provide different viewpoints on how programs can approach this challenge. One of us comes from a private, Catholic, liberal arts college in an urban setting, serving a majority of first-generation college students, with an institution-wide performance assessment orientation. The other speaks from her experience in two different large public universities with distinct missions, one a research-intensive institution, the other with roots as a normal school. Through our collaborations with each other and the other editors of this volume, we discovered deep resonance in our beliefs about how programs can approach the task of creating useful data platforms to intentionally collect candidate and program data, to create different analyses of the data, and to make decisions based on the data and analyses at multiple levels and for multiple purposes. We are not making recommendations for particular products or software. Instead, we want to share ideas, experiences, and questions that may help you make decisions to guide your own selection, development, and use of a data system, including both platforms and practices for their use.

DATA SYSTEM TOURS

We'll describe both of our contexts in order for you to best make use of our learning related to your own context and needs. In sharing the experiences and learnings we have drawn from our institutions' work to gather, analyze, and act upon candidate and program data, we underscore a theme of this entire volume: that the people, tools, and organizations work best when they are intentional and explicit about their interdependence in high-quality educator preparation. We begin by describing how data systems have evolved and been built over time in two very different contexts.

Alverno College: Learner-Centered Institution

At Alverno, a small liberal arts college preparing 50–75 initially licensed educators per year, faculty make extensive use of a data platform rooted in individual student experience and performance. The system is designed to collect student work, artifacts of teaching, evaluative rubrics, and narrative feedback. Alverno students don't receive grades, but are evaluated by their demonstration of evidence of outcomes, as well as external standards and frameworks. In this context, candidates mine their experience, align those experiences to internal and external standards, and demonstrate their readiness for a teaching in a data system that was built to document multiple standards-aligned artifacts of candidates' performance.

Visiting a course on curriculum, instruction, and assessment for 1st-year practitioners of record pursuing licensure, you'd find teacher candidates working in groups focused on a particular course outcome in distinct ways. Two are listening to a podcast on assessment and equity, then recording their own audio reflective response. Four others use a visual thinking routine (Ritchhart & Church, 2020) to represent key strategies to engage students in learning. Three chat with their faculty, looking at student computer-adaptive testing data. Six analyze video representations of accomplished teaching, noting teacher moves, student moves, and their own reflections. After 30 minutes in these tasks, they rotate tasks, transferring into one of three other choices they have made for that day. Over the 3 hours of the class, each teacher candidate visits four tasks of eleven possibilities designed by the faculty, perhaps distinct from any four chosen by another student. Each, however, has the same document open as she engages: a multipage portfolio template in the Alverno assessment data system, documenting evidence of her engagement with each task, reflecting on key resources, self-assessing their performance using a rubric, and setting goals. At the end of class, each submits her weekly portfolio to the instructor in the data system for feedback by her faculty member using the same rubric aligned to the InTASC standards and the Alverno College education "abilities." Faculty can see and act on individual and collective improvements over time. The data system is learner-centered, emphasizing individual teachers' voice, choice, and experience; it also meets and advances the needs of the educator preparation program (EPP) for continuous improvement and external accountability.

The system referenced in the example above and the culture supporting it took time to build, however. Alverno College has had an institution-wide commitment to performance assessment since the 1970s (Loacker & Rogers, 2005). All students are assessed based on their demonstration of "abilities," regardless of major. To gather evidence of students' abilities, faculty and staff developed portfolios with multiple data sources from the 1980s (Mentkowski, 2000). By the early 2000s, external funding led to a custom portfolio system, the Diagnostic Digital Portfolio (DDP), an innovative system at the time. Faculty could design a key performance, aligned with an internal framework and external standards/frameworks. Students could upload their own work and engage in a self-assessment. Faculty could give feedback in rubrics or using narratives. A student could generate her own reports of how effectively she was demonstrating, or, in Alverno jargon, "validating" her abilities (Alverno College Faculty, 2015).

However robust it was for 2003, the homegrown system excluded some elements that later proved frustrating for students, faculty, staff, and administration. For faculty, it was burdensome and time-consuming to generate analyses of performance; for students, they could not remix artifacts from one assignment into others, nor create any externally facing portfolios to support their job searches. While the system did allow video, it required a plugin which had fallen out of use. Most problematically, student access to the data system was not accessible to them after graduation. Those without Alverno network accounts (e.g., cooperating teachers) could not directly add their feedback, instead sending it to faculty or students to upload. The system was not easily accessible by mobile devices for any users.

Over time, an experienced professor and Alverno administrator of academic affairs convened user groups, asking: What do you need of the system? What have been your greatest successes and frustrations? What are our "must-haves," and "nice-to-haves," and how can we prioritize? Should we seek additional external funding to improve the homegrown system? Or have third-party vendors developed sufficiently to support functions Alverno hoped for? How much would it cost, and how could we hold costs down for our majority first-generation student body?

Of three finalist systems, all of which included must-have functions and many of which had the nice-to-haves, campus stakeholders then evaluated, prioritized/ranked, and made a recommendation to the college leadership. The system chosen, a third-party provider called LiveText, provided all of the following features for a cost of about $20 per student: mobile access; student access to their materials after graduation; an easy interface to upload multiple sources of data; the ability to generate multiple forms of reports for internal decision making and external accountability; and permissions for those responsible for evaluating students' performance in the field to directly give feedback.

Change came with growing pains. Though the college need for change was clear and shared, there was not an immediate translation between the two systems. Names of key concepts and underlying structures were

different. LiveText required that assignments "live" within courses in particular semesters. So, while faculty could no longer build a "key performance"
and require that students complete it for multiple semesters in different
courses, in the new system faculty could easily use the LiveText "dashboard" to see which of their students had submitted work, and who had
not. While the system could not support requiring use of the same rubric for
self-assessment by student users, the separate and also critically important
reporting tools played key roles in deepening institutional understanding of
student and program performance.

Any new system also requires processes for stakeholders to learn new
language. In Alverno's case, tutorials were organized with explicit and clear
naming conventions. System training occurred within a context that pre-
sumed regular faculty collaboration. Sister Joel Read, who served as the
Alverno College President from 1968–2003, commented that one of her best
decisions was to create time, space, and expectations for faculty to meet. No
classes in any program are scheduled on Friday afternoons between 1:00
and 3:00. This time was left open and viewed as a faculty requirement, and
can then be connected to needed training, to evaluate program data, and to
create data innovations.

The learning experiences in Alverno's ability-based model are all intended to lead to a point in which the students and the faculty may assess—from
the Latin root, *assidere*, to sit down beside each other—looking together at
the criteria for their performance, and engaging in four key tasks:

1. Observing the evidence or performance
2. Interpreting and analyzing its features
3. Judging its quality
4. Planning for future learning experiences

Faculty must use any data system to create structures for feedback
that are transparent and intelligible to students. Most Alverno faculty do
this through the creation of rubrics that align with levels of expected performance, including going "above and beyond" expectations. Mary Diez,
Alverno alumna and Professor Emerita, taught us that assessments should
have "walls, but no ceiling," with structures to support and guide, but no
limit to how far a student may go. An Alverno student must always know
where she stands in relationship to her gradual demonstration of course
outcomes. Faculty must ensure that feedback and self-assessment are tightly
aligned, and the data system must support this conversation.

Alverno asks faculty and students: What is the quality of the performance, and how is that quality compared to course or program outcomes?
Typically, no single measure can uniquely capture every single outcome
for the course. Instead, multiple demonstrations together create a portrait
of students' capacity. Faculty must ask themselves: How will I know if a

student has met outcomes? What evidence must they show? What learning experiences will generate this evidence? How can I describe evidence that fully meets expectations, that partially meets but does not fully demonstrate the expected level of performance, evidence that may have been omitted by the student and is completely absent, and evidence that exceeds the expected level of criteria, going above and beyond expectations in innovative and distinctive ways?

We use these sources of evidence for external evaluation and accreditation by state (the Wisconsin Department of Public Instruction) and regional bodies (Higher Learning Commission). These organizations and their liaisons may examine certain data—student work and rubrics for self-assessment and feedback—to evaluate how effectively we are establishing our high expectations for students.

Alverno College as a whole may also use the entire body of student learning data to engage in improvement, identify needed changes, and implement and track the impact of changes on student learning. By generating reports about programs, courses, and majors, the college can ensure that we are delivering on our promise to provide high-quality ability-based learning. Though the data system has changed, the proactive commitment to collect, archive, interpret, and share data has remained constant.

East Carolina University: A System-Driven Platform Serving Multiple Needs

As a large EPP in an outcome-focused state, East Carolina University's data system expanded from a strong quantitative focus to a system that (1) integrated institutional and EPP-level data; (2) expanded and enhanced data collection; and (3) actively engaged faculty in program assessment toward improved candidate outcomes.

ECU began as a teacher's college and has long prepared high-quality teachers for North Carolina. Responding to EPP accountability measures, the 21 licensure area programs across five ECU colleges responded to multiple stakeholder expectations: state review, regional and national accreditation, and university-system targets. For our EPP, national accreditation cast a dark shadow—how could we maintain our EPP identity and vision while meeting external demands? Our data system work sought to respond to these pressures with detailed and quality data, to support our claims of successful teacher preparation with evidence.

> Our dean knew what data she wanted—a new system far beyond the scope of our existing system. Her words: "In order to prepare better beginning teachers [who can] perform more like second- or third-year teachers, we need better formative data and valid and reliable summative assessments." Her strategy led to curricular and

clinical innovations that catalyzed, expanded, and enhanced our existing system, moving from compliance to improvement, allowing us to evaluate our innovations' impacts. The new model was rooted in candidate performance data, flexibly meeting and integrating assessment, accreditation, and program improvement needs. (Director of Assessment and Accreditation, ECU, 2018)

With our dean's vision, we set forth to develop a data system that would support the ongoing needs of our EPP, but yield actionable information to continue to prepare high-quality beginning teachers. We started with our basic data needs. After examining requirements for regional (SACS), state (NCDPI), and national accreditation (CAEP), ECU developed five candidate data sets rooted in individual, unique identifier data:

1. Demographic data
2. Course/transcript data
3. Licensure exam
4. Initial licensure formative assessment data
5. Initial licensure edTPA data

Compilation drew from multiple sources and systems: institutional, e-portfolio, licensure tests. The College Office of Assessment team created spreadsheet reports for faculty use. The Office of Assessment added the reports to their annual regional and state reporting timeline. Together, they continue to serve as a powerful repository for program improvement and faculty research.

We expanded the system footprint as we moved from addressing reporting needs to considering EPP goals. Using existing data sources, institutional data (Banner), e-portfolio rubric evaluations (Taskstream), licensure testing (PRAXIS and Pearson), and edTPA rubric data (Pearson), we shifted the ways we were using the data. We added formative data to summative reports to provide more evidence of our initial teacher candidates' developmental trajectories. Now, faculty use these assessment data to assess candidate progress and provide feedback at programmatic check points; at the program level, they could consider course and program coherence and evaluate cross-section reliability.

In time, we found that our system's reliance on quantitative measures provided a great breadth of data, but lacked the rich descriptions evident in the Alverno data tour. As a result, we launched our qualitative data engagement in two stages; first, in data collection and then in data coding and analysis. Both required investment in developing replicable protocols. For example, implementing a new EPP-wide exit survey, we used coding protocols to analyze candidates' open-ended feedback. We conducted a qualitative analysis of candidates' formative assessments and conceptual transference in Video Grand Rounds—a scaffolded model of video observations described in more detail in Chapter 3—studying how they moved from video analysis to clinical implementation. All of these qualitative data sources continue to inform program improvement and faculty scholarship.

Our data system grew through regular and deep faculty engagement, but not all at once. Some faculty exhibited little interest; others were interested in certain aspects of the data system. We took a stance of being invitational with faculty; all received invitations and opted in on their own level and area of engagement. To help unite faculty across diverse program areas (and five colleges), we first sought to build a common language to tear down silos of content-specific jargon and acronyms. Our first success was in unifying the numerous terms we used to describe our students (students, interns, student teachers, teacher candidates) into *teacher candidates*. We built from there. To combat unknown acronyms, we developed a glossary of terms and shared them among faculty. To build a data community, we used humor to build camaraderie when possible, for example by naming a group engaged in edTPA analysis the *edTPALs*, (for edTPA liaisons).

We found collective examination of data to be powerful and generative. As our data system began to provide more opportunities to analyze linked data, faculty shared and discussed more deeply. Our edTPA data summits expanded to include more faculty members and more perspectives. Our annual assessment reporting meetings became more focused on specific programmatic needs and actions to address them. As faculty considered which program data were most valuable and actionable, they became more engaged and discerning.

As assessment coordinator, it was exciting to see the collective assessment literacy of our faculty grow. I worked with faculty who were early adopters and data users as well as those who were data skeptics and naysayers. To both, I asked that we look at evidence-based proof for our claims about our teacher candidates and, if we lacked the data, that we develop the needed evidence. Thus, faculty were positioned to expand our assessment footprint and move toward the data vision our dean provided. Together, we co-constructed a system to support program improvement and faculty research. Through practice innovations, faculty and the Office of Assessment team collaborated in common cross-program project data collection. They designed assessments, analyzed data, and disseminated findings through presentations and scholarly publications. Ultimately, faculty learning increased and generated new assessment ideas and new areas for program improvement. Throughout, the data system continued to serve its function: to assess teacher candidates, to support the EPP, to respond flexibly to emerging needs, and to engage and inspire faculty.

GETTING STARTED

Just as in teaching, there are unhelpful ways to use helpful tools; our hope is that our experiences building robust systems will be helpful to you as you seek to do the same.

As EPPs become awash in data and endeavor to make these data actionable, we found it critical to establish a clear vision for the data system being created, specifically, what issues or activities did our EPPs need to address with our data? When our programs "began with the end in mind," we were positioned to address existing needs and be responsive and flexible to new requirements on the ever-changing landscape of accountability in educator preparation. The vision for your data system must provide equitable attention to your candidates, your EPP needs, and your EPP's goals for the future.

We strongly counsel EPPs seeking to create or refine data systems to begin by assessing your current data use culture, identifying what your program does well, and leveraging those assignments or activities when building your data system. We believe that EPP faculty can develop data systems that provide data for feedback and to feedforward: Useful systems should be both reflective and developmental.

At both of our campuses, we found that our data systems' work was most generative when we began with our missions, visions, and conceptual frameworks, aligned with our assessment design. We identified and considered our outcomes, developmentally leveled, to which we sought to align our various sources of evidence. We made explicit the institutional or system dispositions toward our expectations of student and program data. We have found that launching a data system search or major revision has worked best when we considered how our different systems could support routine tasks and free time for innovation or emergencies.

At Alverno College, stakeholders generated a "*must* list and *wish* list." Faculty and staff engaged in multiple substantive conversations to identify what data were required and available, and began to consider how they were connected with other institutional data and general dynamics of data aggregation from the candidate-level, to the program, and beyond. This conversation wasn't only related to selecting a tool, but was aligned to the overall institutional commitment to assessment (Loacker & Rogers, 2005).

At East Carolina University, because of its large size, leaders and stakeholders considered issues of scale, discussing how to prioritize and engage with data analysis at various levels (individual work samples, sorting and analyzing by course, program, student demographics, regional sources of data, and national comparisons). Because of the North Carolina "value-added model" context, there were also requirements for data use at the state level. Our data system's formative assessment data helped bridge the gap between methodologies embraced externally to assess preparation outcomes and those employed internally to prepare candidates.

In each campus context, we sought to remain true to our institutional mission, our community, our students, and our faculty. We were mindful of accreditation needs, as well as our unique cultures of evidence. We identified common features the sources of data would need to address (e.g., the EPP conceptual framework, external accreditation standards, state value-added measures). We leveraged program documents and key assessments that described candidate growth and progress. We aimed to anticipate equity issues and potential barriers so that our systems would be accessible to all learners (e.g., those with sporadic broadband access) and users (e.g., faculty and students on and off campus, cooperating teachers, certifying officers). Our goals in our different contexts were consonant: Both campuses prioritized the creation of an accessible, inclusive, generative, flexible system that could effectively meet multiple stakeholders' needs over the short and long term.

As you visualize your EPP data system, we suggest that you keep teacher candidates as the focus of the data system; preparing educators is the focus of EPP work, not reporting data on them. Ensure that the system demonstrates the progress and development of candidates' readiness to teach. We further advise developing data systems that address the most urgent needs of your EPP, including the opportunity—the places and spaces—for faculty to ask hard questions of their programs and research their practice. Consumers of EPP data range from the faculty at the program level, to institutional data reports, to state licensure or program approvers, to specialty and national accreditors. The vision for your system must include meeting the EPP's most basic needs.

Finally, as you get started, remember that data systems are not static enterprises, they must be agile and adaptable to changing contexts, such as policy changes, demographic shifts, and local/regional school district needs. Our visions for campus data platforms included flexible, responsive elements that allowed our programs to be nimble and adaptable to change.

Assess and Build Participant and User Capacity

A system that is impenetrable to its users is useless. A system that is generated from a culture of assessment and evidence, by contrast, can grow and thrive in service to the organization and its people. Building user capacity is not simply an issue of system training, but of developing collaborative and inclusive assessment literacy practices that are supported by the system.

If you are a new director of assessment charged with building the EPP's data system, you may understand the accreditation task, but not the instructional technology needed to support it. You may have some programs or faculty who are eager to engage in data use for program improvement, but others who are not. It is critical to build a team that contributes its strengths and perspectives to build an integrated and flexible system. In our contexts, we assessed the strengths of our teams. For example, we sought to identify what colleagues had quantitative data analysis strengths, who were the intrepid technology innovators, and who had strengths in rubric design. Knowing the culture of our EPPs and the strengths of our teams guided our implementation. We also leveraged existing engagement practices (e.g., the Alverno faculty schedule that required time for meeting and collaboration on Friday afternoons) or built new structures that would maximize our teams' strengths in using our systems, including facilitative and analytical strengths.

In both of our institutions, we found that systems worked best when leaders invited stakeholders and users to assess the current system's culture, use, strengths, and weaknesses. Leaders could then connect those needs with the people who would interface with the system and increase or enhance the system's capacity. There is often a misconception that data systems ensure compliance rather than improve practice. If that's the case in your EPP, we propose leveraging your data platform implementation to commence a culture shift. We encourage colleagues in teacher preparation to tell the story of practice and outcomes, as opposed to framing the work solely as compliance and accountability.

Weighing Options for Data Systems

As EPPs consider platforms that will enable the data use practices you want, you will need to evaluate how different systems serve your needs. The size and mission of the EPP will influence data system construction and use. As practitioners, we have worked with homegrown, campus-developed data systems with limitless customization and high-cost and boxed systems with many features but little personality. There are pros and cons to each option: Therefore, our goal here is to provide a series of considerations as EPPs and their faculty and administration are weighing options.

In a small tuition-driven undergraduate institution, there are signature values and assessment structures, (e.g., the ability-based model of assessment and self-assessment at Alverno College) that make designing a homegrown system appealing. At the same time, customized systems may be difficult to keep updated. While the Alverno portfolio system was tailored to meet the mission and needs of the institution, in time the maintenance of the system became costly to the unit, necessitating a shift to consider "off-the-shelf" options.

At a large public institution, service agreements and campus-level data integration may drive selection criteria over data use. For ECU, the idea of an integrable and semicustomizable system was attractive to the EPP and campus, which allowed us to access campus funding to launch and maintain the implementation. This customization–standardization trade-off provided adequate e-portfolio support for the EPP while keeping us aligned with the campus instructional technology vision.

When weighing platform options, another strategy is to seek out your data counterparts in other professional schools or institutions. EPP data needs and desires parallel those in other professional schools. You may find partners or experts on your own campus, which may lead to new assessment partners on your campus and smoother implementations. For example, we found that our colleagues in the College of Nursing also had a need to track clinical experiences, including preceptor sites and clinical hours. Together, we shared needs and concerns that ultimately led our EPP to adopt a placement-tracking product that originated in the nursing education field.

Weighing options also includes considering the roles and workloads of faculty, staff, and administrators engaged in the data systems. Who will be engaged in the data system? The time and effort of these users feed the data system. In a large EPP, a system may require a data office with a team that drives reporting timelines and provides reporting and technical support, all while working closely with faculty. A smaller EPP may be well supported by a lead faculty person who does the work as part of their faculty load and a strong staff support person. Other EPPs may distribute the activities that feed the data system to several faculty leaders. Many options exist, but what is critical is weaving the system into the daily work of the EPP.

Finally, weighing options also includes assessing the affordances and barriers the system may create. Clearly, this chapter focuses more on the affordance of a well-designed data system, but the potential issues must also be considered. One potential barrier is accessibility. Data systems must have entry points, portals, that are accessible where the work occurs. Systems limited to a campus network or VPN may limit faculty engagement and prevent candidate access from the field. EPPs serving rural communities or communities lacking ready Internet access will want to consider this potential barrier to system access and use. Other barriers may emerge once the program implements the system and seeks to make additions or modifications. Will the system be a barrier to future development or help to facilitate it? Inflexibility can be a powerful barrier. The inability to modify the system once implemented leaves the EPP with a strong system for that period of initial implementation, but becomes a barrier to future growth.

BUILDING ENGAGEMENT AND PARTICIPATION

Faculty Engagement

In order to remain useful, data systems must be fed with data like a fire needs fuel. For many EPPs, faculty evaluations of candidates' performance will be a primary data source, relying upon faculty to enter data that can be aggregated and analyzed. Faculty who feel assessment data collection infringes upon their professional role or academic freedom may spar with administrators tasked with driving the data collection on behalf of the EPP. To engage faculty more fully in the "feeding" of the data system we found it helpful (even in EPPs with very different numbers of faculty) to create a sense of "we" in our use of data. At Alverno, this meant that the nine full-time faculty members liaised with adjunct faculty colleagues to gather and engage in analysis. At ECU, this also happened, but within teams nested in programs; at UCSB, within the teacher preparation unit. Faculty often need to "see" how the outcome of their efforts will improve their practice and the outcomes for their students before they buy in (Guskey, 2002). Through faculty retreats like those described in the UCSB case study in Chapter 5, EPP leaders may cultivate a culture of evidence in their units. We encourage you to consider the opportunities that may exist to build a culture of evidence in your EPP, and ask your team how your data can demonstrate its value to faculty for their work—and for their candidates.

In engaging faculty and building their engagement and sense of responsibility, we found it helpful to make requirements explicit. At both of our institutions, leaders clearly outlined the role faculty will play in feeding the assessment system and how their work feeds into other assessment activities. At Alverno, for example, 1st-year faculty engage in a year of professional development that builds their knowledge of the ability-based system and their responsibilities for gathering sound assessment data that provide evidence of students' abilities; only thereafter can it become meaningful to house and interrogate those data in their system or feel a sense of the urgency of yearly reviews or accreditation visits. Once that sense of ownership and responsibility is established, then challenging conversations (e.g., if faculty do not complete needed data or reviews in a timely manner) can emerge from the context of mutual responsibility, common standards of performance, and the value of the data to the EPP and its outside evaluators.

Starting with a culture of developing faculty responsibility worked best for us when it was grounded in recognizing and valuing people's strengths and areas of growth. Some of our colleagues took to a new online, e-portfolio platform with ease, while others needed a guide-on-the side in their first semester of implementation. We identified strengths (not only technical but relational) in colleagues for providing individualized supports for faculty. Faculty innovations could also be shared; if a faculty colleague demonstrated strengths in data use or feedback, we found that inviting them to create a collegial guide or screencast might serve as powerful and accessible resources for faculty needing support.

Candidate Participation

After faculty, your candidates will be the most regular contributors of data to the system. Candidate submissions, their feedback, and use of evaluation from the data system are critical to EPP success. From the start, setting expectations for candidate accountability, like faculty accountability, will help to avoid issues in the future. Just as with faculty, we found that if our candidates understood external requirements (e.g., state assessments), then they could engage more fully in timely completion of required data elements. A midprogram reflective assessment at Alverno, for example, also operated as an initial orientation to the structure and purpose of the state-mandated test of pedagogical knowledge. At ECU, the triad meetings between student teacher, clinical teacher, and university supervisor fed the data system, but more importantly these meetings culminated in documentation of candidate progress and provided valuable mentoring and coaching for candidates.

We discovered that when faculty engaged with each other and deepened their understandings of course assessments and their contributions to a larger portrait of candidate and program strengths, they could then communicate these more clearly and explicitly to students. Faculty and student advisers could then explain the rationale for a key assessment happening in a foundational course, or in a midprogram portfolio, or in a capstone experience. We found that student engagement was improved when we were transparent with students about the assessment requirements, evaluation processes, and why the EPP valued them.

We found that it was important to not only focus on the external assessors' priorities but to critically reflect on the purposes of assessment. At ECU for example, encouraging students to critically reflect on and provide detailed feedback to teacher education leaders and faculty on areas of potential improvement in their preparation was valuable and actionable when analyzed internally. However, when the same data were made public on a state dashboard of "candidate satisfaction" data, the data appeared to be a poor reflection of preparation rather than a powerful tool for improvement. Holding that tension and reflecting on it continues to be a source of engagement for faculty and students alike.

Similarly, we found it important to consider phases of data—not only final evaluations as data points but candidates' and programs' processes of improvement, revision, and refinement. At Alverno, for example, the data system is more robust in generating reports of summative data than it is for analyzing multiple formative assessment points prior to a final project's completion. Faculty and leaders there continue to engage in how best to build all stakeholders' sense of what data points are critical and how they contribute to a larger portrait of program capacity. At ECU, many of the innovations highlighted in the case study in Chapter 3 were key formative assessments developed to provide more data points along a teacher candidate's developmental trajectory.

In both of our contexts, we served candidates with very different lived experiences, cultural funds of knowledge, and day-to-day challenges. The more we developed deep understandings of candidates' lives, the more we have been able to anticipate and address equity issues and potential barriers. If a student's main technological device is her phone, then a data system that is not mobile-friendly is a barrier to her. If a computer lab on campus is only open during the day, that may present a barrier to students with extensive work responsibilities.

Institutional and Program Decision Making

A robust data platform informs robust decision making. Accessible, informative, and actionable data provide the evidence base for institutional or EPP decision making. When you need to make difficult student-focused decisions (e.g., removing a student from a program), you might need to consider that the data system can help inform and provide evidence of performance, such as appeals processes, dismissal, academic status, and so on. The system can be especially useful in making difficult decisions and for addressing external mandates.

In our experiences, we found that it was helpful when designing our platforms to consider what sources of data might not yet be linked, but have potential to inform individual or collective faculty practice. At Alverno, for example, each semester we used data to review candidates for graduation with honors because, as an institution not using grades, a grade-point-average determination was not available as part of determining scholarly and service excellence. Artifacts and rubrics showing how often a candidate for honors had exceeded rubric criteria or attained a "distinctive" level supported evidence-based determinations of scholarly excellence. Feedback from co- and extracurricular experiences, resumes, and letters of reference supported determinations of service excellence.

At ECU when considering new program development or program deletion, leaders tapped into our data system to help inform that decision making. For example, enrollment data, employment data, and feedback data from employers guided program improvement. ECU leaders also tried to avoid using naming conventions or jargon that would limit or date the system; acronyms and organizations change, as our profession has seen in the shift from NCATE and TEAC to CAEP.

MAINTAINING AND ADAPTING THE SYSTEM OVER TIME

We believe that data systems have the capacity to support the lifeblood of educator preparation in higher education—program evaluation, partnerships, and research—and successfully address accountability and reporting needs. In this section, we share a few examples to highlight the breadth and depth of utilizations from campus self-study efforts to university-system initiatives.

Program Evaluation and Partnerships

Van de Walle's (2014) widely-used mathematics methods text encourages elementary teaching candidates learning to teach the concept of data analysis to focus on the "story of the data." We extend this idea to ask, what stories do you want your data system to tell? We believe that EPP data are more complex and nuanced than pass rates and percentages portray. How can data platforms collect and export rich data stories about EPPs? To construct a rich and compelling story about your EPP and its candidates, consider the examples we present in the rest of this section.

In both of our contexts, we incorporated valid and reliable data measures that helped to meet multiple program needs both in the moment and for the future. In both of our states, a required assessment of pedagogical content knowledge was a key capstone data point with multiple rubrics that could be analyzed and compared longitudinally. We leveraged those data for program improvement or strategic planning.

But beyond our use of externally mandated assessments, both of our institution systems allowed us to collect a mix of quantitative and qualitative, direct and indirect evidence of candidate development to construct the story. We engaged teacher educator colleagues and institutional assessment staff to support quality survey development and in quality assessment analysis.

We aimed to synthesize the evidence-based findings in a way that engaged the readers of the story. For example, in a national accreditation visit, ECU used the data to "tell our story." At Alverno, leaders build electronic exhibit rooms drawing on data system reports in order to convey the "story" of continual improvement for the state Department of Public Instruction liaison.

Campus-based program review and regional accreditation demand EPPs demonstrate how they use candidate data as an evidence-base for continuous program improvement efforts. Often on 7- to 10-year cycles, these activities can be a heavy lift for EPP faculty and administrators when not tended to on an annual basis. How will your data system be called on to contribute to a periodic internal self-study while also meeting the day-to-day needs of the EPP? At ECU, we designed the signature assessments collected in the data system to support multiple reporting needs. Each course-embedded assessment was evaluated by the instructor with the evaluation feeding our data system. Through our system, we leveraged rubric design tools to align assessments to state and national standards sets. This allowed us to tailor reports for different audiences without creating new assessments for each requirement.

At the state level, EPP program approval processes, like the State of Wisconsin Department of Instruction's Continuous Review Process (Wisconsin DPI, 2012), examine how the program is learning from data and what we are doing in response to those data to revise and improve teacher preparation. When state reporting criteria shift, so must your data system. How will your data system meet current program review needs? Flexibility is key.

Research and Innovation

Robust EPP data systems not only support the EPP, but also the faculty and schools who collaborate to prepare educators and inform practice. For faculty, it is critical to demonstrate how their investment in the data system will yield dividends for their students, their individual and collective research productivity, and their research–practice partnerships with P–12 partners. For faculty, creating an extant data system for use in their research multiplies their efforts by utilizing data and student artifacts collected and evaluated as part of the program for research. Many EPPs and their faculty strive to use program data for innovation and practice-based research. When used strategically, data systems help support faculty development, promotion, and tenure through practice-based research agenda. For junior faculty, in particular, this approach helps introduce them to the program, its assessments, and a culture that values and utilizes its data. Through this work, junior faculty find new collaborators based on content, an instructional approach, or the data conversations themselves. For EPP faculty working across disciplines, there are incentives to develop new research strategies and implement novel instructional approaches. For more senior faculty, data-driven conversations may serve as rich opportunities for faculty mentoring and leadership.

Many data systems are built to achieve specific goals and accomplish specific tasks, providing essential data and support for the EPP. However, a more impactful data system is one that provides spaces for innovation, such as prototyping new assessments or exploring new feedback mechanisms. At ECU, we wanted the data system to support the dean's vision for innovation through "squishy pilots" (see ECU case study in Chapter 3 for details). Building innovation sandboxes within the data system to capture prototypes and pilot data allowed ECU to iteratively test the design to inform their efficacy and further development. Once a "squishy pilot" proves worthy, migrate it from the sandbox to the operational data system to inform programmatic decision making. This is how new innovations and assessments become institutionalized in EPP practice and culture. We sought to preserve the primary responsibilities and needs for the data system, but also create spaces for our innovations and the artifacts they yielded. These data, in turn, were used to assess the impact and scale of those innovations.

SUMMARY: HOLISTICALLY INTEGRATING PEOPLE
AND TOOLS WITHIN ORGANIZATIONS

As this chapter demonstrates, it is difficult to separate the role that people, tools, and organizations play in driving a transformational change—like developing and implementing an EPP data system. An EPP cannot simply buy a product, a tool, and expect the problem to be solved. An EPP cannot simply provide a faculty member an assessment buy-out and expect a system to be built. And an EPP cannot simply make assessment policies without developing a culture of evidence for data-informed decision making.

Cautions and Considerations

Design work takes time, and time is a limited resource for EPP faculty and administrators. Remember, Rome wasn't built in a day—your data system will grow under your steady, strategic leadership. Are your key, early-adopter faculty available to assist with data system development? Are you able to set assessment priorities to spread design work over multiple semesters or do you have the ability to pilot an assessment and then scale it up? In small EPPs the same faculty or administrators may be responsible for managing the people and the tool. In larger EPPs, an office or committee may be charged with the task. Consider the role of committee work and common scheduling in the Alverno case study in Chapter 4 and the role of distributed leadership in the UCSB case study in Chapter 5. Are you able to leverage current committee structures or leadership models in your EPP to engage more people in the work of the data system?

Trade-Offs

Until now, we posited that all of these elements—getting started, building capacity, and fostering engagement—are essential, required. We think they are. Without some degree of support for each one, confusion, resistance, or frustration may set in among your EPP faculty. We propose that, as an EPP assessment leader, you utilize your knowledge of the EPP, its faculty, programs, and culture, to play to its strengths when implementing a new data system. Each EPP will need to answer some questions; for example, Are we willing to take on some faculty resistance because of a lack of incentives to invest more resources in our data system implementation? Are we willing to bear some frustration by our candidates for the lack of resources now to maintain future system flexibility? Only those in the EPP will know which trade-offs are best for your EPP and allow it to drive a transformational data change forward.

When ECU first adopted edTPA, back in 2011–2012 before its edTPA rebranding, few implementation resources were available. We decided to dive in with edTPA because our data analysis indicated our previous portfolio had little construct validity, lacked reliable scoring, and failed to discern between truly exceptional teacher candidates and those who were proficient. With few portfolio resources available we were forced to stretch our skilled personnel to train and orient others to edTPA, create scaffolds for interns, and prepare for local evaluation in our e-portfolio system. Scarce resources and personnel strain led to anxiety and frustration among faculty, clinical partners, and the interns. We were willing to trade-off the increased anxiety and initial frustration because the edTPA fit the vision of where we wanted our EPP to go with a valid and reliable teacher candidate performance assessment. The incentive of having valuable, actionable data aligned to our EPP vision propelled us past the frustration and anxiety. This was a trade-off we were willing to make.

At Alverno College, despite the many technological affordances of the third-party system, there were some concessions made. For example, many faculty members miss the requirement in the old system that no assessment would be considered complete (or even be able to be submitted) without a student's self-assessment. Because the submission box for a self-assessment was separate, this was easily accomplished. In LiveText, not so. Additionally, because LiveText is built for a graded system and Alverno does not use number or letter grades, some of the features of the data system have required explicit discussion about common naming structures. Lastly, faculty "change fatigue" is a real challenge and some colleagues have yet to fully adopt the new portfolio system—onboarding and invitational modeling about the benefits of its use is an ongoing process.

It can be daunting to envision the processes and practices that may be required to build or improve a system that will support robust and compelling data use in your context. But don't let the size of the mountain deter you from beginning to climb. Every educator wants their work to matter, and what better way to evaluate the impact of our work than by creating strategies and structures to enable compelling, multimodal, longitudinal data conversations? To be sure, neither of us is at the summit of this mountain either—we continue the work of improving and refining our own institutional practices around data systems and their use every day—but we do encourage you to take small steps to begin the work. The challenge of the terrain is real, but the view and perspective that awaits you is worth it, and there are many other explorers out here who welcome you on the journey.

REFERENCES

Alverno College Faculty. (2015). *Feedback is teaching.* Alverno College Institute.

Guskey, T. R. (2002). Professional development and teacher change. *Teachers and Teaching, 8*(3), 381–391.

Loacker, G., & Rogers, G. (2005). *Assessment at Alverno College: Student, program, institutional.* Alverno College Institute.

Mentkowski, M. (2000). *Learning that lasts: Integrating learning, development, and performance in college and beyond.* Jossey-Bass.

Ritchhart, R., & Church, M. (2020). *The power of making thinking visible.* John Wiley & Sons.

Van de Walle, J. A. (2014). *Teaching student-centered mathematics: Developmentally appropriate instruction for grades pre-K–2.* Pearson.

Wisconsin Department of Public Instruction (DPI). (2012). *Wisconsin educator preparation program approval handbook for Wisconsin institutions of higher education continuous review process.*

CHAPTER 8

Making Time and Space for Data Use

Tine Sloan, Kristen Cuthrell, and Désirée H. Pointer Mace

The most powerful reform decision we ever made was to make structures for faculty to meet regularly.
—Sister Joel Read, President, Alverno College, 1968–2003

WHY TIME AND SPACE FOR DATA USE?

Throughout our work with high data use programs we saw that using data for improvement on a programmatic level required engagement from faculty across all sectors of professional practice. This was new work for many teacher educators, and unless you're at Alverno, it usually required new opportunities for engagement. When that engagement was for "continuous improvement" (as per most accountability policy), these opportunities were ideally institutionalized to be, well, continuous. What's more, these opportunities engaged faculty in new collaborations around the data. For these and many more reasons, the success of data for program change required attention to making time and space for this work.

In the three case study programs described in this volume—University of California, Santa Barbara (UCSB); East Carolina University (ECU); and Alverno College—collaborative work was a necessary foundation for program improvement work. Though each approached it differently, we have some take-aways for why it was a necessary foundation. First, it allowed faculty to learn about candidates' practice beyond what they saw in their own teaching or supervision practice. Second, what they "saw" in the data was more informative when analyzed in the company of diverse faculty: Each teacher educator brought their expertise to bear on the analysis; each brought the contexts in which they conducted their work (a particular K–12 school, a university class, and so on); and each could contribute to understanding the data in different ways. Collectively, these analyses resulted in far more powerful understandings about candidate practice, about colleagues' practice, and about the program as a whole. Third, this work expanded opportunities beyond a handful of powerful voices that previously guided program work. It brought faculty on the fringes of such work (especially field supervisors) into the fold of decision making and analysis. It is not difficult to see the advantage to having those closest to candidate practice engaged in the improvement of the program's practice.

Another reason we devote a chapter to "making time and space" has to do with the collective, reflective nature of programmatic improvement work. It is a form of reflection that strengthens our ability for programmatic inquiry, for creating a culture of inquiry (Bunch et al., 2009; Peck et al., 2010; Sloan, 2013, 2015). The concept of reflection from a "social relations perspective" (Høyrup & Elkjaer, 2006) can be helpful to understanding this. Rather than reinterpret the eloquent words of Høyrup and Elkjaer (2006) and Raelin (2002) we reprint their explanation here:

> Raelin associates reflection with learning dialogues. The process of reflection is *collective*; we reflect together with trusted others in the midst of practices:
>
> > Reflection brings to the surface—in the safe presence of trusting peers— the social, political and emotional data that arise from direct experience with one another. [Raelin, 2002, p. 66]
>
> In the social relations perspective reflection develops into a social practice: Reflective practice is according to Raelin:
>
> > The practice of periodically stepping back to ponder the meaning of, what has recently transpired to us and to others in our immediate environment. It illuminates what the self and others have experienced, providing a basis for future action. In particular, it privileges the process of inquiry, leading to an understanding of experience that may have been overlooked in practice. . . . It typically is concerned with the forms of learning that seek to inquire about the most fundamental assumptions and premises behind our practices. [Raelin, 2002, p. 66] (Høyrup & Elkjaer, 2006, p. 36)

Reflective practice opens up for public scrutiny our interpretations and evaluations of our plans and actions. We subject our assumptions to the review of others (Raelin, 2002). The outcome may be the validation of knowledge, assumptions, plans, and actions and a development of these through the dialogue implying individual and organizational learning. This approach—people reflecting together in an organizational context—calls attention to the organization as a context for reflective practice. The collective and organizational perspective are interwoven. In this perspective, disclosure is an important process. An ideal here is a reflective culture that makes it possible for people to be challenged constantly without fear of retaliation

(Raelin, 2002). This is a culture that values continuous discovery and experimentation (Høyrup & Elkjaer, 2006).

Reflection necessarily requires time and space to step back, to open possibilities to see things anew. Collective reflection further requires a mutual trust among participants, where "disclosure" is possible "without fear of retaliation." This culture of collaborative inquiry takes time and space and leadership to develop (we discuss this further in Chapter 9). But our work here and elsewhere supports an investment in creating a culture of inquiry that moves beyond compliance of external mandates for data use (Bunch et al., 2009; Peck et al., 2010; Sloan, 2013, 2015).

All said, the newness of data work, the collaborative element to this work, and the reflective nature of this work are all reasons to approach the work through understanding the value of creating time and space for the work. The following are examples of strategies each case study program created in order to do this. For each, we describe what the program did and why, and how it was (or was not) sustained over time. Every example below is explained in more detail in the programs' case study chapters, and we encourage readers to access these for more information. Here we provide a brief description, focusing on the how and why of making time and space for the activity.

CREATING THE PHYSICAL AND PSYCHOLOGICAL SPACE TO DIG IN

When starting this programmatic data work, many programs began by setting time aside for faculty to learn about and collaboratively analyze data. They did this in different ways, but one important feature was the sustained length of time to engage, often in a "retreat" or departure from normal activity. Sometimes this required suspending normal activity, as UCSB did for one week each spring as faculty scored teaching performance assessments. That week, all supervision and as many course meetings as possible were suspended in order to allow for thoughtful, collaborative engagement throughout the week. At Alverno, this involved (and still does) an annual calendar that sets aside Friday afternoons for scheduled groups, across different faculty, to meet regularly. Both of these options were relatively doable for smaller programs such as UCSB and Alverno, whereas different strategies were implemented in larger institutions. The following describes how ECU began.

As ECU programs engaged in meaningful data use, it became clear that the typical approach of one person submitting all the final reports at the end of the semester did not truly move the dial in faculty understanding what candidates knew and were able to do. In fact, not many were aware of what was in the final reports. On the cusp of adopting edTPA as the unit performance assessment, change was needed in how to examine the data.

We have been trying to get folks together that taught a similar course, maybe across departments or across programs . . . and trying to get some common process of assessment and so forth, because that not only gives you a greater ability to compare and contrast, but it also allows you to start developing these communities of practice where people really start talking about the work from the ground up, and you have to have those real opportunities; they can't be fake. (Linda Patriarca, Dean of the College of Education, ECU)

ECU chose to gather everyone together in an annual data summit. All programs in the educator preparation unit were invited to send representatives to the meeting. Data was compiled by the Assessment Office and included data from recurrent program outcome measures as well as from pilot studies evaluating new practices. The summit brought data into communal view and provided a context in which program members could deliberate alternatives for action and program improvement. As faculty engagement with edTPA increased (i.e., local scoring, integration in coursework), engagement in the annual, full-day data summit grew. This was an opportunity for faculty to collectively analyze both programwide data and unitwide data at one time. Held on campus, leaders made sure to provide accessible parking, rooms for breakout conversations, and most important, food and coffee. The coffee and cookie bar was an especially big hit one year. Over time, faculty attendance grew, and awareness increased about the types of data provided for programs, and about the prospects for analysis. Engagement further increased as faculty saw action as a result of the conversations at the data summit. These summits are still held annually at ECU.

The Alverno College faculty as a whole convenes multiple times during the academic year for "faculty institutes" during which it is common for people to make reference to or engage in analysis of student, program, or institutional data. A recent institute conversation about student evaluation data inspired a year-long faculty work group focused on increasing the cultural responsiveness and inclusiveness of 1st- and 2nd-year courses.

Former President of Alverno College Sister Joel Read, who led the college from 1968–2003 and was at the helm during the institution's conversion to a performance- and criteria-based system, once remarked that the best decision she made in leadership was to create time and space for faculty to meet, and then require that they do so. As a result, beyond the thrice-yearly institutes, no courses are scheduled on Friday afternoons at Alverno, but faculty are required to be on campus (or in equivalent online spaces), focused on different kinds of collaborative work. This time might be used for department meetings, interdivisional ability department meetings, 1st-year faculty support workshops, or all-faculty meetings. This norm, then, helps to ensure that data engagement is possible and regular.

UCSB created quarterly faculty retreats that began as a response to implementing sweeping reforms in California's teacher preparation policy, but ended up a norm that continues to this day. Many UCSB teacher educators are part-time faculty, so scheduling these retreats around family obligations (after school drop-off and before pick-up for instance), or distance to travel, or around traffic considerations, allowed for more egalitarian opportunities to engage (and babies were always welcome). When retreats were held in off-campus locations, it created a psychological and physical break from other obligations, allowing for more focused attention. Often when these were held on campus, there would be faculty hopping in and out just to attend that 1-hour meeting. This made it very difficult for them to re-engage in the conversation. And in fact, as the collaborative work grew, people did not want to miss the conversation (more on this in the UCSB case study in Chapter 5). For several years the retreats were held at the program director's home, a space that could squeeze about forty-five or so faculty into the common living area, and allow small groups to gather in other rooms or outside. This home became the "TEP[1] Retreat Facility" and though the location was less inconvenient than campus, it was the unanimous choice for retreat day. Providing good food for these events was so greatly appreciated that program leaders realized how caring for people in this small way signaled to them in a big way that they were valued. Sometimes it's the small things.

In all three cases, program leadership took great care to structure activity that would engage faculty in worthwhile activity over time. They were strategic in selecting the data for use in these activities, in providing cross-unit analysis opportunities, and in ensuring people from different roles "sat at the table" to collectively make sense of the data. Chapter 9 of this volume provides more detail on leadership practice related to structuring activity in these extended-time spaces. These spaces, and what followed as a result of faculty's analyses, allowed people to discover and experiment. They were critical cornerstones to data work, and they continue to this day in all three programs (annually for ECU, quarterly for UCSB, and weekly for Alverno). Many spontaneous, collaborative opportunities have also cropped up since then (more on this below).

MAKING DATA ACCESSIBLE

To support both structured data analysis work, and more free-form exploration of data, all programs paid attention to ways faculty could access data. We think of this as creating a space for the work. Two programs—Alverno and ECU—created data platforms that served a number of purposes (see Chapter 7 in this volume for more on these platforms). These systems offered more widespread opportunities for all faculty to work with data by, for instance, easing the process for anyone to access it, packaging the data in digestible formats, or expanding opportunities for researchers to work with programmatic data. Throughout our work we saw access to data become vital to faculty's abilities to develop and act on innovative ideas and, in turn, understand its impact on candidates' practice (i.e., the process of experimentation). We also saw how motivating and exciting it was when faculty could "see" candidates' practice change, especially when candidates enacted teaching. This meant that the type of data people could access was also important. Survey results, course assignments, written reflections, all have a place, but artifacts close to the enactment of teaching—video of teaching, lesson/unit planning, case studies, student work—is especially important to ensuring preparedness to teach. Fortified with this kind of evidence, and with opportunities to bring this evidence to programmatic attention, was empowering for people. So creating space for data access was time well spent in our programs. Here we offer examples from ECU and Alverno.

As ECU supported program improvement through data use, it became very important to make a wide array of data accessible to faculty and staff. Their Office of Assessment invested time in preparing relevant data sets for faculty use, as this was seen as crucial to making meeting time feel well spent. And program leaders could pull data for meetings and summits that would allow for meaningful faculty deliberation and decision making. The Office pulled edTPA portfolio samples and shared them with programs. They disaggregated other quantitative measures of program outcomes for faculty use. Use of the college's integrated data management system allowed data to be pulled by the office and then organized in ways that shielded faculty from being overwhelmed by not knowing either the data storage systems or how to pull reports easily. They created an online data request ticket system to ease this process. In the online request, faculty included Institutional Review Board (IRB) approvals, purpose of data request, and types of data needed. This process then allowed the Office of Assessment to serve as the "honest data broker" and maintain the appropriate safeguards for data collection and reporting. This type of data preparation/support was done for all educator preparation program (EPP) areas and was sustained over time as the Office of Assessment expanded and was able to hire a full-time edTPA coordinator. Additionally, graduate assistant resources were committed to the Office of Assessment as the data organization tasks became part of larger faculty-led research.

At Alverno College, the entire institution has had a performance assessment orientation since the 1970s. This "ability-based" model presumes clear and transparently shared criteria that faculty and students alike may use to determine progress toward outcomes and demonstrations of student ability. Thus the structures for engaging in sense making based on data are of critical importance. Student learning portfolios have been gathered, shared, and analyzed regularly for decades: first, as paper-based portfolios, supplemented with large video tapes in the 1980s; subsequently, in a "Diagnostic Digital Portfolio" in the 2000s; and currently, in an online, cloud-based, mobile-device-friendly portfolio system (see the Alverno College case study in Chapter 4 for more on the origins and details of this system).

During a student's course of study, several "external assessments" require them to examine their prior learning data across courses and defend their expertise to experienced assessors. This may mean that literal spaces may need to be reserved (e.g., small meeting rooms for a conversational assessment) or virtual spaces created (e.g., an asynchronous evaluation of a graduate thesis proposal). Alverno College has an Assessment Center staffed by colleagues who are adept in coordinating and running these external assessments.

CULTIVATING COLLABORATION

At its very core, effective collaboration relies to some degree on "shared understanding, agreed purposes, mutual trust, and usually an element of interdependence" (Head & Alford, 2015, p. 725). These are conditions necessary for the collective reflective practice offered earlier by Høyrup and Elkjaer (2006) and Raelin (2002). They are also conditions that are inherent in the work of teacher preparation. The complexity of teaching requires a preparation that pulls apart elements of practice via courses and clinical practice for the benefit of a novice's focused learning. When new teachers enact the integrated practice of teaching they must do so by reintegrating pieces. Hence there is a natural interdependence in the practice of teacher educators. Ideally faculty also have a shared understanding of the work, which is necessary for cohesive programs, which research suggests is important to the efficacy of preparation (Darling-Hammond, 2006; Grossman et al., 2008; Hammerness et al., 2005; Hammerness & Klette, 2015). Finally, we argue that faculty share a mutual trust. This is necessary to effective collaborative inquiry where candidates' performance can be tied directly to faculty's work (specific courses, say) and where it's imperative that conversations on practice are part of data analysis. To truly collaborate for programmatic change means faculty must do so with the trust that experimentation, discovery, and disclosure are necessary to the process. Effective collaboration, in our experience, requires quite a lot of time and space to develop. The following examples illustrate how two programs—Alverno and UCSB—approached the cultivation of collaboration.

At Alverno College, because of the institution-wide commitment to authentic assessment and generation of evidence of student learning, the uses of time and space mentioned above were only possible because of intentional onboarding of new full-time faculty and adjunct faculty colleagues. Led by experienced Alverno educators, the Friday afternoon times during one's 1st year of work at Alverno are oriented to ensure that new faculty understand the ability-based model, can effectively align program outcomes to course outcomes, and can ensure that course assessments generate evidence of course outcomes and that student self-assessments always accompany evidence of outcomes. Thus faculty build a common sense of ownership for the model and commit to their roles in generating the program data that makes robust analysis and evaluation possible. The abilities that students develop at the undergraduate level are also expected of faculty. Faculty work within courses must ensure that assessments include the Alverno criteria used for students to self-assess their own abilities—social interaction, valuing in decision making, problem solving, analysis, aesthetic engagement, communication, global perspective, and effective citizenship—and these abilities must be modeled by faculty so that students can deepen their own. As a result, faculty conversations, debates, and collaboration can draw on the criteria and tools built over decades to support group problem-solving tasks. The Alverno case study in Chapter 4 goes into greater detail about cultivating collaboration within this model.

At UCSB, one strategy leaders relied on to cultivate collaboration was to support existing communities of practice that faculty had already created in the enactment of their work. These faculty had previously created core conditions for collaboration and were well situated to take on new forms of data that might inform their work. There were communities of practice across courses, such as a group of elementary reading and English language development instructors who had cocreated assignments and course experiences to coincide with each other's practice. There were groups of supervisors who shared their practice around observation and feedback. The introduction of new forms of data that revealed candidates' practice, such as that found in the teaching performance assessments, were opportunities to dig deeper into understanding what candidates were doing, and how these faculty communities were and were not as effective as they had hoped. The ability to see opportunities in their own growth as teacher educators required trust, a trust that had already developed in these communities. Supporting them with opportunities to share their inquiries with the larger group allowed for safety in numbers, and the confidence of findings built on multiple rounds of analysis and deliberation among their trusted peers. Faculty retreats then became a place to share this work, for instance, in the form of providing workshops to all faculty whereby they took their other colleagues through a similar process of examining candidate work vis-à-vis their own practice. In this way program leaders relied on local talent to create learning opportunities for all. This created opportunities for deep inquiry in a safe and supportive way. And the retreats provided the necessary length of time to do it well.

SUPPORTING EXPERIMENTATION

The final category of time and space strategy we offer here is that which supports faculty experimentation for the good of programmatic practice. A core piece in reflective practice, experimentation at the collective level requires attention to the organizational practices that will enable it.

At ECU, in an effort to increase innovation development, the college's dean developed very specific policies and procedures for inviting and supporting experimental projects—what they called "squishy pilots" (see the ECU case study in Chapter 3 for an in-depth look into the innovation phases). A memorandum of understanding (MOU) was created to guide and support each proposed innovation, including specification of project goals, needed supports (e.g., faculty release time), an evaluation plan, and project deliverables. The shared terminology in the innovation phases in conjunction with the dedicated college supports for IRB development, research methodology consultation, data storage, analysis and collection tools, and travel support (dissemination at conferences) propelled collaborative program- and college-level experimentation in curricular and clinical experiences with the EPP.

The dean also realized that building a culture of programmatic experimentation required some dismantling of institutional barriers. Within many of our university contexts, one such barrier is the individual reward culture of promotion and tenure structures. The collective needs of programmatic research and collaboration do not fit well within this culture. Changes to the structures of this culture opens space for the work. The ECU dean recognized that personnel policies needed adjustments. Hence, she created a "fourth box" in faculty tenure and promotion guidelines that called for evidence of participation in collective work of the program. In doing so, the dean made it very clear that program improvement work was recognized in its complexity and valued in terms of its contributions to the unit and the field. This was extremely motivating to faculty and enabled a new culture of collaboration to develop.

Alverno continued to innovate opportunities for collaboration and experimentation, even as they had a deep culture set for that work. In particular, they took advantage of virtual space. As technology has evolved, so too has the Alverno College faculty's innovative work with synchronous and asynchronous time and online and virtual space. Preparing unit data for an annual state licensure liaison visit shifted from physical artifacts and binders to an online project management space; those in directorial positions coedited analysis documents, assigned tasks to other faculty, and opened the space to the state liaison when the review visit neared. Conversations to support adjunct faculty in their assessment design made use of asynchronous video discussion tools. Ad hoc collaborations and meetings now occur as frequently via video chat as in physical spaces on campus. The purpose remains the same; the orientation toward formative use of data for improvement is consistent.

SUMMARY

Programmatic data work is not an add-on. For many teacher educators it is a new addition to their practice, and we found that for it to truly change practice on a programmatic level, it required new opportunities to engage. We offer some insights into why the work requires this level of attention—the newness, the collaborative needs, the collective reflective needs—and we offer some examples of how programs created time and space to meet these needs. Throughout this volume we offer different slices of faculty's engagement with candidate evidence, to describe the ways it transformed the programs in which they worked. Creating time and space for that work is one slice. It is a critical one that in our experience is often overlooked. It is also work that loses its potential when conducted intensely for a finite implementation period until accountability policies and reports are satisfied. For continuous improvement—a concept that many of us believe has yet to reach its potential—it requires that the examples we offer above become institutionalized. In some cases, they did. UCSB still engages in quarterly faculty retreats (2 decades after they commenced) which almost always include some form of data for faculty engagement. Alverno and ECU still have robust data platforms and systems in place to allow faculty to access the data. Alverno created a culture of collaboration over several decades, inculcating new faculty into the work, and creating year-long calendars that scheduled cross-program collaboration time. Where did these programs fall short? UCSB still needs to create promotion and workload policies that support this work. Too many research faculty fall away from the work when their own tenure requirements get in the way. At ECU, faculty and administration changes have introduced the inevitable slide in how practices and processes are interpreted and enacted. Further, the shift from local evaluation for edTPA to external scoring reduced the number of program faculty involved in the work (as it also did at UCSB). Alverno can identify substantive ways to more fully engage candidates, and their practices of self-assessment, as crucial stakeholders of data. Candidates' collaboration in this work is an untapped opportunity to systems and practices in all three programs, which makes this work exciting. It is ever evolving, and with the time and space to conduct it, imagine what we can do as a field!

NOTE

1. TEP = Teacher Education Program

REFERENCES

Bunch, G. C., Aguirre, J. M., & Téllez, K. (2009). Beyond the scores: Using candidate responses on high stakes performance assessment to inform teacher preparation for English learners. *Issues in Teacher Education, 18*(1), 103–128.

Darling-Hammond, L. (2006). *Powerful teacher education: Lessons from exemplary programs.* Jossey-Bass.

Grossman, P., Hammerness, K., McDonald, M. A., & Ronfeldt, M. (2008). Constructing coherence: Structural predictors of perceptions of coherence in NYC teacher education programs. *Journal of Teacher Education, 59*(4), 273–287.

Hammerness, K., Darling-Hammond, L., Grossman, P., Rust, F., & Shulman, L. (2005). The design of programs. In L. Darling-Hammond & J. Bransford (Eds.), *Preparing teachers for a changing world: What teachers should be able to do* (pp. 390–411). Jossey-Bass.

Hammerness, K., & Klette, K. (2015). Indicators of quality in teacher education: Looking at features of teacher education from an international perspective. In G. K. LeTendre & A. W. Wiseman (Eds.), *Promoting and sustaining a quality teacher workforce* (pp. 239–277). Emerald Group.

Head, B. W., & Alford, J. (2015). Wicked problems: Implications for public policy and management. *Administration & Society, 47*(6), 711–739.

Høyrup, S., & Elkjaer, B. (2006). Reflection: Taking it beyond the individual. In D. Baoud, P. Cressey, & P. Docherty (Eds.), *Productive reflection at work* (pp. 29–42). Routledge.

Peck, C. A., Gallucci, C., & Sloan, T. (2010). Negotiating implementation of high-stakes performance assessment policies in teacher education: From compliance to inquiry. *Journal of Teacher Education, 61*(5), 451–463.

Raelin, J. A. (2002). "I don't have time to think!" versus the art of reflective practice. *Reflections, 4*(1), 66–79. doi:10.1162/152417302320467571

Sloan, T. (2013). Distributed leadership and organizational change: Implementation of a teaching performance measure. *The New Educator, 9*(1), 29–53.

Sloan, T. (2015). Data and learning that affords program improvement: A response to the U.S. accountability movement in teacher education. *Educational Research on Policy and Practice, 14*, 259–271. doi:10.1007/s10671-015-9179-y

CHAPTER 9

Leadership Strategy and Practice

Tine Sloan, Diana B. Lys, and Ann Adams Bullock

The following is a conversation between the newly established Assessment Coordinator (AC) and faculty (F) head of a program in one of our case study institutions:

> *F:* It's good you are here. What is the state department of education (DOE) making us do now?
>
> *AC:* No DOE mandates at the moment; no changes right now. I would really like to learn about your current assessments for DOE. Could you tell me about the assignments?
>
> *F:* Sure. We call them "artifacts." We collect them in the institutional learning management system (LMS) and then keep a copy in case DOE requests them.
>
> *AC:* That's great. May I have access to the LMS to check them out?
>
> *F:* Of course. (But giving AC a look of wonderment as to why.)
>
> *AC:* So I know your grads do great work and that is a credit to your faculty. So, tell me, how do you assess their artifacts? How do you know they meet the state standards? What does your rubric include?
>
> *F:* Rubric? What rubric?
>
> *AC:* Well, DOE did require them. And certainly, you have some guide for being able to determine who meets or exceeds—or fails to meet—the state minimum standards, yes?
>
> *F:* Looking at me directly and tapping his index finger to his temple. Rubric? The rubric is right here.

SHARED LEADERSHIP CHALLENGES IN EDUCATOR PREPARATION

Skillful leadership is essential to building local capacity and commitment to using data for program improvement. While concerns about leadership often center on the actions of a dean, department chair, or program director, the three program portraits presented in the present volume (Alverno College;

University of California, Santa Barbara; and East Carolina University) indicate how important it is that leadership functions are distributed across all sectors of professional practice within a teacher education program. Course instructors, field supervisors, cooperating teachers, and administrators face a set of shared leadership challenges related to both the contemporary policy context and institutional history of teacher education. In this chapter we begin by identifying some of these common challenges, and then describe what we have learned in our efforts to engage them in multiple program contexts.

Policy Tensions: Accountability and Improvement

Anyone working in a teacher education program over the past 2 decades is acutely aware of the intense public scrutiny and related accountability pressures that have characterized state and federal policy, as well as professional accreditation processes during this period. Programs are now routinely required to collect and report data on a plethora of program features and outcomes, including candidate demographics related to admission and completion, coursework requirements related to state curriculum standards, field placements and hours, teaching performance, and graduate and employer satisfaction. While these data may offer some potential value as resources for program improvement—and in fact are often represented by policymakers as serving the dual purpose of improvement and accountability—the primary purpose for many of these data collection and reporting activities is that they are *exchanged* for program approval/accreditation. Data collection and reporting mandates from state policymakers and accreditation agencies are thus viewed by many teacher educators as facts of institutional life requiring compliance at best, and at worst viewed as unwelcome intrusions that overwhelm resources for local autonomy and decision making.

Viewed from this perspective, the most fundamental leadership challenge related to data use for teacher educators at every level is to imagine, and help others imagine, how program data (including measures required for external reporting, as well as those developed by the program itself) can be useful resources for local learning and program improvement.

Organizational Silos of Practice

Almost all teacher education programs are organized into "silos" of practice. The most fundamental of these, of course, are the silos of coursework and fieldwork. The division of labor within most teacher education programs wherein some individuals (often tenure-line faculty) teach courses on campus, while others supervise teacher candidates in the field, leads to very different perspectives on the learning-to-teach process and related disconnections between the learning going on in courses, and the challenges candidates are experiencing in their practicum classrooms. Program meetings may include campus faculty, but not field-based teacher educators such as student teaching supervisors and cooperating teachers. These organizational disconnections are often compounded by significant differences in power and voice between field-based and campus-based teacher educators, with accompanying challenges in communication and collaboration between educators ostensibly sharing the same goals.

These organizational conditions constitute a second major challenge for teacher education leaders concerned with building program capacity and commitment to using data for program improvement. This is the challenge of building organizational structures and policies that bring teacher educators serving in diverse program roles together for the purposes of communication, collaboration, and joint decision making.

A Culture That Rewards the Individual Over the Collective

The organizational structures and personnel policies of most teacher education programs define program roles and responsibilities, evaluate performance, and reward achievement as matters of individual practice. Faculty teaching courses are evaluated based on student ratings of the courses they teach. Field supervisors are evaluated and compensated based on their individual coaching responsibilities. Research faculty are evaluated on publication and grant records where first authorship, sole authorship, and lead PI status is paramount. Teacher educators identify strongly with the quality and integrity of their individual work, and improvements in individual practice are valuable, to be sure. However, at its core, program improvement is a collective endeavor, which requires collaboration across courses, across coursework and fieldwork, and collaborative research endeavors across practitioners and researchers. The value and importance of this type of collaborative work is often in tension with tenure and promotion policies for teaching and research faculty, and compensation or workload policies for field-based teacher educators.

This means that a third challenge for program leaders is to create shared professional experiences, and accompanying personnel policies, that strengthen program members' sense of collective identity, and collective commitment to collaborative program improvement. This means moving from a sole focus on "my research," "my course," or "my coaching practice," to an expanded focus on improvement of "our practice" as a program. For leaders this may require rapidly adjusting one's lens from the unit they lead to the perspective of program faculty to the view of a clinical partner. In our experience, leaders who are able to negotiate these shifts deftly are well prepared to guide their organizations to develop a collective mindset.

In the remainder of this chapter we highlight themes in leadership action that cut across our three cases. These address the challenges identified above in order to improve the work of programs by moving specific evidence into thoughtful action.

A THEORY OF ACTION IN LEADERSHIP

As leaders engaged with these tensions, we saw them orchestrate opportunities for strategic learning on the part of program faculty. We noticed a theory of action rooted in approaching change as *a learning problem,* where leaders tried to understand who needed to learn what and how, in order to improve their collective work.

Each of our program leaders paid attention to learning and change in different ways. At UCSB, leaders and researchers used an inquiry–action, self-study process (also described in Chapter 5). Figure 9.1 illustrates this inquiry–action cycle of program development:

This repeating cycle included four phases. The "Program outcomes and events" phase captured program-level activity (as opposed to individual practice activity), such as faculty retreats, and the TPA scoring week (for local calibration and scoring that included all faculty). It included smaller groups of faculty coordinating across courses or creating programwide artifacts (such as a lesson-design frame, or a student teaching record). It also

Figure 9.1. UC Santa Barbara's Inquiry–Action Study Process

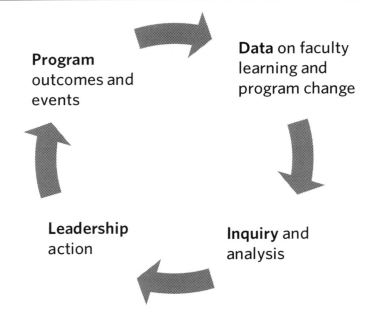

included policy and practice activity such as modifications to workload, development of a research program, or changes to a curriculum sequence. In the next phase, "data on faculty learning and program change" were gathered directly from these events (observation notes, faculty free-writes, workshop materials), as well as gathered outside of them (faculty interviews, course syllabi, other curriculum artifacts). These data were regularly fed into an "Inquiry and analysis" phase where researchers and program leaders worked jointly to make sense of it (note some data were first processed by researchers to ensure confidentiality). These analyses focused on what faculty were learning, how they were learning, and how the program was changing. Sometimes the analysis was short and informal (a few hours), other times prolonged and systematic (with an actual retreat from campus for 2 days). These inquiries would frequently reveal pockets of faculty work that leaders saw as strategic to programmatic growth. These faculty were often asked to join the "Leadership action" phase, during which leaders used data from the inquiry to plan and execute next steps in the program change process. Leaders often shared what they were finding in their inquiries—what they saw faculty learning and where the program was changing. As programmatic work grew, faculty created offshoots of this inquiry–action cycle to lead other areas of programmatic work.

Leadership at ECU approached the program improvement work through a process where experimentation on program practice could begin in a relatively low-stakes way—as a "squishy pilot," as they called it. In a squishy pilot, individuals or small groups could experiment with innovative ideas around practice (say, a series of new course assignments) and take initial steps to understand the efficacy of the innovation. This inquiry might use informal data such as anecdotal student feedback and samples of student work, which they used to refine ideas, processes, or assessments. If the innovation showed promise, leadership supported them to create a more formal pilot in a second stage of work. In all, there were six stages to this process. As illustrated in Figure 9.2 (also included in this volume as Figure 3.1), each stage supported progressively more formal implementation and research (e.g., IRB processes, support of methodologists, conversations with program leaders).

The idea was that such a process allowed faculty to learn and engage at their levels of interest, comfort, and collegiality, but with a clear pathway to developing innovations for programwide research and practice. The ECU dean believed faculty needed a visual heuristic to guide them, in order to orchestrate their efforts as part of the unit's work, not solely their individual academic pursuits. In turn, leadership had access to what faculty were engaged in, how they were doing it, and what they were learning. ECU leaders strategically selected and supported successive steps for faculty's work that would allow it to become better supported with more formal research, and ultimately reintegrated into programwide work. The ECU case study in Chapter 3 describes this process in more detail.

Figure 9.2. ECU's Pirate CODE Implementation Process

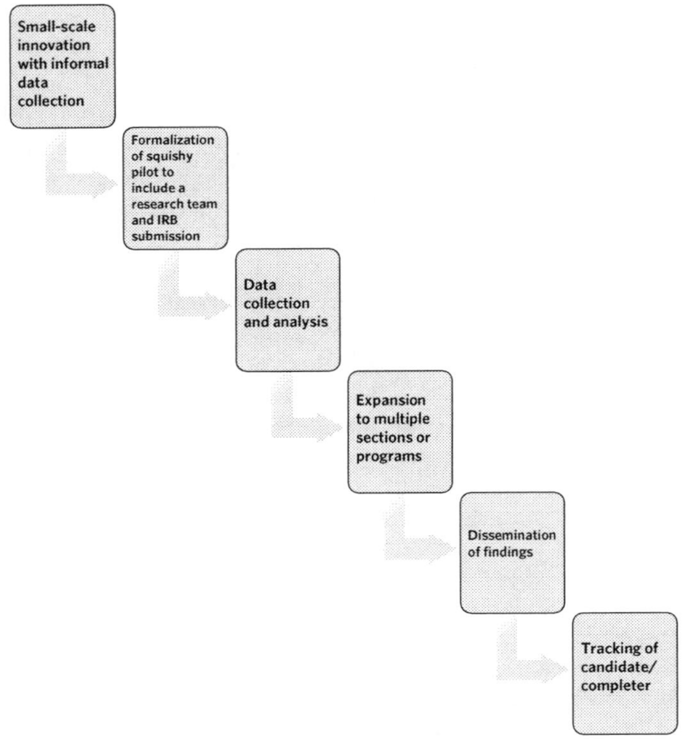

The UCSB and ECU processes illustrate how leaders managed policy implementation as a learning problem rather than a compliance problem, and in doing so, created a culture of inquiry. We characterize a *culture of inquiry* as one where activity is grounded in evidence, and where people have shared understandings of practice and use a shared language in their work (Bunch et al., 2009; Peck et al., 2010; Sloan, 2013, 2015;). In this culture, disturbances to the status quo are a signal for inquiry, as opposed to rejection or absorption that maintains the status quo. Such a culture relies on collaborative work, which at its core relies on some degree of "shared understanding, agreed purposes, mutual trust, and usually an element of interdependence" (Head & Alford, 2015, p. 725). Leading effective collaborative work requires time, effort, and skill in understanding and managing the complexities of the problem space. Early in our work we used Engeström's CHAT framework to understand program learning and change in the organizational problem space (Engeström, 1987, 2001). Later we needed a more accessible framework to understand how leadership practice was interacting with learning and change

ORCHESTRATING LEARNING AND CHANGE

The framework used throughout this volume is an adaptation of Engeström's work that we have found accessible to understanding the transactional nature of key dimensions related to data work (McDiarmid & Peck, 2007). As explained by Charles Peck in the introduction to this volume, these include dimensions "related to the values, beliefs and motivations of the *people* involved, those related to the *conceptual and material tools* used to carry out the work, and those related to the *organizational policies and practices* that shape the way the work is carried out" (see Figure 9.3 for a visual representation of the framework). We found that the People–Tools–Organizational Policy/Practice (PTO) frame anchors an array of leadership actions to a set of practical dimensions that not only help us make sense of the array of actions, but can also guide leaders' action in their future work. Some program leaders within our network began to use the frame to guide their own actions in situ. From their work and others, we extract examples to describe how leaders moved evidence into programmatic action.

Figure 9.3. People, Tools, and Organization Framework

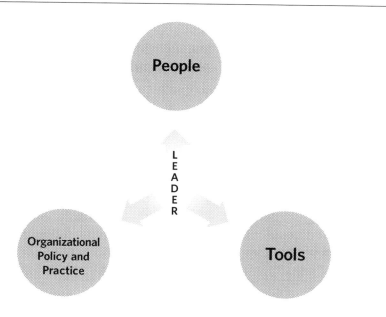

People: Relying on Local Expertise

Program leaders worked diligently to engage people with the work of change. Engagement was not just a matter of having faculty buy in to a vision or blueprint for change. While there may be many reasons why people should engage, mere participation does not adequately harness the expertise of the people doing the work—which is a collective expertise that surpasses that of a single leader or set of leaders. Nor does buy-in consider a key motivating factor that educators share: A high level of integrity and commitment to good practice. Nobody wishes to teach badly. This may be stating the obvious, but it is worth consideration. Of further consideration is the nature of educator preparation; there is a high level of interdependency among courses and field-work that create the whole of a new teacher's practice, which mitigates the effectiveness of any single teacher educator. To do their best work, teacher educators must rely on colleagues to do theirs, and on program leaders to orchestrate across practice, and on organizational policies to support the integrated nature of the work. It stands to reason that having some influence on these programmatic pieces would be important to faculty.

The program leaders in our case studies orchestrated people's expertise in ways that strengthened their opportunities to inform, and even lead, programmatic work. They did this in several ways. For instance, at UCSB when first implementing the programwide TPA, leaders tapped into existing communities of practice where groups of faculty were already planning across courses, or supervisors were collaborating across practice. These communities shared a history, understandings of the work, trust, norms for engagement, and so on, and could more easily get to the heart of working on programmatic implications of the assessment. Then program leaders facilitated opportunities for groups to share their work with the larger group. Quarterly faculty retreats were a primary venue for this, and "sharing" grew to more than "presenting" what we know. It grew into carefully crafted learning opportunities for faculty. Over time, through strategic collaborative data practices (described further below), new cross-practice communities emerged. For example, a group of secondary faculty, methods instructors from each content area, literacy instructors, and supervisors formed a group when they noticed problematic practice in the ways secondary candidates attended to their students' literacy needs. The group worked for several years developing and articulating shared practice, learning about literacy in content areas, developing cross-practice assignments, suggesting a different curriculum sequence, and so on. They even guest-taught in each other's courses, and worked with supervisors on how to support candidates in placements and vice versa (how to teach candidates so they could enact literacy instruction in their placements). Program leaders supported these efforts with an occasional lunch for their meetings, with opportunities to share their work with all faculty (at retreats), with the opportunity to shape the curriculum sequence (which they did), with support from administrative staff, and with pledged support from program leaders to problem-solve institutional barriers to the work (e.g., experimenting with changes to workload for adjunct faculty).

ECU tapped into local expertise in multiple ways throughout their large institution, with collaborative research on planned studies of practice and other studies that emerged in the "squishy pilot" process described earlier. Supported initially by a large federal grant, planned studies of practice addressed both systemic teacher education elements (clinical practice, intern support, and so on), and data-driven program improvement (use of the edTPA, development of a data platform, and so on). Within this process, new faculty leaders emerged, some who developed innovations for their own practice, others who were selected by the dean to lead larger, schoolwide efforts (such as an assessment coordinator). ECU's squishy pilot process also engaged faculty from across the spectrum of professional practice. Program leaders invited faculty participation in the pilots, being mindful to include a range of faculty perspectives from those who were eager to join in, to those more reticent to jump on board. The diversity of perspectives was a purposeful leadership move to engage and not marginalize faculty voices. Each pilot codified their work in a memorandum of understanding that established the team's norms for planning, executing, and studying the pilot. Once in place, the dean seeded the work of each pilot with continuing support to inform the pilot development and later disseminate findings. Supports ranged from refreshments for partner meetings, to specialized methodological supports, to travel funding.

As local talent and expertise became more interconnected, people's activity expanded from a more siloed practice (their own course or supervision practice) to a more programmatic practice (shared assignments, programwide lesson templates, and new curriculum sequences that bridged content and program area divides). Strategic facilitation of cross-practice work was essential to programwide improvement in all three cases, largely because integrated practice would be more effective than disjointed practice in preparing new teachers. Leaders also reported that when faculty across all levels were given the opportunity to understand the whole program—and their piece in it—they developed a sense of programmatic responsibility. This was especially true for program faculty who were previously on the fringes of the decision making (often field supervisors). Leaders in each program were intentional in including and integrating people from cross-practice roles.

Tools: Choosing Data That Enables Programmatic Engagement

One of the most powerful things to get people's attention was evidence of candidates' teaching practice that ran counter to faculty's expectations. Program leaders were very strategic in choosing and managing "attention-getting" data used in collaborative analysis. This strategic orchestration of learning was used for several ends. For example, in an effort to break down silos, UCSB program leaders would vary the types of data used in retreats across the year, so that it would privilege different people's expertise at different times. This meant one data retreat might focus on video of candidates' student teaching—privileging supervisor's expertise of the contextual, school-based factors that course instructors did not have—whereas another might focus on adapting instruction for students with disabilities, and require expertise from another group of faculty.

In North Carolina, the state university system introduced value-added measures (VAM) as part of their teacher quality research initiative, presenting programs with their VAM scores as evidence of the program's effectiveness. This created a great disturbance in the university system, and quite a bit of tension within the ECU faculty. However, the college leadership team sought to transform the external pressures into internal motivation for faculty learning and program improvement saying, "We don't need to embrace VAM, but we need to understand what it is and how others will use it." The assessment coordinator worked with each program to explore the VAM methodology and its affordances and limitations in an effort to assert local ownership of the analysis. Next, program leaders engaged P–12 partners to examine the VAM findings (as they would soon be made public) and to see if their impressions matched the VAM findings. They explored the disconnects and alignments between VAM and partner feedback. The dean then sponsored a collaboration with researchers to undertake a predictive analysis of each program's assessment data to see which of the local assessment instruments predicted VAM outcomes (Henry et al., 2013). When none of the existing program assessments were found to be related to VAM outcomes, program leaders leveraged the findings to bring more valid and reliable assessments, including standardized teaching performance assessments, to the programs as a more valid evidence base for future program improvement efforts. Through these efforts, the faculty expanded their assessment literacy, accepting VAM as one data point, while actively supplementing with others deemed more useful for program improvement and more aligned with the program's mission.

A key to data selection for collaborative analysis was to ensure that data provided access to what candidates were actually doing, in other words, the artifacts of their practice (lesson planning, video of practice, case studies of students, and so on). Aggregated data were important for noticing patterns and trends over time, but understanding practice required data close to practice. It was through this type of data that faculty could envision how their own practice might change. At Alverno, the teacher candidate portfolio contained multiple artifacts of candidates' work from multiple practices (courses, fieldwork placements) in the program. The portfolio was mission-aligned to help candidates demonstrate, or "validate," their abilities as an Alverno-prepared teacher. The portfolio, which candidates would build over time via an electronic platform, was also a collaborative space for faculty to provide feedback intended to support candidates' future teaching practice. The platform allowed faculty to examine their individual contributions to candidates' practice and growth, as well as see other areas of candidate expertise. It was a rich source of data that could facilitate faculty's understanding of how candidates integrated learning from across the program.

In all three cases, evidence of candidates' practice was a significant motivator for changes to individual faculty practice. Changes to programmatic practice, however, were facilitated by data whose scope was programmatic (e.g., the TPAs used in all three programs and the portfolio at Alverno), rather than specific to a course or two (such as an assignment). A holistic assessment such as the PACT[1] or edTPA[2] became a powerful motivator for collective responsibility due to the integrated, authentic nature of the practice it captured. In other words, for these assessments, candidates were required to integrate their learning from across the program and enact it in teaching practice, which meant faculty needed to untangle how the preparation they provided was enabled or constrained by the rest of the program. Although all teacher educators know in an abstract sense that their own contributions are part of the whole, in these programs, it was the TPA data that allowed them to understand specific ways in which their contributions could integrate better with the whole. In choosing data for "continuous program improvement" we found it essential to work with assessments that reflect the complexities of teacher preparation and expand the analysis and evaluation of joint activity to a programmatic level.

Organizational Policy and Practice:
Attending to Supports and Constraints

At this point in the chapter, it would be clear to any program leader that each of the examples provided so far required a set of organizational policies and practices that would enable the work. We recognize that readers may feel overwhelmed by the organizational constraints of their settings. Each setting in our program cases was different: Alverno is a small liberal arts college, UCSB is a midsize, research-intensive university, and ECU is a large regional institution. Alverno had a long-established culture of using candidate evidence to determine candidates' readiness to teach (there is no letter grade system for this), and to guide program development. Nonetheless, during our study the edTPA had been introduced in Wisconsin, and this new data source needed careful integration to make it matter the way the portfolio did. All program leaders created opportunities for data to be accessible and usable and, ideally, meaning-ful. Like Alverno, we saw ECU and UCSB develop processes for shared engagement with data through which faculty developed a shared language of practice. We found that a shared language of practice was integral to program improvement (Peck et al., 2009). Several leadership actions sup-ported programwide use of data. We describe five areas of leadership ac-tivity related to organizational policy and practice.

Providing opportunities for consistent, structured collaborations with all fac-ulty at the table. All program leaders created consistent opportunities for programwide meetings and retreats. These were critical sites of collabora-tion and innovation and required extensive planning and attention to data selection, how activity was organized, and how faculty within multiple roles would jointly engage. Food, camaraderie, and occasional off-site meeting spaces contributed in important ways to building community and space for inquiry. Each program had annual calendars with this time built in. At Alverno College, these policies and practices were particularly well de-veloped, with an institution-wide commitment to collaborative work built into every faculty member's weekly time commitments (see the Alverno case study in Chapter 4 for more on this institutional innovation for cross-practice engagement).

Planning, consulting, planning, and planning some more. Program leaders considered the planning and operation of programwide data retreats or data summits as a critical part of their workload. At times they took weeks to consult with and plan retreat activity in order to ensure that faculty could engage in worthwhile inquiry during the time allotted. Follow-up to these events was equally important, a critical factor to making the retreats worth-while. Hence part of the planning process was considering follow-up pro-cesses that enacted people's ideas. In asking leaders to reflect upon planning for this collaborative data work, one reported that she had not understood how critical those first retreats were in establishing activity that was differ-ent: "This was a honeymoon period that could have failed badly had people not seen them as worth their time. Only years later did I realize how much our work depended on people consistently engaging in these time-intensive retreats."

Creating time and space—suspending normal activity. Program leaders re-alized their inability to squeeze this important work into existing work-load structures. At UCSB, all course- and fieldwork was suspended for a week each spring to allow faculty to collaboratively score TPA portfolios and focus on data analysis. While execution was not perfect each year, it was one of many ways program leaders signaled to faculty that the data work was important, and it required allocated time and space to engage. At ECU, program leadership supported the attendance of faculty teams at national conferences where they presented practice-based research efforts. This investment created time and space for faculty to grow professionally as a team and to consider/problematize/ideate new areas for engagement or improvement. Unique among the cases, Alverno regularized meetings for data-focused work by scheduling weekly time for faculty to meet in different teams across the calendar year. Program leaders utilized the cultural meeting norms of the unit to engage with candidate portfolio data and to focus on program strengths and opportunities for growth. All program case studies (see Chapters 3, 4, and 5) describe their processes in more detail, as does Chapter 8, "Making Time and Space for Data Use."

Attending to workload and promotion policies. We noted earlier that one of the endemic challenges in higher education is the culture of individual entrepreneurship that rewards individual accomplishments over the collective work we saw as essential to program improvement. This is markedly evident in promotion and tenure processes, as well as hiring policies for nontenured instructors/supervisors. Collaborative data work rarely features in these policies, so several program leaders paid particular attention to this. In the UCSB research-intensive context, leaders were not as successful at changing promotion and tenure policy, but they were able to modify non-tenured faculty workload to include some time for data work. At ECU, workload changes included enrollment caps on intensive methods and field-based methods courses that included "gateway assessments" requiring multiple rounds of feedback. To address promotion and tenure policies, the ECU dean introduced a "fourth box" to be added to the traditional three—teaching, research, and service. The fourth box was an effort to place new value on contributions to program improvement efforts, and it captured faculty activity such as leading a program assessment team, serving as a clinical partner liaison, or conducting analysis of candidate data to inform the work of the program. The idea behind the fourth box was that it honored faculty's scholarly contributions to practitioner preparation as more than "service," which is traditionally where this work gets categorized. The fourth box was an attempt to signify distinctions between the type of work conducted in the professional discipline of teacher education and types of work conducted in other disciplines.

Supporting Faculty. In addition to workload, promotion, and hiring, a large part of program leaders' efforts were to find ways to support faculty engagement in this highly collaborative work. Our leaders were naturally concerned with the budgetary needs this work posed, and at times real dollars were used. UCSB had a small grant to support their self-study, and

ECU had a large federal grant to initiate their work. ECU used their grant to create robust research opportunities, whereas UCSB did so on a smaller scale (providing graduate student researchers, for instance). All three programs created budget line items for new positions, some long-term (such as an assessment coordinator) some short-term (such as a 1-year appointment to help supervisors develop and use an electronic evaluation tool). All programs designated administrative staff to support faculty work so that faculty groups could request administrative help with developing new curriculum, planning and implementing workshops for fellow faculty, and so on.

Much of the time, however, leaders supported faculty via their interest and participation in the faculty-led work. This included participating in the working meetings of faculty groups as appropriate (as an interested participant, not as the leader of the meeting) and attending to institutional policy when it constrained people's efforts. It included efforts to make program meetings a place for problem solving, coplanning, and getting feedback on practice, in other words, activity people could not do solo. This meant that presentations of information could get relegated to text for asynchronous consumption.

Leader as Orchestra Conductor

Breaking down leadership practice into the three dimensions of the PTO frame was helpful in making sense of activity that seemed particularly important to programmatic data work. When leaders enacted these practices in real time, however, they were orchestrating activity within and across the three dimensions. A useful metaphor is program leader as orchestra conductor. A conductor orchestrates multiple dimensions of music and musician so they may co-create a performance. Members of an orchestra each have their roles, but they are interdependent. They share understandings of the discipline and each other's roles in it, and operate with the mutual trust that their colleagues will play their parts as required. The conductor supports each of them in their role, simultaneously keeping track of the parts with an eye on the whole, and facilitating movement forward. To stretch the analogy further, the music of a beautifully performed symphony is a sum that is greater than its parts.

Turning to program leaders' coordination of the PTO dimensions, Figure 9.4 provides an example of leadership activity aimed at building effective collaboration.

The analogy of "orchestra conductor" has its limitations, of course. The metaphor doesn't describe the process whereby important leadership functions became distributed over time, across all sectors of professional practice in these programs. Perhaps a jazz analogy works better, where different musicians take the lead at different times and others adapt their

Figure 9.4. Example of a Program Leader Orchestrating PTO

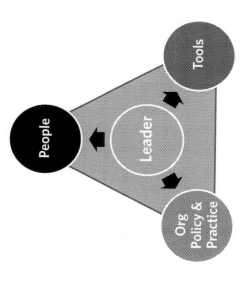

When TPA data revealed candidates' shortfalls in practice, people became vulnerable. Deep inquiry of this data, particularly in the company of others, required mutual trust. One leader selected data that over time would reveal multiple needs and strengths (to spread focus) and allowed different members to be necessary sources of expertise (to build confidence in their contributions and interdependence among colleagues), then facilitated retreat activity to focus on cross-practice strategies (to further build interdependence). This leader explains her thinking: "It was not enough to frame data retreats with 'we're all important, we're all needed here,' I wanted to be sure people *experienced* their contributions as necessary." Using a holistic assessment tool like the TPA facilitated understandings of the integrated nature of the discipline and colleagues' roles in the discipline. The annual calendar reflected time for everyone to attend retreats, which meant program leaders worked to suspend or replace other activity.

parts to co-create. It seems the success of a jazz trio requires the elements of effective collaboration (interdependence, trust, shared knowledge, and so on). Likewise, we believe that successful distribution of leadership required effective collaboration practice as its base. Then we saw groups of faculty taking it upon themselves to develop programwide artifacts, develop new course sequences, determine new cross-practice assignments, and take on new roles. And like a seamless symphony and stunning jazz performance, the sum of these teacher educators' collaborative work was greater than its parts. A cohesive and integrated preparation experience created better opportunities for teacher candidates to integrate and apply learning from their faculty's individual practice (Hammerness & Klette, 2015).

CONCLUSION

The orchestration of people, tools, and organizational policy and practice was a useful way to analyze leaders' practice, and, as we mentioned, this framework offered a guiding heuristic for some leaders engaged in the work. Throughout the study, leaders also navigated the challenges posed by larger policy and institutional contexts. We describe three of these at the start of this chapter: challenges created by tensions between accountability and continuous improvement policies; challenges related to organizational silos of practice in most higher education programs; and challenges posed by an institutional culture that rewards individual entrepreneurship over the collective work conducive to program improvement (see Figure 9.5).

We conclude by summarizing leadership practice across the dimensions of Figure 9.5 (see Table 9.1). We gained several insights as we considered the totality of this work. One of the most important was the consistent effort among leaders to effectively respond to external policy and institutional needs while maintaining local control and autonomy over the work.

In all three cases, program leaders were deliberate in approaching the policy and institutional challenges from a faculty learning perspective. Perhaps this is why one program leader said, "we had the professional time of our lives!" and other program faculty agreed. This excitement and passion for their work was a consistent finding in UCSB's self-study of faculty, as it was in the work of ECU, and in the culture of Alverno, and throughout the cases that were a part of the larger University of Washington study. We believe that the extensive work around developing collaborations and a culture of inquiry was central to why people felt this way. The opportunity for collective responsibility was not just good for program change, but good for people. It created an opportunity to take

control of their work in an era where educators' practice is increasingly criticized and monopolized by outside agendas. It also allowed them
to cobuild the program they invested their professional lives in. Finally,
people had *evidence* that change was working. They had access to consistent evidence that candidates' practice was getting better, and they shared
understandings of what "better" was. Yes, it was an energizing period for
all of us.

**Figure 9.5. Orchestrating PTO to Engage the Institutional and Political Challenges for
Teacher Education Leaders**

Table 9.1. Summary of Leadership Considerations on the PTO Dimensions in Response to Challenges Posed by Key Policy and Institutional Contexts

Challenges	PTO Framework Dimensions		
	Conceptual and material tools used to carry out the work (including data)	Values, beliefs, and motivations of *People* involved	*Organizational policies and practices* that shape the way the work is carried out
Policy Tensions: Accountability and Improvement	There was a tension between the quantity and type of data required for reporting (multiple data points, mostly quantitative) vs. the type of data needed for program work (both disaggregated quantitative with heavy on the qualitative). Disaggregated data was useful for identifying patterns but improvement of practice required data closer to the level of candidates' practice (actual artifacts of practice).	People were resistant to external pressures and feared loss of autonomy. Leadership relied on local talent to engage people in shaping the work; they distributed leadership to empower people; and they allowed dissenting voices to help shape the program's response to policy. People were motivated by what they saw in candidates' artifacts of practice (less so with quantitative data).	Leadership structured opportunities for faculty to learn about policies and data, and provide input on what did and did not work for improvement. They made time for analysis of candidate artifacts. They studied what faculty were learning, and how the program was changing in order to guide their actions. They cultivated cultures of inquiry that moved away from a compliance stance, creating more autonomy and local control over the process.
Organizational Silos of Practice	Use of a holistic assessment such as the TPA challenged silos as it required candidates to integrate their learning from across the program in order to enact teaching. Data made evident that candidate success was contingent upon their ability to make connections among practice silos.	There were power differentials among faculty roles, where some members worked on the fringes of program decision making (usually supervisors and adjuncts). Supervisors are closest to practice and a vital source to program improvement work. Historical silos affected the mutual trust and respect required for deep inquiry.	Leaders created opportunities for cross-practice collaborations in the form of planned research, data retreats with everyone at the table (especially supervisors), and the support of faculty-led working groups. They attended to ways faculty could develop a mutual trust and understanding of each others' practice, and the program's practice as a whole.

| Challenges | PTO Framework Dimensions | | |
	Conceptual and material tools used to carry out the work (including data)	Values, beliefs, and motivations of People involved	Organizational policies and practices that shape the way the work is carried out
A Culture that Rewards the Individual Over the Collective	Use of a holistic assessment such as the TPA revealed the integrated needs of teacher preparation; it revealed the limitations of an individual teacher educator's effectiveness; it revealed the expansion of this effectiveness when practice was connected to others' practice and when practice took place within a cohesive program.	Collaborations became energizing. When peopled learned the whole program, and about each others' practice, it seemed to empower them. We saw people eager to form new collaborations and lead practice. We also saw people torn between commitments of two academic worlds.	Leadership created space and time to do the work; they attended to promotion, tenure, and hiring policies to reward collective efforts; they distributed leadership of the work across the professional spectrum.

NOTES

1. Performance Assessment for California Teachers (PACT) used at UCSB for 12 years prior to edTPA.

2. edTPA was used in all three programs

REFERENCES

Bunch, G. C., Aguirre, J. M., & Téllez, K. (2009). Beyond the scores: Using candidate responses on high stakes performance assessment to inform teacher preparation for English learners. *Issues in Teacher Education, 18*(1), 103–128.

Engeström, Y. (1987). *Learning by expanding: An activity-theoretical approach to developmental research.* Orienta-Konsultit Oy.

Engeström, Y. (2001). Expansive learning at work: Toward an activity theoretical reconceptualization. *Journal of Education and Work, 14*(1), 133–156.

Hammerness, K., & Klette, K. (2015). Indicators of quality in teacher education: Looking at features of teacher education from an international perspective. In

G. K. LeTendre & A. W. Wiseman (Eds.), *Promoting and sustaining a quality teacher workforce* (pp. 239–277). Emerald Group.

Head, B. W., & Alford, J. (2015). Wicked problems: Implications for public policy and management. *Administration & Society, 47*(6), 711–739.

Henry, G. T., Campbell, S. L., Thompson, C. L., Patriarca, L. A., Luterbach, K. J., Lys, D. B., & Covington, V. M. (2013). The predictive validity of measures of teacher candidate programs and performance: Toward an evidence-based approach to teacher preparation. *Journal of Teacher Education, 64*(5), 439–453.

McDiarmid, B., & Peck, C. A. (2007, March 16). *Theories of action and program renewal in teacher education* [Paper presentation]. Northwest Association of Teacher Educators 2007 Conference, Seattle, WA, United States.

Peck, C. A., Gallucci, C., & Sloan, T. (2010). Negotiating implementation of high-stakes performance assessment policies in teacher education: From compliance to inquiry. *Journal of Teacher Education, 61*(5), 451–463.

Peck, C. A., Gallucci, C., Sloan, T., & Lippincott, A. (2009). Organizational learning and program renewal in teacher education: A socio-cultural perspective on learning, innovation and change. *Educational Research Review, 4*(1), 16–25.

Sloan, T. (2013). Distributed leadership and organizational change: Implementation of a teaching performance measure. *The New Educator, 9*(1), 29–53.

Sloan, T. (2015). Data and learning that affords program improvement: A response to the U.S. accountability movement in teacher education. *Educational Research on Policy and Practice, 14*, 259–271. doi:10.1007/s10671-015-9179-y

CHAPTER 10

What We Learned About Getting Started With Data Use Through Self-Study

Aaron Zimmerman, Tabitha Otieno,
Jahnette Wilson, Chase Young, Jessica Gottlieb,
Benjamin Ngwudike, and Marcelo Schmidt

In this chapter we will describe the process that we (seven faculty members across four institutions) used to engage in the process of self-study as a means to better understand and improve data use practices within our respective teacher education programs. The objective of this chapter is to provide the reader with an introduction to the self-study process, with a focus on how to get started. By outlining specific steps in our process and by highlighting particularly fruitful strategies, this chapter serves as a resource for teacher education faculty and administrators who, themselves, want to get started with self-study work within their respective departments.

The chapter is organized around four essential questions:

- What are some different ways to frame the purpose of self-study?
- Who should be involved in the self-study process?
- How does one engage in the self-study process?
- What are some of the challenges and benefits to engaging in self-study?

The recommendations presented in the chapter are the product of the experience of a 2-year self-study cycle at our respective institutions. These institutions (Texas Tech University, Jackson State University, University of Houston, and Sam Houston State University) were brought together within a network of teacher education programs, University–School Partnerships for the Renewal of Educator Preparation (US PREP, https://www.usprepnationalcenter.com). At each institution, one or two researchers led the self-study efforts. Supported by US PREP—through both stipends as well as opportunities to convene multiple times during each year—research leads (the authors of this chapter) conducted self-studies at their respective institutions while checking in with one another and sharing results every other week. We also shared our findings formally (with each other as well as with other teacher educators, scholars, and higher education administrators) during the official conferences hosted by the US PREP network. This work was supported by US PREP for 2 years. It is in this context that we describe our 2-year process of learning about our own institutions as well as learning from one another.

WHAT ARE SOME DIFFERENT WAYS
TO FRAME THE PURPOSE OF SELF-STUDY?

Deliberating Purpose at the Outset

Although self-studies can be conducted in a variety of contexts and can explore a variety of topics (Zeichner, 2007), we use the term *self-study* to refer to studying the process of collaboration for continuous improvement around data use practices within our respective teacher education programs. By self-study, we are referring to the process of collaborating with program faculty in an attempt to better understand how program stakeholders utilize and make sense of data.

We recognize that every organization has its own unique structure and its own unique concerns, and thus one of the guiding principles to our work was the premise that a self-study cannot be guided by a set of predetermined or standardized questions. Instead, we believe that it is critical that faculty concerns (including the concerns of clinical, field-based faculty) should frame the guiding questions of any given self-study. Although self-study projects can be valuable for accountability reporting functions such as those required by the Council for the Accreditation of Educator Preparation (CAEP) or Teacher Preparation Inspectorate (TPI), the self-study work that we describe in this chapter is not motivated by compliance with external mandates. Instead, the focus, goals, and findings of the work described in this chapter are intended to guide efforts toward making data use practices within each local program more meaningful to the program's faculty and stakeholders. In order for this to occur, it is critical that local program faculty own and drive this work.

In our collaborative work together, we often referred to this principle as the "North Star." For us, the North Star represented our commitment to the values that undergirded our work. Our work was not motivated by accountability pressures, but rather by a spirit of inquiry that was focused on better understanding how and why our local program stakeholders made sense of data as a tool for improving their practice. Likewise, perhaps the most fundamental piece of advice that we can share in this chapter is that we believe the framing of self-study work must be developed through deliberation. It is rare that program administrators, faculty, and staff members possess a shared understanding of the goals for data use activities (Peck et al., 2010). Thus developing a shared sense of priority and purpose related to data use work cannot be achieved simply by stating goals or issuing mandates, but, perhaps, is only achievable through an ongoing process of discussion and deliberation about the values and purposes of the work. We have found that unless this deliberation takes place, it will be difficult for a self-study to maintain its momentum.

It should be noted that this process of deliberation can take place in both informal and formal spaces. Informally, faculty can meet and talk with one another about what they are observing as they work with their teacher education candidates. These informal conversations can be a productive launching pad for future questions (e.g., What data do we have that might answer this question? What data do we need in order to investigate this question further?). Indeed, if the self-study process is genuinely motivated by the North Star (i.e., a set of collective values and commitments), then many of these conversations will occur spontaneously.

One cannot, however, overstate the importance of formal opportunities for deliberation. Unless department leaders (i.e., department chairs and deans) dedicate time and space for faculty to share, analyze, and discuss data, such opportunities may remain an afterthought in the mind of faculty. In other words, department leaders must demonstrate to faculty through their actions, and not just their words, that getting better at data use is an institutional commitment. Thus department leaders should consider organizing department-wide and collegewide meetings focused exclusively on providing the opportunity for faculty to engage with data. As we will discuss later in this chapter, we found that some of the most productive moments during our respective self-studies occurred when multiple stakeholders were brought together in conversation through the efforts of department leaders. Indeed, the organization of these opportunities communicated, to all stakeholders, the respective department's commitment to this work.

PTO as Theoretical Framework

As we began our self-study inquiries at our respective institutions, we developed our research questions using the PTO (People–Tools–Organizations) theoretical framework (McDiarmid & Peck, 2012). We found the PTO framework to be especially useful for the framing of our work because of the way that it accounts for the interaction between how teacher education programs are organized, what tools teacher educators use to evaluate teacher growth and teaching effectiveness, and the beliefs, knowledge, and values of individual program stakeholders.

In order to understand data use within a given program, it is critical to understand how individuals make sense of data use, what data use tools are available to them, and how communication and collaboration among these individuals are facilitated and encouraged (Mandinach & Gummer, 2019; Miller et al., 2015). Hence, with this framework in mind, each research lead began by developing a unique set of questions at their respective institution. These questions were specific to local context. The next step at the outset of our collaborative work was to pool together these research questions in order to find common ground, that is, a set of more general, underlying questions that could constructively guide our collective inquiry. Having a common set of research questions provided us with a common reference point throughout the self-study process. We found this to be especially valuable as we consulted with one another and gave each other feedback and advice throughout the self-study process. Had we each been studying our own individual set of research questions (with little overlap between them), it is doubtful that our conversations throughout our 2 years of collaboration would have been as productive.

The following represent the shared research questions that guided our respective self-studies:

People:

- What ideas, beliefs, and feelings shape the way program members engage data?
- To what extent do program members see data use as an inquiry process? As a compliance process?
- To what extent do people in our program see their work primarily through the lens of individual practice (e.g., *my* course, field placements) or as a collective practice?
- What common goals and values are shared among program members? How strongly?

Tools:

- What methods are used to collect, archive, and analyze the data?
- How accessible are the data to individual program members? To role-alike groups (e.g., field supervisors, foundations faculty)?
- To what extent can the data be disaggregated to address issues of concern regarding specific students, groups of students, performance over time?
- To what extent do students have access to data related to their progress in the program?

Organizations:

- What program policies and practices affect data use?
- To what extent are data use practices integrated into regular faculty/staff/partner meetings?
- To what extent are roles and responsibilities related to data use well defined and coordinated vs. ad hoc?
- To what extent are expectations related to data use work identified in personnel policies (e.g., job descriptions, promotion and tenure criteria, compensation)?

WHO SHOULD BE INVOLVED IN THE SELF-STUDY PROCESS?

Selecting a project coordinator, or team of project coordinators, was the first critical step in our self-study process. We recommend that the project coordinator(s) be faculty with established professional relationships within the given college of education and, preferably, part of the teacher education faculty (whether tenure-track research faculty, clinical faculty, or field-placement coordinator). Having active lines of communication with colleagues is not only important for the purposes of gaining access to interview participants and policy documents but also because the ultimate goal of the self-study process (guided by the North Star) should be to leverage the findings of the self-study to effect actual change toward improving data use practices within the program. Additionally, project coordinators should be familiar with the methodological procedures of qualitative research, given that the majority of the self-study project will most likely consist of collecting and analyzing qualitative data (including interviews and focus groups). Project coordinators should have experience with conducting qualitative interviews as well as analyzing interview transcripts for themes. Project coordinators, therefore, should not only be individuals with strong organizational skills and, preferably, with qualitative research experience, but also individuals who deeply understand the concerns and aspirations of the faculty within their respective teacher education program.

We recommend that program administrators (e.g., deans and department chairs) not play a direct role in leading the self-study work. We found that the power relationships associated with these roles sometimes made it more difficult to obtain candid feedback about data use policies and practices from our respective program faculty. Having said that, we found that it was critical for project coordinators to keep administrators, as well as other faculty, informed about the findings of the self-study as it progressed. We found that unless department leaders were aware of the emerging findings of the self-study, it was unlikely that the self-study findings would effect meaningful change within the program.

Once project leadership is established, it is important that relevant stakeholders in the teacher education program be identified. We began by contacting a variety of people who worked at and with our respective institutions in order to collect information regarding data use from multiple perspectives. We collected data from faculty who serve various roles (e.g., faculty who teach methods courses as well as faculty who supervise teacher candidates in the field) as well as faculty who represent different levels of experience, expertise, seniority, and leadership. We found that collecting data from a wide range of faculty produced a more holistic understanding of the data use practices within the program. Additionally, we recommend interviewing teacher candidates and/or recent graduates of the program, as well as administrators (e.g., deans, associate deans, department chairs, and directors of assessment) within the teacher education program, as we found that their perspectives tended to yield unique insights.

We found it valuable to learn about the perspectives of individuals outside of our institutions, as well. For us, these individuals included cooperating teachers, mentor teachers, and school and district administrators (e.g., principals and superintendents). We do want to emphasize that, as contexts differ, so do the important stakeholders. Thus it is the responsibility of project coordinators to develop a comprehensive list that represents data use throughout the program. We believe that learning from all of the relevant perspectives increases the likelihood that the given program's data use practices will be improved (and made more useful for all parties involved). Furthermore, and as we shall discuss in a later section of this chapter, the multiple data sources collected during these self-study projects were, indeed, able to provide useful data for the purposes of external reporting requirements.

HOW DOES ONE ENGAGE IN THE SELF-STUDY PROCESS?

Timeline

As we began to engage in the self-study process, we found it beneficial to establish a set of targeted dates for key steps in the completion of the project. Based on our experience, our suggested timeline for an initial self-study cycle is one semester, approximately 5 months. A timeline will help pace the project coordinators throughout each phase of the work. Amendments to the timeline may be necessary as the coordinators move through the process. The following represents our timeline for our self-study work:

January:

- Begin planning and coordination of project

- Review self-study questions

February:

- Demonstrate that data sources have been identified
- Finalize research questions (understanding that these may evolve over time)
- Get IRB approval (or equivalent permission to conduct this research) if you choose to seek publication
- Identify from whom you are collecting data from and by when

March:

- Begin data collection
- Keep records, including digital recordings, field notes, interviews, and other documents

April:

- Continue data analysis
- Present evidence of initial stages of data analysis including descriptive, thematic analysis, quantitative analysis (as applicable)

May:

- Present results of data analysis

June:

- Provide evidence of a first draft of the self-study report
- Be able to communicate evidence-based information and recommendations based on the self-study

Data Collection

We gathered data from a variety of sources including interviews, observations, focus groups, surveys, and artifacts. Interviews were the main source of data in our self-study work. Interview protocols were adapted for specific stakeholders so as to capture the many differentiated voices: administrators, teacher mentors, school principals, faculty, and site coordinators. Sample interview questions included the following:

- When you hear the word *data,* what do you think about? What does the term mean to you?

- What are your main responsibilities with regard to collecting data?
- Of the data that is available to you, which data do you find most useful in your work in mentoring teacher candidates?
- What kinds of data do you wish you had? Why would these data be valuable to you and your work?

Observations were another valuable data source that we collected during the self-study process. At our respective institutions, we strategically selected meetings that we thought it would be informative to attend. These involved department meetings, course planning meetings, and days that the department had specifically set aside to discuss programmatic data. As project coordinators, we observed these meetings and took field notes, paying particular attention to issues such as who speaks, what they speak about, what data is shared, how the data is discussed, and what the outcomes of the meeting are.

A third data source that we found to be particularly productive was the focus group. Like interviews, questions during these sessions can focus on issues of what data is used to make programmatic decisions, who has access to that data, and so on. What makes the focus group a unique method of data collection is that a focus group can involve individuals who all share the same role, or the focus group can intentionally bring together individuals with different roles. For example, a focus group could bring together instructors of the same methods course; alternatively, a focus group could bring together a group of course instructors, site coordinators, directors of assessment, mentor teachers, and district administrators. In particular, we found the latter configuration to be especially effective at not only soliciting multiple perspectives but also at providing a forum to brainstorm programmatic innovations as a result of having multiple stakeholders in the same room at the same time.

The following is a sample from the transcript of one of these focus group interactions:

> *Research Lead:* So what can we do better at [our university] related to data use?
>
> *Assessment Office Representative #1:* Something that I would like us to work on is regular routine review of data. Because we get a lot of ad hoc requests to look at data, like somebody has an interest and so they all want to look at that [data]. But we have a lot of data that never gets reviewed because it's not a concern. . . . So I would like to put in more routine review and use of data.
>
> *Assessment Office Representative #2:* And I would also say that . . . often data-related tasks fall to program coordinators. And so there are certain expectations for daily usage that just, it's a nonnegotiable.

Data are collected in campus labs for multiple reasons, but if you ask people they will say that it is collected for [accountability and compliance reasons]. And so we could get better at changing the mindset, and we've really been working to shift the thinking around this and help people to get that it's more than a report that's completed for compliance, but that it is a repository of data and a process where programs can sit together, as a group, and review the data, review the goals, for the program and what it is that they want to collect, and how they want to use that to make decisions. But often it falls to a program coordinator to try and make a deadline sitting in an office. . . . We really want to be much better at changing the way [people] think about that. We keep trying in the center for assessment to send that message, that you get to decide what you want to measure, you get to decide how to make that meaningful, and you as a team of program faculty can decide what you want and how you use that data to make decisions. We try to get away from compliance-driven data assessment usage to really meaningful assessment.

Assessment Office Representative #1: [It is also about] shifting the mindset on accreditation, because we have a group of faculty that don't mind, like [an earlier speaker] said, "I like being able to prove to other people that we meet those standards and that we're a high-quality program." And then there is also the group of faculty that, if you say anything about accreditation, [they] have very negative thoughts toward accreditation. And so, for that, I think accreditation got a really bad rap, instead of being a way to demonstrate how amazing your program is, like this is your chance to brag about yourself. Some of our faculty have gotten a really negative [image] . . . attached to accreditation. I think that's why we have tried really diligently [to spread the message that] this isn't just for accreditation. Even though, what's wrong with it being for accreditation?

Faculty Member: Well, in terms of data and also what we're measuring, I think one thing I'd like to see, I'd be more interested in working on and getting closer to the goal, is assessment of [teacher] dispositions and the data on dispositions. In preparing teachers, we cultivate knowledge on dispositions and I am the first to acknowledge [that] those skills traditionally and historical have been easier to grade and assess, but dispositions have not been so. And I hear a lot at . . . conferences how dispositions are gaining traction . . . and how teacher education programs should cultivate and measure how we are cultivating dispositions. How our preservice teacher is going to develop the skills, like let's say, willingness to learn about other cultures, openness to learn about other cultures, or being able to communicate more effectively with students and their parents who may not be speaking English. I don't really have data on that, other than . . . isolated studies that I would be doing in [my] class. I don't know how they're doing . . . after my class. So I think collecting data on dispositions would be quite important, critical for if we are looking for more data, to collect more data is area for growth.

Assessment Office Representative #2: It sounds like [we] have a [new] committee member. [Let's] get him on the assessment committee.

In this selection from the focus group session, we see different stakeholders sharing their different perspectives on data use from different components of the program. Furthermore, as this selection from the transcript illustrates, the focus group session was an opportunity for the different stakeholders to give their input about what they perceive to be the challenges and opportunities related to data use in the program. Furthermore, the transcript seems to indicate that the conversation was able to open up new collaborations.

A fourth data source that we utilized was surveys. In particular, we created surveys that were designed to solicit unique input from various stakeholders. For example, we asked P–12 administrators, "What data have been shared with you that have informed your work with mentor teachers?" and "What data have been shared with you that have informed your work with teacher candidates?" We also used surveys to pose questions to teacher candidates such as, "What data that have been collected by your supervisor have had the most impact on your practice as a prospective teacher?" We found that surveys have the advantage of being distributed via online systems that expedited the gathering of data from many participants.

Finally, artifacts served an important role in our data collection process. Certain documents (e.g., policy documents, meeting agendas, rubrics) provided insight into the policies and practices that influence the data use practices within our respective organizations.

Data Analysis

The first step in our qualitative data analysis began with coding interview transcripts, observation notes, and textual artifacts using low-inference codes (Erickson, 2004). Once a few data sources had been coded, we began to develop a list of low-inference coding tags from the coded documents. We used these tags to create categories inductively. Once these codes were consolidated into a manageable list, we used this reduced list to code the remainder of our data sources. Codes that turned out not to be useful were dropped. Preferred software packages such as Dedoose, NVivo, or RQDA can be employed to do the coding.

It should be noted that although each research site followed the same qualitative data analysis procedures, we did not pool our data together nor did we attempt to create generalizable, cross-case conclusions. Rather, there were four different analyses conducted on four unique sets of data, one corresponding to each research site (see Table 10.1). This approach corresponded with our motivation to use the self-study data that was collected as a means of informing the practices at each institution, unique to the specific people, tools, and organizational structures in place within each given program.

To this point, we want to emphasize that methodological choices should be expected to vary depending on the institutional context of the study. At each institution, the self-study research coordinators developed a methodological approach that was aligned with the aims of the self-study inquiry at that institution, developed in response to the guiding questions and concerns at the given institution (i.e., the North Star). Although, at each research site, we elected to utilize the conceptual framework of people, tools, and organization (PTO), there exist other potential conceptual and methodological approaches that could be considered. Indeed, adopting an alternative methodological approach to the self-study may yield novel insights. For example, researchers might experiment with ethnographic approaches to answer questions related to the culture of the teacher education department; with phenomenological approaches to investigate the lived experience of collecting, working with, and talking about data; with narrative approaches to learn about the stories that are being told regarding data and data use within a given teacher education department; or, with statistical modeling grounded in social network analysis to answer questions about communication focused on data. Although these approaches were not utilized during our initial set of self-study inquiries, we, as project coordinators, collectively discussed the potential application of these different methodological options as viable approaches for follow-up studies.

WHAT ARE SOME OF THE CHALLENGES AND BENEFITS TO ENGAGING IN SELF-STUDY?

Challenges

The first challenge that we want to highlight related to conducting a self-study involves being discouraged by the sometimes seemingly overwhelming nature of the task. The nuances and demands of self-study work seem daunting, particularly at the outset. A quote from one of the self-study research leads reflects this sentiment: "The 1st day we met and discussed the self-study, I was so overwhelmed and intimidated by the scope of the work

Table 10.1. Summary of Data Sources and Findings

	Data Sources	Findings
Jackson State University	Interviews: Interviews were the major source of data in this self-study. A total of 23 individuals were interviewed in the process of data collection. All interviewees played different and significant roles in the teacher education program. Focus group: During the process of conducting interviews for self-study data collection, a focus group of nine individuals was formed that included one associate dean, three departments chairs from the teacher education programs, assessment coordinator, site coordinator, three faculty members from three Teacher Education departments, and two researchers conducting the interview. Secondary data sources: Selected documents were analyzed to determine the frequency and time devoted in discussing data in any agenda items in various management meetings. The documents reviewed included Specialized Program Association (SPA) reports, faculty meetings, and the teacher education sample syllabi.	To enable faculty members and other stakeholders to see data use as a process of inquiry, the teacher education leadership team needs to create regular time and space to enable stakeholders to see data use as a process of inquiry rather than compliance. The leadership team also needs to develop policies that define how data use should be integrated into job descriptions, promotion and tenure, and salary increments.
Sam Houston State University	Fifteen interviews were conducted with various stakeholders in the program, including practicum professors, foundations professors, site supervisors, academic leaders in teacher education, the office of assessment, deans, and K–12 personnel including a superintendent, a principal, and two mentor teachers. Based on the initial interviews, focus groups were intentionally constructed to promote action as a result of the discussions. Finally, the researcher took detailed notes at college, department, and program meetings.	Four themes emerged: (1) context, (2) data, (3) engagement, and (4) outcomes. Within the theme of context, the researcher noted that national, state, and organizational standards are constantly changing, and thus EPPs are often forced to be reactive instead of reflective. In any given year, one entity is likely updating their standards, which means institutions have little chance to examine the effects longitudinally. For the data theme, there was an issue related to whether analysis was defined as a team responsibility or an individual's responsibility. As an individual, it can be difficult to collect and analyze data effectively, and the results may be less likely to result in collective action. When considering engagement, everyone involved in EPPs should have a shared understanding of data use practices and tools. In terms of outcomes, at this point, there are differing views on what data is important and how it should be used.

University of Houston	The study used the following sources: 24 individual interviews, 1 focus group, observations of program meetings, and artifacts of data use (e.g., meeting agendas, accreditation reports, and contents of databases). Participants in the interviews and focus group included individuals involved with teacher education, specifically leadership, faculty, field supervisors, data managers, and EPP partners	The data from the study supported the use of self-study and examination of program data to move from simply "compliance" to "collaborative inquiry" for sustainable programmatic transformation. Analysis of these data revealed themes that were used to generate actionable plans and promising strategies related to program improvement activities around data use and collaborative practices. An improved communication plan focused on data collection practices, analysis, and use was formulated and disseminated to all stakeholders. Collaborative efforts were used to engage faculty in transforming the culture and data practices of a program through collaboratively constructed programmatic outcomes and a data plan to guide programmatic decisions.
Texas Tech University	Ten members of our teacher education department participated in the self-study. These participants came from all aspects of the program, including program leadership, faculty anchors, instructors, professional development facilitation, site coordinators, and those responsible for assessment and accreditation processes. Interviews were conducted, focusing on how (and how often) individual teacher educators utilized tools related to data use, as well as how the organizational structure of the department shaped the manner in which teacher educators understood their work and their data use responsibilities. Documentary evidence was also collected, including mission and vision statements, CAEP documentation, documents describing the alignment between the college goals and CAEP requirements, and data reports.	We found that teacher educators in our department were often forced to adopt multiple roles when collecting, managing, and analyzing data. Specifically, teacher educators, at different times, must use data for research, for program improvement, and for providing teacher candidates with formative assessment. We also found that the teacher educators within the department had a common rubric for assessing teacher quality; however, not all teacher educators endorsed this rubric as a valid assessment of teacher quality. They noted that they are rarely afforded the opportunity to discuss what they believe to be quality teaching (or how to measure it).

that I wanted to run out of the room. From time to time, reference was made that some of our team members had qualitative method experience and that their expertise would be essential along the way. I had a plan to fade out gradually so they could get someone else with a qualitative method background to replace me. Though I was discouraged and helpless, I did not quit." It should be noted that this team member later became one of the most active and enthusiastic participants in the self-study work.

A second challenge worth highlighting relates to the lack of a shared understanding related to the goals of the self-study, especially at the beginning of the project. One of the most important findings from our self-study efforts was that program administrators and faculty seldom begin the self-study process with a shared understanding of what the goal of data use is within the program. This underscores the need for active communication regarding the purpose of the self-study and the importance of what is being learned about the needs, questions, and concerns related to data use within the teacher education program.

A third challenge that we encountered involved keeping stakeholders informed and engaged throughout the self-study process. As mentioned earlier in this chapter, administrators and faculty should be informed and engaged with the self-study process throughout the duration of the inquiry. We found that keeping everyone involved and informed throughout the process was important to maintaining the momentum of the self-study and ensuring that its findings would be used to make changes in program policy and practice.

Benefits

As illustrated in the focus group transcript presented earlier, we found that one benefit from the self-study process is that practical solutions and new innovations may be generated organically through the inquiry process. We discovered that when representatives from diverse stakeholder constituencies were brought together in conversation, they were often spontaneously able to generate new opportunities for increased collaboration. As the participants listened to one another, it was not unusual for these participants to recognize problems that they had not previously recognized or fully understood, and, almost intuitively, they began to work together to brainstorm solutions. Returning to the conceptual framework of PTO (People–Tools–Organizations), we began the self-study process with the assumption that the manner in which a given teacher education program is organized (including opportunities for collaboration) will affect the manner in which stakeholders collect, discuss, and utilize data. In the case of the focus groups, not only did these focus groups help us learn more about the nature in which the teacher education program's structure was supporting or inhibiting data use, but we found that the focus groups themselves served as an intervention, that is, the focus group discussion provided a unique opportunity for collaboration between various components of the program. In this way, the self-study inquiry itself was, modestly, able to reshape the organization of the program.

One of the most beneficial outcomes of the self-study process was the creation of program reports that we provided to our respective programs. Our program reports included the following:

- A description of program context
- A description of our methods of data collection and analysis
- A summary of the findings (including brief excerpts from interviews and observations)
- Insights using the People–Tools–Organizations (PTO) framework
- An action plan for next steps designed to address each of the needs identified from the self-study
- A report to stakeholders

These program reports and action plans for follow-up proved to be one of the most fruitful outcomes of the self-study process. For example, at Jackson State University, the program report highlighted that certain valuable program data were not reaching all program faculty. This motivated the creation of a new assessment team charged with collecting, analyzing, and sharing data within the teacher education program.

At the University of Houston, stakeholder surveys (sent to principals and mentor teachers) motivated the University of Houston faculty and administrators to revise the assessment tools that were used to evaluate teacher candidates. This helped the program and its stakeholders take an important step toward developing a shared language in relation to the assessment of their candidates' process of learning to teach. The self-study research leads from the University of Houston presented the following conclusions to their program leadership:

- Differentiated perceptions of data collection, analysis, and use are inherent within faculty and staff roles and responsibilities.
- A shared vision regarding data collection, analysis, and use should be the foundation for collaborative data use practices.
- Coordination of an intentional data use plan that includes time and space for the work will support building a culture that engages in inquiry-based data use practices, as opposed to one of compliance.
- Context matters: Quantitative data is made more palatable and meaningful when accompanied by the qualitative story.

- Levels of concern and perception of use matter in the face of change and transformation.

Based on these conclusions, the self-study research leads from the University of Houston presented the following recommendations to their program leadership:

- Develop an improved communication plan focused on data collection, analysis, and use.
- Collaboratively construct programmatic outcomes with all stakeholders: leadership, institutional effectiveness, faculty, site coordinators, and district partners.
- Co-construct a data plan with stakeholders: "What data should guide programmatic decisions?"
- Use the collaboratively constructed programmatic outcomes and the data plan to inform continuous programmatic improvement efforts.

These conclusions and recommendations not only informed the University of Houston program leadership about the nature of data use within the program but also provided the program leadership (and, indeed, the entire department) with a specific and actionable set of recommendations based on the results of the self-study inquiry. This, in turn, provided a clear pathway for follow-up and improvement during the subsequent semester.

Using the Self-Study to Address Accountability

It should also be mentioned that, although the North Star of our self-study projects was most certainly not abject compliance with accountability measures, our self-study reports were, in fact, able to provide useful data for the purposes of external reporting requirements. For example, the Jackson State University project coordinators analyzed data use practices related to several different types of data, including ACT scores for admission to teacher education program, Praxis I and II scores, Foundation of Reading scores, candidate portfolios during field experience, mentor teacher evaluation of teacher candidates, field supervisor evaluation of teacher candidates' performance, and site coordinator evaluation of candidates' performance during the field experience. CAEP Standard #5, specifically, states: "The provider maintains a quality assurance system comprised of valid data from multiple measures." Thus in addition to helping to answer the research questions of the Jackson State self-study inquiry, this collected data was able to serve as documentation for CAEP accreditation.

FIVE CONSIDERATIONS FOR GETTING STARTED

1. Each teacher education department is unique; thus project coordinators should pay careful attention to the unique concerns and aspirations of the program's faculty and stakeholders.
2. Deliberation around the emergent findings and future directions of the self-study inquiry should take place throughout the self-study process (not just at the outset). Continuous deliberation can serve to maintain the motivation and momentum for the inquiry, whereas prolonged periods without communication can cause motivation to wane.
3. It is critical for local program faculty to own and drive the self-study inquiry; otherwise, faculty may interpret the self-study process as just another mandate that is divorced from their authentic concerns.
4. Different data sources (including policy documents, observation field notes, meeting agendas, surveys, individual interviews, and focus groups) each provide unique opportunities to gain insight into the data use practices of the program.
5. Having critical friends is valuable. Although we worked at four separate institutions, as six project coordinators, we benefited greatly from being able to communicate regularly and collaborate with one another. We were able to share our developing insights, our common challenges, and our innovative solutions. Furthermore, we found that we were less likely to be discouraged by our setbacks when we were able to discuss our experiences together.

Our self-studies at our respective institutions provided us with an opportunity to build unity within our respective programs. We were, in this sense, able to leverage the reality of increased accountability for data use (Coburn & Turner, 2011; Spillane, 2012) as an opportunity to work together to improve our collective work. We believe that the self-study process, focused on data use, is an opportunity to build a culture of inquiry within teacher education programs. This process is not without its challenges, nor should it be considered to be a quick fix. Our experience, however, has taught us that the self-study process (when initiated by faculty and guided by faculty concerns) can help programs learn how to make programmatic data play a role in making our collective work more effective and more meaningful.

REFERENCES

Coburn, C. E., & Turner, E. O. (2011). Research on data use: A framework and analysis. *Measurement: Interdisciplinary Research and Perspectives*, 9(4), 173–206.

Erickson, F. (2004). Demystifying data construction and analysis. *Anthropology & Education Quarterly, 35*(4), 486–493.

Mandinach, E. B., & Gummer, E. S. (Eds.). (2019). *Data for continuous programmatic improvement: Steps colleges of education must take to become a data culture.* Routledge.

McDiarmid, B., & Peck, C. A. (2012, April). *Understanding change in teacher education programs.* [Paper presentation]. American Educational Research Association Annual Meeting, April 14–19, Vancouver, BC, Canada.

Miller, M., Carroll, D., Jancic, M., & Markworth, K. (2015). Developing a culture of learning around the edTPA: One university's journey. *The New Educator, 11*(1), 37–59.

Peck, C. A., Gallucci, C., & Sloan, T. (2010). Negotiating implementation of high-stakes performance assessment policies in teacher education: From compliance to inquiry. *Journal of Teacher Education, 61*(5), 451–463.

Spillane, J. P. (2012). Data in practice: Conceptualizing the data-based decision-making phenomena. *American Journal of Education, 118*(2), 113–141.

Zeichner, K. M. (2007). Accumulating knowledge across self-studies in teacher education. *Journal of Teacher Education, 58*(1), 36–46.

Part IV

NEW DIRECTIONS

CHAPTER 11

Improving Programs Through Collaborative Research and Writing

Joy N. Stapleton, Diana B. Lys, Christina M. Tschida,
Elizabeth Fogarty, Ann Adams Bullock, and Kristen Cuthrell

If everyone is moving forward together, then success takes care of itself.

—Henry Ford

Teachers spend only 3% of their day collaborating with their colleagues (Mirel & Goldin, 2012). This isolation associated with teaching is not new. Lortie documented it as early as 1975 in his book *Schoolteacher,* and it remains evident today (V. Strauss, 2013; Webb, 2018). This culture of isolation follows teachers as they move into faculty positions in colleges of education where they often work in academic silos, especially early in their career (Jones, 2013; Norrell & Ingoldsby, 1991). Academic silos can be difficult to navigate for faculty in small educator preparation programs (EPPs) where faculty take on many administrative roles, and in large EPPs where faculty carry heavy teaching loads and navigate increasingly intense standards for promotion and tenure. One potential way to offset academic isolation is through the formation of vibrant intellectual communities to support teaching and scholarly production. These communities can leverage collaborative research to improve programs and, ultimately, to contribute to the research base on teacher preparation.

In this chapter current and former faculty from East Carolina University describe our roles as collaborative researchers who developed a collective and program-focused research agenda that contributed to the improvement of our teacher candidates as well as programs. As faculty at a large regional EPP, we balanced heavy teaching loads and increasing demands for promotion and tenure as our institution pivoted to be more research-intensive. Specifically, we describe the collaborative process surrounding three key program innovations and highlight informal networks, program improvements, and collaborative research efforts to sustain innovations.

COLLABORATION TO BUILD COMMUNITY

In colleges and universities, faculty consistently balance the requirements to teach courses, provide service, and publish research. In our experience, teacher education faculty take on additional responsibilities, including supervision of clinical practice, teacher candidate support, and continuous improvement activities. In many regional institutions the workload is considerable. Faculty teach six to eight classes a year in addition to other responsibilities. The stringent requirements on new faculty to establish a research agenda while fulfilling all other job requirements can be overwhelming in a new context with new school partners and colleagues, especially when engaging in larger issues related to program improvement. These factors can slow the publication pipeline, ultimately disadvantaging tenure-track faculty in their efforts toward pretenure review. One way for new faculty to alleviate "publish or perish" stress is by joining a collaborative writing group. One of the valuable things about the work we have been doing is that it shows a pathway for managing both pressures for tenure, and also collective program-level policy pressures for continuous improvement.

It is typical to start a career in academe with a focus on one's own research agenda. This is a natural evolution for a researcher extending out of graduate school where a singular research focus based on interest is common and reinforced by the dissertation process. This research is often driven by publication benchmarks for tenure and promotion. Contextual factors like individual interest, time, money, research releases, and university politics influence individual faculty research. As new members of the academy, it is not unusual for a faculty member to research in isolation. To combat unproductive isolation, our dean's goal was to develop collaborative writing groups to pool resources, engage colleagues, and most importantly, to center research efforts around issues of EPP concern and improvement.

A collaborative writing group in which faculty come together to publish research is especially helpful for early career faculty (Austin, 2010) but can be just as beneficial to motivate a faculty member in their mid- or late career (Dronzek, 2008). Creating collaborative writing groups of individuals with complementary skills can lead to writing success for the entire group (Staffileno et al., 2016). Finding individuals who are interested in the same topics, are willing to collaborate, and follow through with tasks can lead to more completed projects. Productive writing communities have individuals who are willing to give their time, ideas, and feedback (Golde, 2015). This willingness of individuals to invest their valuable time is based on the belief that everyone is working toward the same goal and the entire collaborative writing group will succeed as a result of this work (Golde, 2015). Over time, individuals within the collaborative writing group begin to build what Bhavsar and Ahn (2013) call total accountability. When a writing group achieves total accountability, members follow through with assignments and meet deadlines. It also means admitting when one cannot meet the deadline and asking for help.

Developing a Collaborative Research and Writing Approach

When faculty function within silos, their research is done with little regard or planning for how the research will affect the program mission or contribute to program graduate knowledge. One way that leaders can encourage collaborative writing is by providing time and resources. Typically, there is a catalyst—a leader who encourages collaboration through provision of tools. Tools can include buyouts that afford the time to do the work or money to fund projects or travel. Sometimes leaders can be people in positions of power, such as a chair or a dean, but leaders can come from all areas regardless of title. Leaders also provide organizational structures that enable cross-program or cross-college collaboration. The collaboration may result from a need to improve or a focus of continuous improvement in the EPP.

Incorporating collaborative writing teams in a university setting invites faculty to shift their research to focus on concerns and issues associated with the university at a college or even a program level. As collaborative writing groups focus on research associated with curricular issues and share their findings, they change practice at the program, department, and institutional level (Bass & Bernstein, 2008). This collaborative approach to attacking research problems can transform educational activity (Gale, 2008; Huber et al., 2005) while reducing the feelings of isolation faculty often experience by being a part of a larger institutional community (Sorcinelli, 2004).

As faculty members advance their research agendas, they find other like-minded individuals who are engaged in similar or adjacent research. Often, collegial friendship over coffee evolves into scholarly conversations and collaborative projects. Faculty become energized through increasing the number of individuals involved with a project as they continue and even expand their research. Think of this research as silos with multiple researchers working together in program improvement. While faculty may still be working together in program area silos, faculty begin to share the work among a larger set of writing colleagues and their work is done for the benefit of enhancing their program or college at large. In an imperfect analogy, we liken this movement away from silo work to the interconnectedness that defines an entire farm as a shift, so to speak, from "silo to farm."

As collaborative writing groups meet and talk about the research project, individuals express their thoughts and opinions (Golde, 2015). Being exposed to a variety of opinions can challenge and inform thinking (Golde, 2015). The conversations within the group result in richer thinking and more complex writing (Franklin et al., 2016). Individuals within the group have different abilities and move into roles and responsibilities as they engage in the writing process. Collaborating with individuals who have different strengths leads to opportunities for mentoring (Houfek et al., 2010), which can be especially helpful for new faculty members. In addition to improving writing skills of individual faculty members, the added expertise improves the overall quality so that the "outcome is greater than the sum of its parts" (Axelrod & Cooper, 2010). As individuals continue to write together over time, they develop what Cramer, Hurst, and Wilson (1996) refer to as the "fourth voice" (p. 26).

In doing this research and writing work together, we found our "fourth voice." We witnessed the impact of our program and college-level collaboration on our collective practice, and we sowed seeds for the improvement of teacher preparation through contributions to the research literature. We reached beyond our university to collaborate with others in the field doing similar work. This unexpected outcome of collaborative research and writing allowed our work to continue even as individuals moved to other institutions. Coming back to our imperfect analogy, we think of this expansion and movement as "farm to table"—sharing the fruits of our labor with others. As we've spent the last decade working through various research and writing projects, we've also affectionately dubbed the messiness of our work: *CollaborWriting* (see Figure 11.1).

In the next section, we present three cases that tell the story of how we leveraged a focus on continuous improvement and evidence-based program improvement to develop research and writing teams using three different collaborative models. We share the messiness of our CollaborWriting. Much of the impetus for the collaborative work discussed in this chapter resulted from two critical changes in our EPP: the award of a Teacher Quality Partnership (TQP) grant to improve clinical practice of student teachers in two partnering school districts and a pushback from the field on traditional approaches to clinical practice.

Figure 11.1. CollaborWriting: Silo to Farm and Farm to Truck Analogy

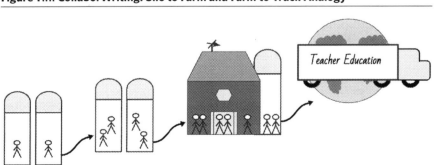

COLLABORATION CASE ONE:
USING INSTRUCTIONAL COACHES TO IMPROVE PRACTICE

Shared Collaboration

Our Teacher Quality Partnership grant had a strong focus on clinical practice innovation and improvement. The dean tapped four tenure-track faculty as coprincipal investigators (co-PIs) to lead aspects of the grant alongside two public school partners. As part of the TQP grant, the co-PI for clinical experiences hired multiple coaches from the school district to work with student teachers in three different program areas in the College of Education. Coaches were trained using the Big Four framework (Knight, 2008)—(1) classroom management, (2) content planning, (3) instruction, and (4) assessment for learning—and the Teachscape Classroom Walkthrough (CWT) Standard Look Fors walkthrough observation instrument (Smith et al., 2013). Instructional coaches conducted walkthroughs and in-class observations, mentored student teachers in best practices, and provided individual coaching and targeted professional development.

The introduction of instructional coaches during student teaching had a strong impact on student teachers' use of effective instructional practices. The use of instructional coaches significantly increased the number of instructional practices student teachers were able to implement in each teaching episode (Smith et al., 2016). In keeping with the People–Tools–Organization framework described in Chapter 1, we will share specific actions related to each in this case.

People

The co-PIs were the first group to gather data for the emerging research agenda. The team grew to include a tenure-track assistant professor, a tenured faculty member and a late-career professional—all teaching in the elementary program. The shared collaboration model worked for this group, as a common problem of practice united their efforts. The benefit of equal multiple voices helped with the large scope of the problem of practice and implementation. By taking this on in a group, this dynamic and large-scale partnership project allowed faculty to focus on different components of research.

Tools

Tools employed to support the collaboration included:

- Reassigned time for co-PIs
- Graduate assistant support

- Data collection and analysis technology tools such as a web portfolio to store Teachscape walkthrough data
- Additionally, the team identified a need for statistics support, so external funding extended the collaboration to engage BioStatistics faculty as consultants with data collection and analysis support with district partners

Organization

The faculty met monthly with the instructional coaches in the school districts. Agenda setting included equal voice to all district coaches. The team also expanded with the additional Biostatistics faculty. The shared collaboration recognized the strengths of each participant and sought to strengthen areas of need. Co-PIs also met with each other on a monthly basis and provided updated reports.

How the Project Expanded Beyond Its Original Purpose

As the elementary program found the coaching to be beneficial to their teacher candidates' ability to reflect as well as to the quality of feedback faculty were able to provide, faculty began to explore coaching in junior-level coursework. Because grant funding did not provide additional personnel in the junior-level courses, faculty explored the use of video coaching tools to provide similar feedback to teacher candidates as they completed practicum hours across the region. After an initial pilot with the virtual coaching software in the elementary program, the College of Education bought a site license for the platform to be used across the college. With expanded tools and college support, principal candidates utilized the software to video coach junior teacher candidates. Other program areas utilized the video coaching software in their practicum settings.

Research Outcomes

Overall, the coaching framework improved and systematized feedback to our teacher candidates. The coaching framework and the process improved the feedback for candidates, including the structure, specificity, and timeliness of feedback for teacher candidates. After a year of implementation, faculty and coaches shared their work at local, regional, and state conferences. Following process refinements, the faculty began publishing the findings in multiple scholarly articles such as these listed below:

Smith, J. J., Stapleton, J. N., Cuthrell, K. C., Brinkley, J., & Govington, V. M. (2016). Improving the internship model: Instructional coaches for teacher candidates. *Teacher Education & Practice, 29*(2), 344–358.

Stapleton, J., Tschida, C., & Cuthrell, K. (2017). Partnering principal and teacher candidates: Exploring a virtual coaching model in teacher education. *Journal of Technology and Teacher Education, 25*(4), 495–519.

Tschida, C. M., Gallagher, J., Anderson, K. L., Ryan, C. L., Stapleton, J. N., & Jones, K. D. (2019). Using video capture and annotation technology to strengthen reflective practices and feedback in educator preparation. In T. Heafner, R. Hartshorne, & R. Thripp (Eds.), *Handbook of research on emerging practices and methods for K-12 online and blended learning* (pp. 314–332). IGI Global.

Why Was This Collaboration Successful?

This shared collaboration project embraced "equal 1st authorship," meaning that lead faculty rotated being "first" on articles and presentations. The collaboration evolved overtime with co-PIs expanding their collaboration with additional faculty members from different departments with similar interests across the campus. Other guiding principles for shared collaborations included the following:

- All members contributed equally.
- The group determined their boundaries and ways to be fair in the beginning with each taking the lead. They set and met deadlines as a group.
- The group allocated time and space to meet and write. Sometimes these were on campus and sometimes, more informally, off campus.

COLLABORATION CASE TWO: USING VIDEO TO PREPARE TEACHER CANDIDATES

Facilitated Collaboration

In most EPPs, the program requires an early experience course for elementary candidates with field experience. At our university the course included a 16-hour field placement requirement. Given the large scale of the program and multiple delivery models including an online option that expanded across 100 counties in the state, approximately 250 early experience candidates completed the course each year. Teacher candidates seemed at times to be merely clocking hours in the course without consistent activities or opportunities for observation. Further, placing candidates for observations was problematic given the rural nature of the region and the need to preserve placement sites for student teaching. To capitalize on teacher candidates' first classroom observation experience, a small elementary faculty group, comprised of tenure-track and non-tenure-track faculty, sought to enhance what the candidates saw, and more importantly, to encourage them to develop the observation and reflection skills that they would need throughout the program. As a result, the Video Grand Rounds (VGR) model was developed.

The VGR model introduces a conceptual framework for novice teacher candidates' observations using video clips as common, shared texts for guiding classroom observation experiences. VGR was piloted with one faculty member in the early experience course. Findings across both the treatment and control groups coalesced leading to iterative model refinements, specifically the simplification of observation protocol and the development of video clip faculty guides. Following refinements, the elementary program faculty discussed piloting the VGR model in multiple sections with multiple willing faculty. Over time, six or more faculty groups continued to collect qualitative and quantitative data in a quasi-experimental design. As we delve into specifics, we will break it down in the People–Tools–Organization framework.

People

One faculty member, the associate chair in the Department of Elementary Education and Middle Grades Education, led the collaboration, leading calendaring of meetings, data collection, and collaborative analysis of findings. The focus on the lead faculty member allowed this research project to have a champion and keep the project in the forefront of their work. Over time, other faculty members took the lead on this innovation in their licensure area, fostering new collaborative spaces.

Tools

Support was provided to the faculty implementing VGR through the following:

- Graduate assistants
- Conference travel support for presentations for both tenure-track and non-tenure-track faculty
- Coding structure in a data system to track VGR participants
- Video selection and compilation support
- An electronic portfolio data collection tool
- Meeting space on campus

Organization

Once the pilot expanded, faculty voluntarily agreed to meet throughout the semester to discuss implementation and data needs. Following a few summers of analyzing data, further refinements were made and newly engaged programs developed materials for piloting VGR. In subsequent years the facilitated collaboration grew as five additional programs piloted and adopted VGR in their early experience course. The leadership model within the collaboration consisted of internal sharing and centralized data collection to support the effort. For each program, a memorandum of understanding (MOU) was drafted to set common expectations and meeting schedules, to identify a key faculty to implement VGR with fidelity, and to support continued data collection in the VGR process.

How the Project Expanded Beyond Its Original Purpose

After analyzing the qualitative and quantitative data from across programs, formal recommendations at the EPP level were developed to adopt VGR as a recognized option in the early experience course. As program outcome data were linked back to VGR candidates, programs were able to discern whether additional areas of focus were needed in the VGR process as well as to determine the appropriateness of the selected videos in exemplifying key elements in the protocols. This deeper analysis occurred over the summers when additional graduate assistant research support was available and faculty taught fewer courses. This evolution of collaboration culminated in faculty across the colleges sharing VGR as a transformative practice in educator preparation in our national accreditation site visit.

Research Outcomes

The informal network of faculty implementing VGR, coupled with the formal support of administration to fund conference travel and data collection and analysis, resulted in a productive 8-year shared research agenda that benefited the individual faculty, program, and EPP. See below for a sample of publications:

Cuthrell, K., Stapleton, J. Bullock, A. A., Lys, D. B., Smith, J. J., & Fogarty, E. (2014). Mapping the journey of reform and assessment for an elementary education teacher preparation program. *Journal of Curriculum and Instruction, 8*(1), 67–85.

Cuthrell, K., Steadman, S. C., Stapleton, J., & Hodge, E. (2016). Developing expertise: Using video to hone teacher candidates' classroom observation skills. *The New Educator, 12*(1), 5–27. https://doi.org/10.1080/1547688X.2015.1113349

Why Was This Collaboration Successful?

This collaboration was successful because one faculty member, who also served as an administrator, facilitated the work and led the group. Guiding principles for facilitated collaboration also included:

- The group relied on one organizer to increase efficiency in data collection and analysis support.
- The organizer provided clear communication about roles when individuals were invited.
- Pilot data and expanded data was shared so as to grow interest in collaboration.
- A distributive model with a common facilitator supported replication of the research.

COLLABORATION CASE THREE: BUILDING A NEW CLINICAL CO-TEACHING MODEL

Administrator-Led Collaboration

Although research projects often emerge from the interest or scholarly agenda of one researcher, they can also begin with a problem of practice. This problem came as a threat to our clinical practice as the state-increased accountability standards caused more and more classroom teachers to decline the opportunity to mentor our teacher candidates. It was an administrator, the Director of Teacher Education, who realized the potential scope of this problem and quickly engaged faculty and clinical partners in conversation to search for possible solutions. The goal was to find something that was just as good as what we were already doing to allow teacher candidates to have a successful experience. One potential answer examined by the group was co-teaching, a model used successfully for student teaching by researchers at St. Cloud State University (Bacharach et al., 2010). First and foremost, the group wondered whether teacher candidates assigned to co-teaching would be as well prepared as those candidates who were assigned a more traditional placement. The group refined the model to include placements where two interns could co-teach with one teacher, hypothesizing that a 2:1 co-teaching model leveraged the benefits of co-teaching while lessening the total number of field placements.

The first step in transitioning from the original problem to more formalized research began with providing professional development to a group of clinical partners and interested faculty. After this opportunity, one faculty member was interested in exploring what would happen if two teacher candidates were placed in a classroom with one cooperating teacher at the elementary level. This small implementation indicated that 2:1 co-teaching placements could potentially be used to reduce the number of clinical placements needed, thus alleviating the problem of decreasing numbers of available placements. Let's take a look at this through the People–Tools–Organization lens.

People

Joining the administrator initially was a group of five faculty members, with one focusing on research and implementation on a pilot project. Then, six additional program areas joined the implementation and study of co-teaching. This administrator-led collaboration found success because the administrator practiced asset-based leadership by choosing the right people who were interested in and could be passionate about the project. This was done through conversation and gauging interest of faculty through various formal and informal conversations. Once the initial group was established, the administrator let the faculty lead with their voice and network with their colleagues through internal presentations and conversations to "spread the word" about the project. In each presentation, the original problem of practice was reviewed, as well as the data collected at each point. By keeping the data and project in front of faculty, expansion and buy-in were easier. The administrator took the opportunity to use the "tight and loose" leadership strategy. By being "tight" about the parameters and overall direction and keeping the problem of practice, it allowed the project to stay on track. The "loose" component was allowing faculty to have buy-in and take the lead with data and pedagogy in the project. By using their expertise, the faculty felt vested in the project but could focus on a subgroup of work because the administrator took the lead on many of the logistical components.

Tools

Two tools proved critical to the success of the co-teaching collaboration:

- Reassigned time for lead faculty
- Funding to send the co-teaching team to attend professional development as a group, which also helped build community

Organization

In order to continue implementation in a formalized manner that could yield data, an MOU was developed with each program area about the methods for assignment to either the co-teaching or traditional conditions and to standardize other aspects such as training. Monthly meetings, collaborative study design, and data collection planning meetings, as well as yearly data summits to analyze and discuss data at program and college levels, were facilitated by the administrator. Since the original goal of the innovation/activity was to have a model "at least as good" as the original, these findings buoyed the collaboration among faculty and, perhaps more importantly, with public school partners who wanted more co-teaching. Further, data

results across programs were utilized to frame a recommendation at the
EPP level to adopt co-teaching as a recognized option for student teaching.

Research Outcomes

Program areas were encouraged to utilize the data in their own writing,
presentations, and programmatic decision making. IRBs were created for
multiple phases of the work. See below for select publications.

Tschida, C. M., Smith, J. J., & Fogarty, E. A. (2015). "It Just Works Better": Introducing the 2:1 Model of Co-Teaching. *The Rural Educator, 36*(2), 11–26.
Fogarty, E. A., & Tschida, C. M. (2018). Using Co-Teaching as a Model of Professional Learning. In A. Novak & C. L. Weber (Eds.), *Best practices in professional
learning and teacher preparation: Methods and strategies for gifted professional
development.* (151–171). Prufrock Press.
Stapleton, J., Cuthrell, K., Tschida, C. M., & Fogarty, E. (2017). The PDSA over-
haul: Approaching reform in teacher candidate support. In D. Polly, M. Put-
man, T. Petty, & A. Good (Eds.), *Handbook of research on innovative practices
in teacher preparation and graduate-level teacher education programs* (pp. 87–
105). IGI Global.

How the Project Expanded Beyond Its Original Purpose

Quickly the problem of placements began to impact both the large elementary and special education programs. Early career faculty from these
programs were asked to join the co-teaching research and implementation
groups. The results then resulted in a collegewide implementation in various
licensure areas under the facilitative leadership of an administrator.

As the co-teaching project evolved, the collaborators' work expanded to
the national level. Networked colleagues interested in using co-teaching in
student teaching led the group to host a collaborative webinar on best practices in co-teaching. Conversations that began during the webinar continued over the next year and resulted in the formation of the Co-Teaching in
Clinical Practice Topical Action Group (TAG) of the American Association
of Colleges for Teacher Education. This TAG allowed faculty from across
the country to share research, dialogue with one another, and explore
cross-institutional work. Two of the faculty were asked to give the keynote
address at a state conference focused on co-teaching as a reform initiative
in teacher education at Brenau University in Georgia. The group presented
at the inaugural National Conference on Co-Teaching and cultivated partnerships that led to collaboration across five institutions on an IES grant
proposal focused on studying how co-teaching is being implemented across
the country in teacher education. Some of the faculty were involved in the

establishment of the National Association for Co-Teaching, a group of educators committed to transforming education through co-teaching in 2019.

Why Was This Collaboration Successful?

Guiding principles leading to the success of this administrator-led collaboration included the following:

- The impact of a problem of practice on various licensure programs was crucial. We should never waste a crisis.
- It is important to coordinate the work of seeking clinical partners input.
- Data was shared regularly to move the work forward.
- In order to write collectively, time and space was provided.
- The research logistics were clearly communicated.

THEMES ACROSS COLLABORATIONS

To truly transform how faculty members approach their work in research and writing, the cultivation of a shared vision, the intentional use of reliable and valid outcome data, and the strategic development of an infrastructure supporting and extending collaboration is critical. A shared vision among faculty and administration can result in more focused research efforts in shared spaces which, in turn, strengthens partnerships and leads to improved outcomes for teacher candidates. The collaborations also supported EPP faculty through the promotion and tenure process. In sharing our collaborative journey together, we highlight here several themes we believe support high-quality, sustaining, and sustainable collaborations.

Networks

We found—and continue to find—power in the networks developed as part of our collaborations. The collaborative writing, aka CollaborWriting, team behind this chapter formed as a team at East Carolina University's College of Education. Today, we represent six EPPs in three states and we continue to uplift each other's work. And our networks have expanded to state and national opportunities to leverage our research to inform practice.

Proximity

Shared spaces create collaborative spaces in which faculty grow their knowledge and expertise in areas that were not originally an expertise. For us, leveraging the mundane task of office moves yielded value-added outcomes

for faculty. Some collaborative writing teams were (re)located in close proximity in our building, which allowed them to sustain conversations between
meetings. Now that some of us have moved to new EPPs, we employ technology to sustain our proximity. Video-conferencing tools facilitate conversations across the miles within our network. Informal and formal writing
retreats occur regularly with the team. These range from multihour to multiday. Time together builds collaboration.

Shared Expectations

While the vision for our EPP guided much of our collaborative energy, the
use of MOUs as a tool to establish and maintain shared expectations for
participation, implementation, and research allowed participants to hold
one another accountable. Further, policy was adopted in the EPP's govern-
ing council that allowed for innovations that were part of program improvement collaborative research to be institutionalized beyond individual faculty
or program adoption. This policy encouraged more program-level collaboration in research, writing, and implementation.

Trust

Over time, relationships were built and trust was established, allowing the
work to grow and expand beyond the original purposes of the work. This
cross-program support results in rich professional growth and developing
rapport for faculty and administrators. Reliance on valid and reliable data
to guide innovation decisions provides authentic avenues for accountability
within EPPs.

CONCLUSION

Together, our CollaborWriting team has been working on these shared
problems of practice for almost a decade. Over this time, we found meta-
phors to be powerful guiding heuristics for our work. The metaphor of a
school of education or EPP as a farm is powerful to us. Our EPP is situated
in a small city that serves a large rural area in eastern North Carolina. We
are the destination city surrounded by farms just a few miles from our
campus. Initially, we viewed our work as siloed, with individual faculty
who worked alone. As we've shared, we took on the common analogy of
"breaking down silos" as a theme in our collaborative writing groups.
Embracing an alternate meaning for silos helps faculty store up their research, their insights and partnerships, and often that harvest only feeds
the individual faculty member and not the broader community. "Breaking
down silos" is about sharing insights and expertise with others in order

to broaden the impact of individual research and contribute to collaborative efforts. In the end, these collaborative efforts elevate the practice of the entire EPP rather than being stored up for the benefit of one faculty member alone.

As a result of these collaborative projects and their writing groups, our team of faculty witnessed the benefit of approaching work in a team-oriented way. It became a natural component of our work. The "ivory tower" of the university can be a lonely place. Through collaborative efforts, programs were improved, and other collaborative work projects began that are not mentioned here. By creating a trusting environment and a "we" mentality, this group of faculty and administrators did something in higher education that can be replicated in other sites by other faculty. At this university, the results were significant. By working together, the faculty and staff represented in these three collaborative efforts produced over 46 scholarly presentations and publications in 7 years. Over 2,000 teacher candidates have benefited from the three collaborative research projects described above. Their improved programs result in creating a better teacher in some way. More than 100,000 students in grades kindergarten through 8th grade have been taught by these teachers. The power of impacting multiple children as they matriculate through school provides a compelling rationale for collaborative projects around problems of practice.

REFERENCES

Austin, A. F. (2010). Expectations and experiences of aspiring and early career academics. In L. McAlpine & G. Akerlind (Eds), *Becoming an academic* (pp. 18–44). Palgrave Macmillan.

Axelrod, R. B., & Cooper, C. R. (2010). *The St. Martin's guide to writing*. Macmillan.

Bacharach, N., Heck, T. W., & Dahlberg, K. (2010). Changing the face of student teaching through co-teaching. *Action in Teacher Education, 32*(1), 3–14.

Bass, R., & Bernstein, D. (2008). The middle of open spaces: Generating knowledge about learning through multiple layers of open teaching communities. In T. Iiyoshi & M. S. V. Kumar (Eds.), *Opening up education: The collective advancement of education through open technology, open content, and open knowledge* (pp. 303–317). MIT Press.

Bhavsar, V., & Ahn, R. (2013). Lessons learned from the collaborative writing process. *The Journal of Faculty Development, 27*(3), 12–16.

Cramer, G., Hurst, B., & Wilson, C. (1996). *Teacher study groups for professionals.* Phi Delta Kappa Foundation.

Dronzek, A. (2008). The academic generation gap. *Academe, 94*(4), 41–44.

Franklin, K., Hurst, B., & Wallace, R. (2016). Elbow to elbow: Collaborative writing with colleagues. *English Journal, 105*(4), 91–93. https://www.jstor.org/stable/26359235

Gale, R. A. (2008). Points without limits: Individual inquiry, collaborative investigation, and collective scholarship. *To Improve the Academy, 26*(1), 39–52.

Golde, C. (2015). The formation of scholars: Insights of the Carnegie Initiative on
the Doctorate. *GeoJournal, 80*(2), 209–213.

Houfek, J. F., Kaiser, K. L., Visovsky, C., Barry, T. L., Nelson, A. E., Kaiser, M. M.,
& Miller, C. L. (2010). Using a writing group to promote faculty scholarship.
Nurse Educator, 35(1), 41–45.

Huber, M. T., Hutchings, P., & Gale, R. A. (2005). Integrative learning for liberal education. *Peer Review, 7*(3/4), 4–7. https://www.aacu.org/publications-research
/periodicals/integrative-learning-liberal-education

Jones, G. (2013). The horizontal and vertical fragmentation of academic work and
the challenge for academic governance and leadership. *Asia Pacific Education
Review, 14*(1), 75–83.

Knight, J. (2008). *Coaching: Approaches and perspectives.* Corwin Press.

Lortie, D. C. (1975). *Schoolteacher: A sociological study.* University of Chicago
Press.

Mirel, J., & Goldin, S. (2012, April 17). Alone in the classroom: Why teachers are too
isolated. *The Atlantic.*https://www.theatlantic.com/national/archive/2012/04
/alone-in-the-classroom-why-teachers-are-too-isolated/255976/

Norrell, E., & Ingoldsby, B. (1991). Surviving academic isolation: Strategies for
success. *Family Relations, 40*(3), 345–347.

Smith, J., Cuthrell, K., Stapleton, J., & Brinkley, J. S. (2013). *A model for improving
clinical practice: Using observational data to support clinical intern effectiveness* [Poster presentation]. American Educational Research Association Annual
Meeting, April 28–30, San Francisco, CA, United States.

Smith, J., Stapleton, J., Cuthrell, K., Brinkley, J., & Covington, V. (2016). Improving the internship model: Instructional coaches for teacher candidates. *Teacher
Education & Practice, 29*(2), 344–358.

Sorcinelli, M. D. (2004, March). The top ten things new faculty would like to hear
from colleagues. *National Teaching and Learning Forum Newsletter, 13*(3).
https://academicladder.com/top-ten-things-new-faculty-members-would-like-to
-hear-from-colleagues

Staffileno, B. A., Murphy, M. P., & Carlson, E. (2016). Overcoming the tension:
Building effective DNP–PhD faculty teams. *Journal of Professional Nursing,
32*(5), 342–348.

Strauss, V. (2013, August 19). Why teachers feel so alone. *The Washington Post.*
Retrieved from https://www.washingtonpost.com/news/answer-sheet/wp/2013
/08/19/why-teachers-need-free-coffee-at-school/

Webb, D. (2018, January 11). Surrounded by kids, but still alone: Confronting the
surprising loneliness of teaching. *We are Teachers.* https://www.weareteachers
.com/loneliness-of-teaching

Building Capacity and Commitment of Future Faculty to Program Improvement Research

Jenny Gawronski and Starlie Chinen

In this chapter we describe a Teacher Education Research Internship (TERI) developed by faculty, doctoral students, and program administrators at the University of Washington. TERI was designed to (1) support local research aimed at the improvement of our teacher education programs (TEPs) and (2) provide doctoral students with experiences in doing the kind of collaborative research that could be valuable in their future positions as teacher education faculty. This chapter provides a description of TERI's collaborative approach, with specific focus on the personal experiences we had as doctoral students participating in TERI, and what we have learned and gained as a result of participating in the course sequence. We begin by narrating TERI's evolution over 2 years as a group of senior faculty, program leaders, and doctoral students who collaboratively designed and implemented the TERI "course." Then we focus on our learning as doctoral students participating in TERI. We discuss the ways TERI's collaborative design afforded us avenues for personally meaningful participation through our contributions to the group's practices as well as the expansion of our personal and professional networks. While we write primarily from our point of view as doctoral students who participated in the internship, we also use excerpts from interviews with participating faculty to give readers a sense of the goals, opportunities, and challenges that faculty experienced with the process. These excerpts are presented in "Faculty Perspective" boxes throughout the chapter. We conclude the chapter with recommendations for others who may wish to engage in work that simultaneously supports doctoral student learning and teacher education program improvement.

TERI IN YEAR 1

The 1st year of TERI was structured through a year-long internship course in which faculty and doctoral students worked collaboratively to design and implement a research study that could be useful for improving our teacher education programs. The composition of our TERI group began with three teacher education faculty, one assistant dean, three program directors, one visiting scholar, and six doctoral students. As a group, we met once a week across three consecutive academic quarters. Our research focus began with the assumption that collecting information about the contexts and practices of our recent graduates would help our programs identify better ways to prepare preservice teachers for their work after graduation. We developed a conceptual framework to guide our joint work, settled on two research questions, and designed the study. During Year 1 we designed the study, collected data, and conducted preliminary analyses of the data. Below, we provide elaboration on each of these phases.

Designing the Research Study

We began our study design process by identifying research questions that spanned our collective interests related to teacher education. These included improving teacher education programs, defining social justice education, and studying teachers' practice. Our interests came together at the intersection of preparing teachers to implement classroom practices informed by commitments to equity and social justice. We began building a shared foundation for our work by reading and discussing both conceptual and empirical articles on teacher education and teacher learning. The faculty drew on their expertise to suggest several major works in the field of social justice education that could further our understanding of teacher learning in teacher education programs and methodological approaches used in follow-along studies of teacher education program graduates (e.g., Cochran-Smith et al., 2009; Cochran-Smith et al., 2016; McDonald & Zeichner, 2009; Nolen et al., 2011). After defining our research problem, we developed a conceptual framework for investigating multiple influences on teachers' practice. Our framework identified three central influences on teachers' practice: personal history, teacher education programs, and the contexts and culture of their schools and districts. Then we developed research questions through a process that began with independently writing research questions of personal interest. Next, we clustered questions that had similarities in topic, commitment, or language. Finally, we created two research questions that were broad enough to capture most members' personal research interests and also contributed to improvement of our programs, namely: (1) What is the role of an individual's prior and ongoing learning experiences, teacher education program, and school and community contexts in shaping their early teaching practice? and (2) What role does social justice/equity play in graduates' thinking and teaching practices?

These two research questions set the stage to tackle the next step in the process: designing the methodological components of the study. We collectively discussed and wrestled with the methodology in terms of participant selection, data sources, and data collection protocols. We discussed the affordances and constraints of specific criteria for participant selection and weighed what their experiences could teach us about our programs. In particular, we prioritized the commitment of our teacher education programs to prepare teachers to work with students who have been historically marginalized. In the end, we selected participants who had graduated from our program within the past 2–4 years and were currently teaching in Title 1 school settings.

Working from our conceptual framework, we next considered possible data sources. After much discussion about the merits and feasibility of different data sources, we chose to collect five types of data for each participant in the following order: (1) a focus group interview with an arts-based component (focus on past and present influences on current teaching practices), (2) an initial individual interview (focus on personal history, experiences, current teaching context), (3) an observation of the teacher's classroom at their school (focus on practice in context), (4) a post-observation interview at the school site (focus on teacher thinking and instructional decision making), and if possible, (5) an interview with an administrator at each school (focus on school context). TERI members then divided into groups with both experienced faculty researchers, program directors, and graduate students to develop protocols for the focus group, individual interviews, and observations.

FACULTY PERSPECTIVE

From a faculty perspective, the prospective research was intended to focus on *both* program interests and the extant research interests of the doctoral students. Over time, it became clearer to us that we had neither conceptualized nor articulated the concept of *program-improvement research* clearly enough. This aspect of the research plan remained somewhat vague to the doctoral students involved and was underrepresented in our research questions, as well as the literature review and methods planning work we undertook early in the investigation.

Collecting Data

In the latter half of the 1st year, we carried out the data collection phase of the study. We gained consent from 18 graduates across four teacher education programs: elementary, secondary, residency, and alternative certification. We held a large-group data collection event on campus that included hour-long program-specific focus groups and individual semistructured interviews. Next, the TERI members individually traveled to participants' schools and conducted a classroom observation and a follow-up interview. In addition to interviewing the participants, we attempted to interview an administrator in each building to get a leadership perspective on the school context.

Preliminary Data Analysis

Upon completing our data collection phase, the TERI group engaged in preliminary discussions about our prospective data analysis work. For example, during our whole-group meetings, we articulated our wonderings and what we learned from conducting the interviews and observations. Beginning our formal data analysis, we engaged in a process of open-coding our individual interviews. Next, we shared our open codes, highlighting those that came up in multiple interviews, then reorganizing codes into categories. After settling

FACULTY PERSPECTIVE

Although the majority of data collection activities were carried out by doctoral students as part of their seminar responsibilities, faculty also participated in all of the activities described. We felt it was important for faculty to directly participate in all aspects of the study, in part to allow us to better understand the research experiences doctoral students were undergoing in the field, and in part to make our moral and intellectual commitment to the work visible to the doctoral students and to the program graduates we recruited as informants for the study. Our direct participation also provided a valuable opportunity to situate teaching activities in the context of our practical activity as researchers, as we worked with doctoral students to jointly develop interview protocols, negotiate access to informants, collect and analyze data. In some cases, we developed minilessons or short workshops to demonstrate and practice specific skills (e.g., data analysis), but our predominant pedagogy was participatory, with graduate students taking up increasingly central roles in the work as it progressed (Lave & Wenger, 1991). These "teaching" opportunities were particularly important because the doctoral students had a wide range of knowledge and experience conceptualizing, planning, and carrying out research.

on a set of preliminary codes, we individually coded the data using a web-based software. Despite the collaborative development of the codes, there was a lack of shared understanding of what each code embodied and this resulted in some data left uncoded or incompletely coded. While the collaborative data analysis was left incomplete, a few doctoral students used slices of this data set for their own graduate program projects and conference presentations.

TERI IN YEAR 2

At the start of the 2nd year, our work shifted to focus on learning about potential uses of our data for program improvement.

Identifying Local Uses of Data

Under the guidance of the faculty mentors, the TERI group recognized the data collected were too thin to fully address our original research questions. We pivoted our work to focus primarily on identifying how the data could be used for program improvement purposes.

Using our conceptual framework, we developed descriptive case studies of each participating program graduate. The case studies were organized into three sections: personal history, teacher education program, and current teaching context. Each section included short explanatory narratives and direct quotes from the teachers. While writing the case studies, we wrestled as a group with how these follow-along case studies could inform program improvement efforts. We developed a protocol for conducting meetings with program faculty in which we shared these case studies with each program's director, faculty, instructors, staff, and doctoral students.

FACULTY PERSPECTIVE

While some doctoral students experienced this sense of "pivot," faculty did not. Our intention from the beginning was to make the data available for *collective* use in programs, as well as for more individual use relative to specific research interests and needs of doctoral students. However, we found again and again how foreign the goals, discourse, and methodology of *program improvement research* was to the experience and training our doctoral students had received. This was, of course, no less true of our own training as researchers. Indeed, in TERI we were jointly trying to figure out how to make research for program improvement a useful part of doctoral preparation.

As we conducted these meetings, we learned more about the utility of these data for program improvement. First, we became aware of the kinds of questions related to program improvement the case studies raised for the programs' teacher educators. Second, we learned from the program directors, faculty, staff, and other doctoral students about additional data sources needed to make sense of the data. For example, teacher education program members requested more academic content-based examples, such as information on the content of specific methods courses, in order to make sense of the teachers' practices described in the case studies. Third, we gained knowledge about how to more effectively and efficiently facilitate these meetings to support focused discussions about program improvement. For example, we originally asked questions that were broad (e.g., what is standing out to you across these cases?), and we found that it took too long, even in a 2-hour meeting, for conversations to proceed from these general conversations to focus on issues related to program improvement. Based on this observation, we began embedding more pointed prompts (e.g., based on your case and what you heard about the other cases, what are your questions or ideas for further inquiry about the program structure, curriculum, instruction, or partnerships?). These more pointed and specific prompts allowed us to focus the conversations on program improvement quickly, which was important for the time constraints of the meetings.

Upon completion of the meetings with each of the four programs, the TERI members created program-specific summary documents that synthesized case study findings for each program, as well as the insights and questions that had been raised during each program meeting. We aimed for these summaries to provide each program with potentially actionable foci for program improvement. These summary documents were delivered to each program as resources for continuing their use of the case study data for program improvement. Several of the findings from the TERI cases were subsequently incorporated into a proposal for improving the programs' induction-year supports related to the program graduates' aspirations and commitments to social justice-oriented teaching and advocacy.

Sharing the TERI Experience

As we concluded Year 2 of TERI, we considered what we had learned from engaging in TERI that might be valuable to share with the broader teacher education community. We identified two (intertwined) topics for conference proposals and publications: (1) doctoral student learning and (2) strategies for evidence-based teacher education program improvement. We then went through an iterative feedback process with faculty to develop and submit proposals for both research-focused and practitioner-focused conferences.

Building the TERI Community of Scholar/Practitioners

Our motivation to participate in TERI stemmed from our interest and commitment to learn about and conduct research on teacher education. We were eager to be part of a community of doctoral students and faculty who shared these interests. The community was built, over time, by valuing all members' ideas and by openly discussing and grappling with the different steps of our study process. TERI's faculty members established a culture where doctoral students could openly ask questions, share their opinions, and take on increasingly meaningful roles in the group. This occurred through group discussions where doctoral students were encouraged to actively participate and take initiative to move the work forward. The faculty members intentionally created space for us as doctoral students to respond to their ideas by using language such as "that's just my thinking" or "I'm curious what you all have to say about this." This collaborative approach encouraged doctoral students to become contributing members and know that faculty valued our thinking and contributions.

Throughout the 1st year of TERI, we experienced fluctuations in group membership in terms of numbers and prior experience in teacher education. TERI began with an even balance of faculty, program directors, and doctoral students. In the middle of the year, we saw a spike in membership with more doctoral students joining the group. The rise in membership appeared to have been the result of the doctoral students recruiting their peers to join the group with positive descriptions of our study. The increase in members required time to orient the new members to the research project and allowed us to collect data from a larger number of teacher participants.

FACULTY PERSPECTIVE

Faculty were quite intentional about encouraging and supporting the doctoral student participation, and subsequent leadership in deliberations about the focus, methodology, and presentation of the research. However, this stance also required that we invest a considerable amount of what was always scarce time to provide opportunities for these discussions. Additional planning time, also scarce, was needed for the three faculty leaders (who taught this year-long course as an overload) to coordinate productive learning experiences for the doctoral students.

The second year of TERI began with another significant shift in membership. Specifically, many of the doctoral students were unable to continue their participation in TERI and the program directors altered their role in the group. The program directors' role shifted from researchers to recipients of the data summaries we provided. However, two new doctoral students joined the group. The change in TERI's membership created both affordances and constraints. In terms of affordances, the smaller group allowed for more efficient decisionmaking processes and higher levels of accountability for completing tasks. Because many of the logistics of the study had been developed, new members were able to participate in ways that allowed for more central participation more quickly than in Year 1. As a result, our new members experienced a sense of having a voice and being able to contribute ideas and questions. Doctoral students also advocated for specific training sessions to address methodological topics such as "what counts as an evidence-based claim?" In terms of constraints, the smaller number of TERI members meant that each member had to take on more work. The shifted role of the directors meant the absence of their perspectives and active participation in decisions about the case studies and data-sharing protocols. At this point, we often felt like we were unsure whether our work was going to be beneficial to program improvement.

In the next section of the chapter we describe our experiences as graduate students engaged in the TERI process. We detail how we increased our participation over time by moving from peripheral to more central positions as members of the research group.

FACULTY PERSPECTIVE

In retrospect, we believe the TERI process would be strengthened by focusing more explicitly, from the beginning, on specific program improvement goals articulated by the faculty and program directors. While TERI was clearly organized around shared values related to program outcomes (e.g., social justice-oriented teaching practices), these were abstract enough so that they did not necessarily connect well with the more immediate and specific concerns of program directors. For example, during this period of time several of the UW teacher education programs were initiating a series of racial-affinity group caucuses aimed at exploring issues of racial identity in relation to teaching and equity in the program. This initiative, while clearly aligned with social justice concerns, represented a highly experimental intervention that could well have been the focus of our follow-along case studies, and which would have been more likely to focus and sustain the engagement of our program directors.

WHAT WE LEARNED AS PARTICIPANTS IN TERI

In this section of the chapter, we discuss our experiences in TERI as doctoral students, paying particular attention to our learning through participation in the work. It is important to note that while we are coauthors of this chapter, we come to the work of teacher education with distinct histories as teachers, orientations toward research in teacher education, phases in our degree completion, and research interests. In the development of this chapter, it became clear that our prior learning histories influenced how we participated in the group and what we hoped to learn.

Preceding her entry into the University of Washington, Jenny was a ceramic artist and art educator in high school and university settings. As a doctoral student, she is an instructional coach and instructor in the Elementary and Secondary Teacher Preparation programs. In her dissertation research, Jenny studies how preservice teachers use technology and digital media to support their learning as they navigate the multiple roles and contexts of their teacher education program. Jenny joined TERI because she was eager to become part of a research community and learn how to design and implement longitudinal teacher education studies.

Before coming to the University of Washington, Starlie was a middle school environmental sustainability and high school mathematics teacher. Her work as a doctoral student began as an instructional coach and mathematics methods teaching assistant in the Elementary Teacher Preparation program and then shifted into a research assistantship position focused on improving middle grades mathematics instruction in a research–practice partnership. Starlie's current research work focuses on doctoral student learning in mathematics teacher education. Starlie joined TERI because the group's research interests aligned with the research question she was exploring in her qualitative methods course.

TERI's intentional design as a group of educators with differing levels of experience in research afforded us, as graduate students, unique learning opportunities that were not present in our other doctoral work at the time of our participation. In what follows, we theorize TERI as a space for our development as graduate students and prospective researchers through legitimate peripheral participation (Lave & Wenger, 1991). In this way, we describe how we moved from peripheral participants to more central members by taking up the language and practices of the group and, in some cases, contributing to the group's practices. To illustrate our progression as group members, we will focus on three themes in our learning as we deepened our knowledge about teacher education: (1) engaging in the literature on social justice teacher education research, (2) developing knowledgeable research skills, and (3) expanding our understanding of the work of being a teacher educator. Next, we will also discuss how the collaborative approach of TERI afforded us opportunities to learn through participation by contributing to and shaping the group's practices and developing academic, professional, and personal relationships. Lastly, we identify the ways in which the TERI model did not meet all of our research needs as prospective teacher educators.

Deepening Our Knowledge in Teacher Education

Our participation in TERI broadened our knowledge of teacher education. For us, TERI served as a conduit that extended our learning from our teacher education courses to actual research experience that aided us in developing a complex vision of teacher education.

Engaging the literature. The research base on doctoral student learning in teacher education emphasizes the importance of becoming familiar with the literature (Dinkelman et al., 2012; Dunn, 2016; Goodwin et al, 2014; Zeichner, 2005). At the University of Washington, doctoral students are able to take a series of courses that explore current teacher education issues in relation to the United States, global perspectives, community-based social justice teacher education, and special topics such as pedagogies of professional education. Our participation in TERI extended our coursework by providing opportunities to further examine literature in teacher education while also pressing us to engage in research. Additionally, because of the variety of stakeholders in TERI, we were able to have conversations about teacher education with faculty, an assistant dean, program directors, visiting scholars, and other doctoral students. Our membership in TERI afforded us the opportunity to engage in practice-oriented discussions about teacher learning with a wider range of people than we had previously interacted with in our classes.

Developing knowledgeable skills. Doctoral students aiming to conduct research as prospective teacher education faculty benefit from firsthand experience in designing and conducting research studies (Golde, 2008). In line with this view, TERI operated as a community of researchers in which we

---

FACULTY PERSPECTIVE

In our view, the experiences of prospective teacher education faculty, including those of our own doctoral students, are too often limited to those they have as teaching assistants in specific courses, or in the field supervision work situated in a single program or partner school. One of our hopes was that TERI would afford participating doctoral students a broader, program-level perspective on the work of teacher education.

could learn what Lave and Wenger (1991) term as *knowledgeable skills*. In relation to this work, we conceptualize *knowledgeable skills* to mean the specific qualitative research skills we developed through our participation in TERI. These skills include the fundamentals of designing methodologically sound research that is meaningful for teacher education practitioners and learning to work collaboratively on a year-long project involving many people. Through our cultivation of these skills, we were able to take on increasingly central roles in the group. For example, we developed skills to work collaboratively with others in the group to write research questions, select participants, develop data collection protocols, collect data, write case studies, and share the data back with programs. We then used our knowledge of these processes to take up leadership roles for developing new protocols as well as inducting new members into our collaborative work.

Learning through observation. In the beginning, we both took more peripheral roles and learned through observation of more advanced members. For example, Starlie began her participation in TERI knowing little about the literature on teacher education or how to effectively conduct qualitative research. As a result, she engaged in *intent participation* when she would "observe and listen with intent concentration and initiative" (Rogoff et al., 2003, p. 176) to the TERI members with more sophisticated knowledge about the content of our study and experience with research. In particular, as the group grappled with ways to define *social justice* and *equity*, the faculty suggested that these terms be eliminated from the protocols and probed only if they came up organically during the interviews. This decision meant that the definitions of these terms were left up to the participants. Jenny began TERI with some familiarity with the literature on teacher education but was less clear about how to write effective research questions for specific areas of inquiry. For her, contributing ideas for research questions and then observing the collective process of discussing and finalizing the research questions supported her understanding of formulating strong research questions, including the particular academic language used in the field.

Applying research knowledge to other studies. While we learned research skills directly connected to our TERI study, there were also opportunities for us to apply our new knowledge to other research projects. For example, in the scenario described above, Starlie learned that defining concepts can be left open to the study's participants. Starlie grappled with this same question in her own research project on mathematics teachers' perceptions of equity and the relationship between those perceptions and teaching practice. Hearing established researchers describe how to design a research project that allowed participants to explain what *equity* meant to them enabled Starlie to use participant narratives to define a specific construct in her own study.

Learning data collection skills. As TERI members, we had the opportunity to develop data collection protocols. We self-selected into smaller doctoral student groups led by a faculty member. In Jenny's case, she worked with the focus group team and learned about the types and sequence of questions needed to engage the participants in self-reflection and group sharing using a visual representation as an artifact. In particular, we began with more general questions about the influences on their practice to encourage participants to enter the conversation at a place that made sense to them and their visual representations. A year later, Jenny leveraged her experience with developing the focus group arts-based protocol to aid in the development of the protocols for sharing the follow-along case studies with program directors, faculty, staff, and doctoral students.

At a different table, Starlie worked with the interview group to create the individual interview protocol. Once completed, a few doctoral students proposed a mock interview to provide folks who had little to no experience conducting interviews to see what it might look like to ask these particular questions. As the mock interview unfolded, it became clear that the purpose of each question was not clearly communicated in the protocol. This led Starlie to collaborate with another doctoral student to develop an annotated interview protocol that included information about the purpose and goal of each interview question and information about how to know when each question has been satisfactorily answered. It was through this experience that Starlie learned the value of an interview protocol as more than a collection of questions, but rather as a document that supports a pointed and considerate gathering of data for specific purposes.

Expanding our understanding of being a teacher educator. The university-based field of teacher education is a large and complex community of practice that involves teaching, professional learning, service, and research. Doctoral students entering this teacher educator work from teaching in K–12 settings have much to learn about the various activities involved in teacher education. Prior to Jenny's participation in TERI, she thought the work of teacher education included supporting teaching candidates in developing their practice, conducting research on preservice teachers in general, supporting doctoral student learning, and engaging in service (e.g., serving on committees). As the goals and focus of TERI shifted in the 2nd year, she saw the improvement of teacher education programs as an important element of the work of teacher educators. She had not previously considered improvement research as a major focus of her work as an art teacher educator. Jenny's participation in TERI supported her in developing a more holistic understanding of the work of teacher education which allowed her to expand her engagement in teacher education in ways that have better prepared her for a faculty position in teacher education.

Our experience with TERI also expanded our conceptions of teacher education programs. Prior to enrolling in TERI, we had limited experiences with the variations in teacher education programs. As graduate students immersed in our coursework and siloed into content area teaching experiences, we both had generated assumptions about the similarities and differences across the five teacher education programs offered at the University of Washington. TERI became a place for us to interact and learn from a variety of faculty, staff, and graduate students from our five teacher education programs. This supported us in developing a broader understanding of the various ways that programs prepare future teachers. Conversations about similarities and differences across programs extended to topics such as funding, course structures, communication, methods courses, partnerships with school districts, and collaboration. For Starlie, being able to hear about the affordances and constraints of different approaches to these structures from individuals who have done this work for multiple years allowed her to see the variety of ways teacher education programs can be organized. Furthermore, it was particularly striking for Starlie to learn about the variation between teacher education programs that shared similar values with regard to preparing teachers to work with students from historically marginalized groups.

Increasing our contributions. TERI's collaborative approach afforded us the opportunity to learn as participating members of the group as well as contribute to the group's practices and tools. During our first few months as TERI members, we found ourselves transitioning from sideline to contributing members. Initially, we both engaged by listening as more experienced faculty and program directors discussed readings. We gradually began to contribute to the discussions and eventually to the group's practices. Our contributions to the group included three solutions to address organizational issues that arose during our research process: (1) a shared note-taking process, (2) graphics to visualize our research process, and (3) an organizational strategy for our data and communication practices.

Upon reflection, we realized that our suggestions to the group's practices aligned with our personal learning preferences that we refined before joining TERI. When TERI began, the group did not have a system for recording the main points of our discussions as well as documenting our collective decisions. This led to many moments of confusion and some unproductive meetings. Starlie offered to share her personal class notes with the group and became the unofficial note-taker. Starlie's notes for our weekly meetings cataloged our research process, describing the nature of our conversations about social justice in teacher education, research, and program improvement. Ultimately, the class notes evolved into an artifact referenced by new and returning members about the group's decisions, future assignments, and our research agenda.

Jenny leveraged her prior experiences as an artist to create graphics illustrating the conceptual framework (see Figure 12.1). The visual was presented to the TERI group in Year 1 in an effort to coalesce the members around a shared conceptual understanding of teacher learning. Similar to Starlie's notes, TERI members continually referenced the conceptual framework visual throughout the research process to focus the discussions, answer data protocol questions, and onboard new members. We also presented the graphic during our data-sharing meetings to orient the faculty to the conceptual framework. Jenny's illustration of our conceptual framework became an integral tool in the TERI process that was positively received and subsequently provided her with the confidence to suggest an art-based protocol for the focus group.

Figure 12.1. Our Conceptual Framework for the TERI Work

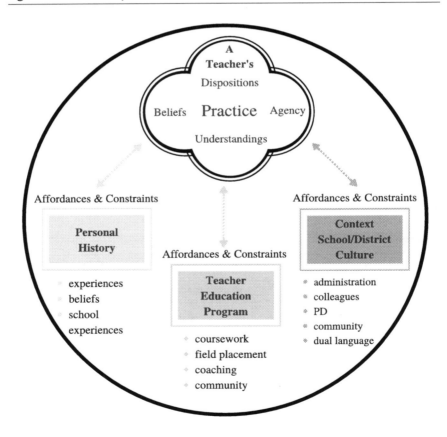

THE POWER OF TWO

Thus far we have outlined our individual contributions to the TERI process; now, we will describe how our work together not only increased what and how we learned knowledgeable research skills but also propelled us to be more central members of the group. Our work in TERI extended past the scheduled meeting times as we often talked about our weekly tasks across the half-wall separating our campus office cubicles. Early in the 1st year of TERI, one such discussion centered on the logistics of working in a large collaborative research team. We realized we would be collecting a large amount of data that needed to be organized by the teacher education program, school, and individual participants. This looming issue had not been discussed adequately in TERI, and we supported each other in thinking about how we could propose a web-based method for organizing our data. Starlie drew upon her previous experience working on a large research team and her familiarity with effective data organizational systems to offer suggestions about naming conventions for files. Jenny's experience with the organization of data on Google Drive led her to take on the responsibility of creating the folder structure for our TERI files.

It feels crucial to note here that TERI was a space where its members were actively attempting to disrupt traditional power dynamics by creating a truly collaborative space where academic status and roles were muted. However, status and roles were challenging for us to ignore as we felt "imposter syndrome" about the value of our contributions. As a result, during the TERI meeting, we coordinated our participation to create openings for each other to share our ideas.

We combined our proficiencies and proposed the creation and use of a Google Drive folder system for the remainder of our study. The founding TERI faculty supported our suggestion, which further positioned us as graduate student leaders in the group. While we may not have originally seen ourselves as having prominent roles in the group, we began to take on more responsibility related to data collection, transcript maintenance, group communication, and membership recruitment.

Expanding Our Roles. Through our developing roles, we moved from peripheral members to more central positions in the TERI group. Other doctoral students and faculty shared with us that they saw our participation as central to the ongoing sustainability of the project. This positioning of us as integral to the project solidified our identities as TERI members with a strong sense of responsibility to the group. Evidence of our identity and commitment is found in our continued enrollment in the TERI class as we were, at the time of this writing, the only remaining doctoral students from Year 1 still with the project in Year 2. As such, we took up more leadership roles by drafting templates for the follow-along case studies, finalizing the protocols for the program meetings, and taking the lead on writing sections for conference proposals. However, it is important to note that our rise as graduate student leaders in TERI was made possible by the collaborative culture established by the founding faculty members. They played an instrumental role in gradually releasing responsibility to us over time and throughout the research process.

Advocating for Our Needs. As we occupied more central roles in TERI, we felt comfortable advocating for our needs as prospective researchers in and outside of the group. By our needs, we mean gaps we identified in our understanding of the research process. Working together, we encouraged each other to speak up and ask for help during our meetings. For example, we wanted to learn more about the kinds of research questions that can be answered by particular data sets and the ways in which one analyzes data to make claims about teacher learning. We felt that our lack of knowledge in these areas prevented us from becoming full participants. However, our participation in TERI supported us in becoming open to asking the group for support around data analysis. Not surprisingly, the established research faculty were receptive to our questions and devoted time during our meetings for discussing the topic, even bringing in guest speakers to help further our understanding of data analysis. As a result, TERI continues to evolve as a group responsive to its members' needs as prospective researchers.

Developing a Professional Network. Lave & Wenger (1991) suggest that a diverse membership is important for sustaining a community of practice. TERI had a diverse membership, and therefore it afforded us opportunities to develop personal and professional relationships in the teacher education community. TERI's focus on working collaboratively with faculty, program directors, and graduate students, created a rare space for us to work side by side with people with whom we would not normally interact. Some of these collegial relationships with fellow TERI members led to additional opportunities for mentorship. For example, we received opportunities to teach courses, serve on a faculty search committee, become a guest speaker, write and publish articles, and have conversations related to career decisions. In addition to these professional connections, TERI grew into a place for us to develop friendships with graduate students that led, in some cases, to writing support and joint attendance at collegewide events. Over time, it became clear to us that TERI was more than a sequence of courses; rather, we used it to cultivate a supportive group of teacher educators.

Gaps in Our Research Skills and Knowledge. As we reflected on what we learned as participants in TERI, we also recognized the ways in which TERI did not meet all of our needs as prospective teacher education faculty. In particular, TERI primarily focused on how to design collaborative research and conduct data collection. Less attention was given to the subsequent steps of the research process, and we continued to struggle with how to carry out data analysis in our individual research projects. We certainly feel we need additional experience with data analysis including coding, categorizing and theme development, identifying findings, and framing the results within a discussion of the literature and gaps in existing research. We hope to make progress on learning these research skills through continued mentorship in TERI's ongoing work, and the development of the present chapter represents one example of that ongoing work. These gaps in our experience may reflect the challenges of trying to plan and carry out a large collaborative research project across 2 academic years with TERI members who represented divergent research interests and experiences. This may have implications for future iterations of TERI.

FUTURE ITERATIONS OF TERI

In the previous sections of this chapter, we described how our participation in TERI offered us unique experiences that advanced our learning as prospective teacher educator faculty. Below, we identify some key elements we believe are likely to be useful to future iterations of the TERI model for doctoral student learning. These factors include, but are not limited to, (1) faculty leadership,

FACULTY PERSPECTIVE

As faculty members responsible for launching and executing TERI, we too learned a great deal from the experience. At a practical level, we learned that a TERI research project must not extend more than 1 academic year (we needed a better articulated syllabus and schedule for each phase of the research) and that it is important to try to keep group membership stable over this time. Equally important, we learned about the strengths and weaknesses of the research preparation in our own doctoral programs, especially for those students whose assistantships did not include a research component. Essentially, our work in TERI led us to think about our own doctoral program improvement as well as improvement for our teacher education programs. Finally, we learned that if TERI work is going to inform teacher education program improvement, then program directors, lead faculty, and doctoral student members need to deliberate the pressing problems and questions that are the focus of TERI research. Everyone involved must understand and sign onto the research and feedback loop that drive program improvement.

(2) opportunities for personally relevant participation for doctoral students, (3) diversity of membership, (4) size of membership group, and (5) logistics.

The foundation of the TERI model rested on the leadership of several faculty members committed to working with a group of doctoral students for at least the duration of an academic year. Central to our experience was the consistent guidance of specific faculty members through the research steps while simultaneously providing an atmosphere of joint inquiry. The core group of faculty planned the course sequence and made pivotal decisions about the study design process, and worked with us to design and plan meetings with TEP program members aimed using the data we had collected for program improvement.

A second attribute needed to produce an effective TERI model was offering ample opportunities for doctoral students to participate in ways that are meaningful for their own learning and research interests. We found these opportunities in TERI primarily because the faculty valued our learning experience alongside the goals of conducting research related to programwide improvement. TERI faculty leaders included doctoral students in the group's decision making around identifying research gaps, our organizational structures, data collection protocols, and conference proposals. While the founding faculty met outside of our TERI meetings to plan our weekly steps, they also organized our class periods using agenda items for us to work on collaboratively. For example, in our 1st year during the winter quarter, they suggested we spend the class period establishing the first round of data collection protocols. We then discussed as a group how best to accomplish this task. The flexibility of each class meeting afforded doctoral students the opportunity to ask questions and develop research-specific skills through active participation in the joint inquiry process. Above all, this process allowed us to see the complexities of research design and planning that were often described only in very abstract terms in our methods courses and textbooks.

A third major component of an effective TERI model was the presence of a range of people currently working in teacher education including the assistant dean, program directors, staff and instructors, and doctoral students who worked as instructors, teaching assistants, and instructional coaches. The diversity in experience of TERI's members allowed for design decisions that could illuminate practical actions for program improvement. We recognize that recruiting and retaining this diverse membership in TERI may be challenging. However, it may be possible to strategically invite various members of a teacher education community to join a TERI group during different phases of the research study. For example, while an assistant dean may not be able to join a TERI group for the entirety of the course sequence, they might be asked to join for specific weeks to provide feedback to the group on the structure and content of the case studies.

A fourth aspect to consider when designing a TERI group is the number of doctoral students that can be effectively supported during the research process. While we do not have a specific ratio for how many faculty to doctoral students is preferable, we did notice that the greater the number of doctoral students, the more difficult it was for them to find personally meaningful ways to participate that supported their individual learning needs. For example, in TERI's second quarter, enrollment increased from five to twelve doctoral students. While this rise in participation allowed us to collect more data than we had previously planned, it also made it challenging for everyone to find ways to participate in personally meaningful ways. For instance, the constraints of having a 2-hour-long meeting each week with 20 or more people made it challenging for everyone's ideas to be taken up while also moving the research agenda forward. To ameliorate the issue of meeting the research needs of a large group of doctoral students, it may be preferable to assign faculty mentors to lead smaller groups of doctoral students focused on specific areas of research.

Lastly, developing and sustaining a community of practice like TERI will require some financial and material resources. Consideration must be given to which faculty will be responsible for the logistics of setting up the course sequence and registering the class, organizing and coordinating meeting times, scheduling meeting rooms, and taking the lead on teaching and administrative tasks. In addition to human resources, some financial resources were needed to support the research project. In the case of our TERI study, one faculty member generously offered funding from their indirect cost recovery account to support monetary and clock hour incentives for the teacher participants. While providing some financial and clock hour incentives to support program graduate participation in the study was an aspect of our study's design that was helpful, we do not view it as a sine qua non for carrying out this type of research. Nevertheless, a consideration of the resources the group might need is important to doing this work.

Altogether, our experience in TERI afforded us many opportunities to learn and grow as teacher educators who see program improvement as a crucial part of our work. In addition to gaining firsthand experience in designing and conducting a collaborative research study, we also came to understand the value of cultivating a supportive and diverse research team. Our TERI experiences will continue to inform our work as we move closer to graduating and moving to the next phase of our work as teacher educators.

ACKNOWLEDGMENTS

We would like to extend our thanks and gratitude to TERI's founding faculty members, Cap Peck, Sheila Valencia, and Kenneth Zeichner, for their role in creating the course series and providing mentorship over the years. We are particularly grateful to Cap and Sheila for their ongoing encouragement and support of our participation in TERI and in the writing of this chapter. We are appreciative of the role Patrick Sexton played in advocating for us to reflect on our learning throughout the TERI process. Lastly, we extend our thanks to the other TERI members and the teachers who participated in our study.

REFERENCES

Cochran-Smith, M., Reagan, E. M., & Shakman, K. (2009). Just measures: Social justice as a teacher education outcome. *Teacher Education & Practice, 22*(3), 237–263.

Cochran-Smith, M., Villegas, A., Abrams, L., Chavez-Moreno, L., Mills, T., & Stern, R. (2016). Research on teacher preparation: Charting the landscape of a sprawling field. In D. H. Gittomer & C. A. Bell (Eds.), *Handbook of Research on Teaching* (5th ed., pp. 439–547). American Educational Research Association.

Dinkelman, T., Cuenca, A., Butler, B., Elfer, C., Ritter, J., Powell, D., & Hawley, T. (2012). The influence of a collaborative doctoral seminar on emerging teacher educator-researchers. *Action in Teacher Education, 34*(2), 172–190.

Dunn, A. H. (2016). "It's dangerous to be a scholar-activist these days": Becoming a teacher educator amidst the hydra of teacher education. *Teacher Education Quarterly, 43*(4), 3–29. https://doi.org/10.2307/teaceducquar.43.4.3

Golde, C. (2008). Creating a broader vision of doctoral education: Lessons from the Carnegie initiative on the doctorate. In R. Reys & J. Dossey (Eds.), *U.S. doctorates in mathematics education: Developing stewards of the discipline* (pp. 53–62). American Mathematical Society.

Goodwin, L., Smith, L., Souto-Manning, M., Cheruvu, R., Tan, M., Reed, R., & Taveras, L. (2014). What should teacher educators know and be able to do? Perspectives from practicing teacher educators. *Journal of Teacher Education, 65*(4), 284–302.

Lave, J., & Wenger, E. (1991). *Situated learning: Legitimate peripheral participation.* Cambridge University Press.

McDonald, M. A., & Zeichner, K. M. (2009). Social justice teacher education. In W. Ayers, T. Quinn, & D. Stovall (Eds.), *Handbook of social justice in education* (pp. 595–610). Erlbaum.

Nolen, S., Horn, I. L., Ward, C. J., & Childs, S. J. (2011). Novice teacher learning and motivation across contexts: Assessment tools as boundary objects. *Cognition and Instruction, 29*(1), 88–122.

Rogoff, B., Paradise, R., Mejía Arauz, R., Correa-Chávez, M., & Angelillo, C. (2003). Firsthand learning through intent participation. *Annual Review of Psychology, 54*, 175–203. https://doi.org/10.1146/annurev.psych.54.101601.145118

Zeichner, K. M. (2005). A research agenda for teacher education. In M. Cochran-Smith & K. M. Zeichner (Eds.), *Studying teacher education: The report of the AERA Panel on Research and Teacher Education* (pp. 737–760). American Educational Research Association; Erlbaum; Routledge.

CHAPTER 13

Looking Back, Leaning Forward

A Conversation About Current and Future Challenges for Making Data a More Useful Tool for the Improvement of Teacher Preparation Programs

Kristen Cuthrell, Diana B. Lys, Charles A. Peck, Désirée H. Pointer Mace, Tine Sloan, with G. Williamson McDiarmid

We end this volume in much the same way as we began: reflecting about the lessons we have learned about how to make data more useful and more regularly used in our work as teacher educators. We enlisted the assistance of Bill McDiarmid to facilitate our conversation, in which we explore this question:

> Looking forward, now, what do you see as the most significant challenges and possibilities related to this work? For teacher educators? For policymakers? For researchers?

In the dialogue below, we offer perspectives on these questions from our multiple regions and types of universities across the United States.

Bill: Well, a good place to start might be to have people talk a little bit about two or three things they felt like they've learned in doing this work together.

Désirée: I think one of the things that's pretty interesting about this work is that, despite contexts and specific systems being really different among the home campuses of the lead authors of this work, there are some things that are really consistent. I would say that one of them is about developing relational practices that center possibilities around data use. That seems to be something that has really been a thread among these various programs—the data are generated by and for people and the outcomes they value. That it's not like data are somehow external or apart from the people and their shared visions of outcomes.

Kristen: To me, that concept is a foundation for any program vision going forward and bringing folks together around the idea that, let's not just have this list of outcome data over here and rubric scores here, but let's see how this data can be used in our programs, and then let's make sure the data we're collecting can help us move forward. The only way you do that is building relationships and having conversations with program faculty and staff. It's not just a "great leader" kind of thing. This is a shared work—a joint venture. For program improvement to truly be impactful and meaningful, there have to be shared conversations around the data and those conversations always come back to how is the data useful and how can we use it?

Diana: One of the most important things that I've learned is how important it is to be very strategic and thoughtful in developing data collection processes that undergird all those conversations, the good conversations that you want to have. Then, those data collection processes continue to evolve in the same way as your conversations evolve.

Tine: What's been most valuable for me was also having the opportunity as a leader to do collaborative analyses of what was happening in our programs through a self-study, inquiry–action process where a researcher was collecting data on what our faculty were learning and how the program was changing. It gave me the opportunity to examine how my actions were interacting or facilitating our collective learning or not. And then in our work together over time, I was using a framework for understanding that work—the People–Tools–Organizations framework—which not only helped me understand the work, but which then became a framework by which I could more deliberately plan my leadership actions and pay attention.

Désirée: What was really striking for me in learning from the other programs that are showcased here is that power really matters, and if, for example, there are graduate students, doctoral students, field supervisors who are contributing to data conversations, they may have a different frame for entering into relationship than tenure-line faculty, deans, and so on. I think when we know that power matters, then inclusive and invitational moves and deliberation on the part of leaders really open up possibilities or, one might imagine, could close them down as well.

Cap: Continuing along the line Désirée was just offering us, one of the things that's become clearest to me as a crosscutting theme was that these three programs have all developed a culture in which dissent is welcome. Now, as we all know, that isn't always easy. I think one of the things that's really important to notice about each one of these programs is that it's possible to communicate and believe, and then experience the value of dissenting points of view as a resource and restrain the very natural impulse to repress that stuff.

Diana: I remember our dean had these great names, and they were always in some kind of quotes. So there were the "naysayers," there were the "fence sitters," but it was never the "complainers." The issues were always framed as "concerns," and the assumption was that they were very well grounded in professional perspective and you had to understand what it was and how people were feeling either engaged or marginalized as part of the work.

Kristen: Diana, I think back to those early days and kind of how we were using the edTPA . . . and when we started doing local scoring and everyone scored and it wasn't just, "oh you have interns, so you score." But no, everyone across the program from early experience instructors to those who taught grad courses, who didn't even teach in the undergrad program primarily. That really opened doors and conversations about what we were looking at and what we were expecting. And it really showcased that we value everyone at this table. And that's something that I'm most proud about with some of our data work is that we shifted that power structure. We said, "No, everyone is important at this table. Everyone has value." Our supervisors helped us develop different reflection instruments and it was all based on "this is what we're seeing and how can we improve, what do we need to do next?" And that was just so powerful. It took a while to get there though and it started with some dissent. There were some conversations in the beginning of "why do I have to look at this piece of data? I don't have anything to do with it. I don't agree with it." I think we had some folks saying that they were "morally and ethically opposed" to some of the outcome data we were looking at. That was a whoa, okay, let's talk about this. Fast-track a couple of years later and we're meeting with the part-time supervisors and faculty at the downtown tavern talking about our students and the things that we've tried and we can do. And look at what our teachers are doing, look at the clinical teachers and the student teachers—the partnerships they have and the impact that's happening with the kids. And that wasn't happening before. So you kind of have to go through growing pains.

Tine: Yes, and when we did go through those growing pains, we ended up in this place where instructors bring drafts of a course assignment for vetting in a program meeting with supervisors and colleagues to ensure not only that it is incorporating all of the elements that the course instructor had wanted, but that it also links to what is happening at the right developmental point in time of a candidate's practice, and so that it gets further supported in practice when supervisors are working with candidates.

Bill: So, looking forward, what are the biggest challenges programs face in making data a useful resource for program improvement?

Cap: I'd kind of like to lead off on this one if I could, just because this has really been worrying me: University policy for me is the biggest challenge to any kind of collective or collaborative program improvement agenda, and I am sorry to say that we have made unfortunately few inroads in the policies that drive people apart in this work, the policies that sustain a highly individualistic, competitive, and entrepreneurial way of relating to the work of teacher preparation. Even though those policies are most strongly articulated and enacted in a place like UC Santa Barbara or UW, almost every institution of higher education in the country is to some extent affected by that culture. We're still rewarding people for individualistic grant getting, publications in their little tiny silos of intellectual interest. This makes me deeply respectful of the effort that people make to swim against the stream of those policies. But the bottom line seems to me is that we can't expect heroic upstream swimmers to do this work everywhere, or forever. We have to find ways to make policy support the work

Bill: Are you referencing primarily promotion and tenure policies or do you have other policies in mind?

Cap: I think the promotion and tenure policies and the value system that privileges the abstract over the concrete, the theoretical over the practical, centralized over distributed leadership—all of those things are part of the problem. But also, the way we underpay the people who are closest to the P–12 classroom mentoring work, which candidates typically say is most influential in their learning to teach process.

Désirée: Alverno doesn't have a research mission as much as we have a teaching mission. We are a tuition-driven school that serves a 75% first-generation student population with about the same percentage of students who are Pell-eligible. So everyone is always mindful of "Do we have the resources for this?" For example, the idea of having as many supervisors in every part of the data decision making process as we can would be so good. But we compensate their time currently by "visit completed." So our challenge is in part a unit compensation structure problem. I think it's really critically important for us to consider how we send messages about how people are valued, and that if we aren't able to value them with finances, then we better value them with inclusive practices and appreciation for their work.

Tine: And there's this whole movement of networked improvement communities in teacher education now, and this work can't happen in any important way without engaging all of the people who are doing the work. And we're struggling with the opportunities for the people closest to the work to help shape this improvement process because they don't have the time built into their appointments.

Bill: Diana, do you want to chime in on challenges?

Diana: I am concerned about the way data use has been kind of overwhelmed by state policy, which has stepped into this data use space. Not for program improvement, but for accountability and sanctioning. Several years ago, we created a recent graduate survey, and it was meant to be a tool used by the UNC system institutions to provide feedback to programs after candidates had been out for one year. Right? It's now part of a sanctions model, and I just keep beating the drum that this is not what this assessment, this tool, was designed for. It's being misused.

Tine: Building on that, you all are making me think about the challenge around the amount of data required now for accountability. I think 20 years ago when we were starting this work and the whole data and accountability movement was coming forward, there was more opportunity at that time to *use* the data we collected. For example, we didn't have so much data required that it overwhelmed our opportunity to use the TPA as a lever for engaging in the work of program improvement. But fast-forward 20 years and now just the sheer amount of data required for accreditation purposes has so tipped the scales to the other side that it's harder to really engage deeply with data that matter.

Kristen: Well, one of the things that has been running through my head while listening to the conversations about challenges for sustaining data use practices: turnover. There's just a lot of movement in university positions and folks go to different places for different reasons. There's so much changeover in terms of leadership and faculty, that it's hard to keep momentum going. So I think sustaining momentum and change goes back to university policy and the PTO framework, and the tools and organizational supports that are put into place. And when you do have kind of like-minded folks together that have grown and evolved through the data use, and understand the different things that are coming at us, you can build some policy, some infrastructure that can last when maybe someone takes another job or moves to a different position. And I think that's one of the things that we were trying to do at ECU, in our Educator Preparation Council and things like that. We were trying to put structure around the innovation and data use process. So that regardless of who was in leadership roles, there is consistency in how the work is supported and how folks go about that work.

Cap: I am also concerned, in terms of looking to the future, that we bring the data movement together with the equity movement in teacher education in ways that I don't think we have yet. Particularly at a practical level—how we use data to develop more effective practices for recruiting and supporting candidates of color, for preparing

White candidates to understand the kids, and the families, and the communities they're serving well enough to do right by them. We're not making so much progress around those goals that we couldn't benefit from a healthy dose of evidence-based feedback.

Désirée: Right. Alverno is so relational and responsive that it is highly appealing to our community, as our students are the best ambassadors for this model. They get their moms and their sisters to come to Alverno as well. But honestly, our context matters: This is all happening in Milwaukee, which is ranked among the most segregated cities in the entire country. Right now, if you looked at the city map of Coronavirus, it is also a racial and socioeconomic segregation map of Milwaukee. Our entire practice is inherently intersectional all the time, which means that we have a tremendous opportunity to provide much-needed diversity in the teacher pipeline. But it also means that our students are existing in this kind of zone of fragility. Where all of them know somebody with Coronavirus right now, and they also have car payments that they're missing, and maybe they're the only person in their family with an income right now, and a family member has a medical vulnerability, and another is undocumented. But that's the reality for the children in the communities that we're preparing teachers for. Right? If we are only creating teacher education programs led by those who can work only with students who are coming from privilege, then that's a big problem. I think there's a kind of moral mission commitment among the programs that we come from, that's really important.

Tine: I'd like to build on that. We share values, but I don't think we share a language for understanding all of the nuances of equitable practice at all. And I think that is a problem. It shows up in conversations where understandings are different, and sometimes those different understandings are not revealed and processed carefully enough to bring people together in the collective work. And that's what used to happen before we were really using data on what candidates were doing in practice to make sense of it together. And it makes me think back to the issue of tools and what data you put on the table, and the kind of tools that we would use that would foreground the kinds of equitable practice that we'd want to see or that we're not seeing and then engage in the same kinds of interrogation and analysis across people's practice—you know, with everybody at the table to really help all of us understand what we're seeing and what we want to see and share a language for what that is and how we get there.

Désirée: I've been fortunate to be part of a conversation that's been ongoing this whole year because about two years ago was the first time that Alverno was recognized as a Hispanic Serving Institution, HSI, which is a federal designation based on demographic enrollment that provides opportunities for the institution and for students—*all* of our students, interestingly, not just our Latinx students—the ability to apply for different kinds of funding sources. It wasn't like we went out and were trying to get HSI designation, but once it happened, we could ask what we need to understand regarding implications for our practice. It's a big part of the institutional assessment culture, these regular professional development for faculty, and a lot of those have been focused on culturally responsive practices with this new designation in mind. It doesn't mean that we're just reading about implications about how to serve Latinx students, but how to hold onto our African American students who might feel like, what does this mean for me? At Alverno, like many places, the teaching faculty is not as diverse as the student population. So we're just engaging in ongoing conversation, learning, book talks, in ways that I hope model for all of our students, not just our teacher education students—that kind of important conversation that you're talking about, Tine.

Diana: And we need to kind of keep focusing on that as an issue of equity and help prepare the teacher educators who are in those pipelines to be attuned to the issues of equity data, use of data for program improvement or program development. And then also, even in the face of these firmly entrenched university policies, support new teacher educators to think about developing their own communities of practice where they can take some collective action in order to improve those programs. I mean it's a whole lot more than just what goes into coursework in a doctoral program. I mean it's like the extracurricular, it's the something else that goes on top of all the courses. What I'm finding in the group with doctoral students with whom I have the opportunity to work is that they have all their silos, particularly within their programs. The ones who have the opportunity to work in the teacher preparation space as university supervisors, they sometimes have to unlearn practices from their coursework and then learn some new things about how to engage collaboratively in this space. And I'm finding that a lot of our doctoral students who are in positions as instructors or supervisors in our teacher education program don't want to work at an R1 institution when they graduate. They want to be doing the kind of work we're talking about in this book. So I'm concerned that their preparation is not giving them all of those experiences, and I find myself trying to start small projects with them so that they can see what a group like this is and how it might work so that they can seek one out for themselves. It's hard. Because those positions . . . we talked about the hierarchy, those positions, like being a university supervisor, can be put off to the side a little bit. It's different from being on somebody's big NSF grant as an RA, a research assistant. That's a different kind of assistantship than being a university supervisor in an educator preparation program. So we continue to further entrench that hierarchy in how we prepare doctoral students and so we're not undoing anything, unfortunately.

Cap: I'm really glad you put a focus on this, Diana. Louis Menand argues that if we want to change the way the work is done in the university, we don't change it by producing new knowledge, we change it by changing the way we produce faculty.

Bill: So, thinking in this broad way about the future, what else do we need to change? In university policy? And in research?

Cap: Well, perhaps it goes without saying that we need research that continually tests our assumption that data matters for program improvement and research that clarifies the conditions under which that assumption is warranted.

Kristen: I would agree, Cap. And I would add that research is needed on the links between equitable practices and data use in educator prep. What differences across types of programs/regions/communities exist? What are equitable ways of involving stakeholders when resources are diminishing? And in what ways are programs resourcing this work?

Tine: We need program improvement research that engages practitioners in true partnership with people who know more about researching practice—I think of the work that Diana and Kristen did at ECU with Kevin Bastian, as an example. We need to create a research design process that gets to the questions that matter for people who are doing the daily work of teacher education. I think also we need large collaboratives that do research on policy questions that matter. One of the papers I often turn to for inspiration is one Christine Sleeter wrote in 2014 that said that most education research is based on the individual interests of researchers, not the needs of the policy or stakeholder community.

Cap: I'm not sure it's even faculty interest so much as the press within university culture and policy for faculty to produce "new knowledge" as individual scholars. And that culture is distributed across universities—it's not just in the R1s. Faculty are quite aware that not only is individual research and grant productivity prioritized for internal promotion and tenure, but the same values are front and center in competition for career moves across institutions, including institutions that don't really have missions centered on research. So, what to do? One college-level policy I have seen used to support the kinds of collaborative, program-centered research that is needed to drive program improvement is the creation of a "fourth box" in promotion and tenure criteria. Kristen, I think you referred to that practice at ECU, and I worked under a great dean, Bernie Oliver, at Washington State University who developed "fourth box" promotion criteria related to diversity and P–12 collaboration that really supported faculty work in those areas. I also think Linda Patriarca's strategic use of her budget at ECU to support faculty course releases related to program improvement projects was really smart. I don't think we can wait for the larger university cultures to change on this—this is an issue that deans have to take on, in collaboration with faculty, to be sure, and I think that many faculty in teacher education would welcome these supports for work they can see needs to be done.

Bill: Are there state policy changes that could better support data-informed program improvement?

Cap: Tine, you said something earlier that I wanted to pick up on, and maybe it branches into another piece of this future-oriented conversation. I can't imagine a future where we don't have more data and more surveillance. So how do we help people understand that problem and cope with it in ways that keep the focus on learning and getting better at the work we care about, rather than just spending all of our time writing reports.

Kristen: We need to develop data systems that are more flexible and responsive to community and EPP needs—not just state reporting requirements. And we need reduction of redundancy in reporting requirements. We need policies that recognize and affirm local EPPs' efforts to support collaborative data use work at the same levels as individual grant/research productivity. It would be helpful if support for these efforts were inscribed in state policies more clearly than they are at present.

Tine: Kristen's response is making me think of the difference between state policy and institutional policy. Both are critical to consider here I think. So I'm going to try and separate them.

In terms of state policy, As Kristen suggested, I think accountability reporting has reached a tipping point, where the quantity of data reported in assurance of program quality has become a deterrent to improvement of quality in practice. And I say this as a person who's been a part of setting these policies in California for the past 15 years. We need to find a "sweet spot" where we report on what is truly at the essence of quality teacher education and allow for programs to devote more of their time and energy to improvement of practice through the *use* of those data. I don't know yet what that balance is, but I do know that all the data we collect for teacher education and the 40-plus proficiency standards we require new teachers to meet, is not getting the attention it actually requires to be useful and used. In other words, at the state level we've set an impossible bar and, while we're getting back programs' best efforts to comply, their best efforts could be better used for digging more deeply into issues that matter for their practice. We've barely moved the bar on equity, on diversifying the teaching force, on ensuring the opportunities and success for students of color. We need to determine what is most essential and let go of the rest.

In regard to institutional policy, we've talked earlier about changes needed in promotion and tenure policy in order to support the collective work of program improvement, and there is no place this is more needed than in our R1 institutions. In the university, we need to distinguish between disciplines that serve professional practice, and those that serve other purposes. I am often reminded of David Labaree's work on the uneasy relationship between education and the university. In our effort to establish education as a discipline on par with the sciences, the humanities, and so on, we have in many ways marginalized the professional practice of preparing teachers. In many R1s we've managed this tension between research and practice functions by introducing nonresearch lines—teaching professors and lecturers—whose work in the rest of the university is usually to teach large courses to relieve research faculty time. The work of teacher educators is not this. And, at least in the University of California, these practice-based lines do not address the scholarly function of research-based teacher education. So the irony is that the field suffers from both inadequate attention to its programmatic- and policy-level research needs, and simultaneously unstable support for the operation of the program itself.

Cap: Bill, do you have any wisdom to share on these matters?

Bill: I don't know about wisdom, that's a pretty high bar for me. But there are a couple of things I was thinking about as I listened to your discussion. One is about doctoral preparation for teacher education. John Goodlad came up with this idea years ago of the "hybrid educator"—folks who have a foot in the P–12 world as well as in the university. I would say that at Michigan State, at UW, and at UNC, I had students who clearly fit that category, and they really agonized over the idea of having to give up their connection to the P–12 world in order to be part of the higher ed world. John, Ken Zeichner, and I actually did some work planning a doctoral program around that idea.

Another of the things that we talked about that deserves more attention is about which evidence do we need to get in front of a specific set of constituents, right? And particularly identifying the kind of evidence that is most likely to both motivate and inform different groups, including supervisors, cooperating teachers, as well as faculty. So thinking about evidence in relationship to these different subgroups within the community, I think, could be enormously helpful to the field.

And, finally, what role do we take as leaders? I work with new deans a lot around that. Because a lot of them want to jump in and be the one who's driving the whole thing, and I actually have to pull them back and get them to think more strategically. And I say to them: "The kiss of death is for a dean or even a director to take over and say, 'I want this' or 'the dean wants that.'" I remember the conversation we had to have with our dean around the transnational education (TNE) work. I remember specifically having to tell her that she had to back off, and let the faculty do the work. So I think the conversation about what does leadership look like here, what kind of leadership is needed, is really important.

Cap: Bill, you and I had a conversation recently with Linda Patriarca, who did such splendid leadership work at ECU . . . and part of that conversation was about how hard the work of systemic change is . . . but the thing I remember most about that conversation was how each of us felt about the experience of doing the work. I think we all commented in one way or another on how exciting and rewarding the work was, and it might have been Linda who referred to the work as "the most rewarding time of my life as a professional." I thought we might close by inviting each of us to comment on our personal experiences of undertaking the kinds of program improvement work that is described in this book.

Désirée: OK, I think that what is exciting about this is that once you do that, once you decide to get in the same boat with other people, there's something that can happen only if you're in that kind of collaborative dynamic that makes everybody better and makes the work better and makes it exciting, even when it's hard, and maybe it's exciting because it's hard.

Cap: Just riffing off that a little bit. It seems to me that one of the unfortunate facts of life in higher ed is that we work primarily alone. We work in these silos that the organization has structured for us. So one of the things I've noticed each time I've been involved in this kind of work, not only with you all, but when I was working with Bill at UW and when I was working with Tine and others in Santa Barbara, is that recovering that sense of the collective and being part of something larger than your individual teaching or research was exciting and motivating. It makes you want to come to work on Monday morning, and then stay late Monday night.

Diana: I'd add one more thing about that. I remember Linda always brought us back to this moral imperative, right? It was a very powerful way of uniting us when it was easy to get deep into just your own piece of the work. But, you know, if you're really concerned about preparing the best teachers to meet the needs of students, then that can be very unifying; and she did such a great job of reminding us of that perspective and kind of keeping us focused on those goalposts.

Tine: No teacher wants to teach badly, and no teacher educator wants to teach badly. And I think one of the things that we've learned in a real way is that all of our work is so interconnected. The practice of teacher education is ultimately a collective practice: In order for my course to be effective, it has to be connected with what others in the program are teaching, and connected to what is going on in the field. So understanding that somebody else is supporting my piece while knowing that my piece is only as good as my colleagues' pieces . . . and that's part of the motivation.

Désirée: It's just like in a garden, there's this sort of organic diversity that makes the growth, makes the garden more fertile. Makes all of us that are connected with it healthier.

Cap: We'd like to thank you, Bill, for your help with this conversation and with the book. And I've just got to say again, every time this gang gets together, I just learn so much. It's remarkable. Finding ways to support folks to work together . . . that turns out to be the sine qua non of program improvement.

About the Contributors

Dr. Kristen Cuthrell is a professor in the Elementary Education and Middle Grades Education Department and director of the Rural Education Institute at East Carolina University. Kristen has presented and published extensively on program improvement approaches while developing and refining innovations in educator preparation. During her tenure at East Carolina University, Kristen has also served as elementary education program coordinator and associate chair. During that time, Kristen was responsible for cofacilitating edTPA candidate support to over 1,800 elementary teacher candidates and leading program improvement in the college's largest initial license program.

Dr. Diana B. Lys serves as assistant dean for educator preparation and accreditation in the School of Education at the University of North Carolina at Chapel Hill. She leads program assessment and accreditation efforts in the school. Prior to joining UNC, she served as director of assessment and accreditation in the College of Education at East Carolina University. Diana played a pivotal role in implementing edTPA at East Carolina University and across the state. She continues to be a key partner in research linking edTPA data to graduate outcomes in the field, including student achievement scores and principal evaluations. Her work has been published in the *Journal of Teacher Education* and *Teaching and Teacher Education*, and she serves as chair of the Accreditation, Assessment and Program Evaluation in Educator Preparation special interest group of the American Educational Research Association.

Dr. Désirée H. Pointer Mace is a professor of education and director of graduate education programs at Alverno College. She has led professional development and educator preparation at the local, state, national, and international levels. She has done advanced work in Argentina, Peru, and Uruguay focused on reform and renewal in teacher learning, reaching hundreds of educators from multiple Latin American countries. Désirée has served on the design team and national academy of the edTPA, the most widely implemented preservice teaching performance assessment in the nation. She has presented on several major panels at the annual meetings of the American

Association of Colleges of Teacher Education (AACTE), and has worked with the U.S. Department of Education as a national peer reviewer in the 2012 and 2013 Race to the Top–District grant programs and as an invited reviewer of the 2015–2016 National Educational Technology Plan. Désirée holds an MA and PhD in education from the University of California at Berkeley and a BA in cognitive science from Vassar College.

Dr. Charles (Cap) Peck is currently a professor of teacher education and special education at the University of Washington. Cap's research work over the past decade has focused on policy implementation and systemic change in teacher education. He has been particularly concerned with factors affecting the extent to which programs of teacher education take up opportunities for learning and program improvement that are afforded by new sources of outcome data. Cap served as associate dean for professional studies at UW from 2014 to 2017, and as director of teacher education from 2003 to 2010. Prior to his work at the University of Washington, Cap was director of teacher education at the University of California, Santa Barbara, where he and his colleagues conducted one of the first studies of the implementation of the Performance Assessment for California Teachers (precursor to the edTPA).

Dr. Tine Sloan is a teaching professor and former director of the Teacher Education Program at the University of California, Santa Barbara. Her research focuses on programmatic issues in teacher preparation including the study of interventions of practice and the use of data in programmatic change. She is the lead investigator for the California Teacher Education Research and Improvement Network (CTERIN), a large research center across nine University of California campuses. She is interested in international contexts for teacher preparation and works with partners from several countries on research and practice collaboratives. This work grew from her position at the National Institute of Education in Singapore, where she served as faculty prior to joining UC Santa Barbara. Tine has a long history with teaching performance assessments, serving on development and implementation teams (for PACT, edTPA, CalTPA), and as a consultant to states and other institutions. She is also active in state policy and is the current chair of the California Commission on Teacher Credentialing.

Ann Adams Bullock is dean, director of teacher education and professor in the School of Education at Elon University. Her research focuses on improving teacher education through data-driven conclusions.

Starlie Chinen is a doctoral candidate in teaching, learning, and curriculum at the University of Washington. Her work focuses on issues related to equity in mathematics education at the classroom- and teacher-education levels.

Her dissertation research investigates how doctoral students transition from roles as classroom teachers to equity-oriented mathematics teacher educators in university settings.

Susannah C. Davis is a research assistant professor at the University of New Mexico. She holds a PhD and MEd in education from the University of Washington. Her research explores how postsecondary institutions, their faculty, and their administrative leaders navigate organizational change and reform efforts and learn in the process. Her current research focuses on how institutions of higher education create more equitable and inclusive policies, practices, and climates, as well as how systems of power shape reform efforts.

Elizabeth A. Fogarty is an assistant professor in literacy at the University of St. Thomas, where she teaches reading methods and foundations classes. She holds a PhD in educational psychology from the University of Connecticut. Her research interests include co-teaching, social justice, and effective practices for teachers in differentiation and literacy.

Jenny Gawronski is a ceramic artist, arts educator, and doctoral candidate in teaching, learning, and curriculum at the University of Washington. Her research interests are in art education, preservice teacher learning, technology, and digital media literacy. Her dissertation research examines how preservice teachers use technology and digital media to support their learning as they navigate the multiple roles and contexts of their teacher education program.

Jessica Gottlieb is an assistant professor in the educational leadership policy program in the Texas Tech University College of Education. Her research focuses on how policy can be used to expand K–12 student access to high-quality learning opportunities, with a particular focus on teacher education policy and STEM education policy.

Patricia A. Luebke is the dean of the school of professional studies at Alverno College in Milwaukee, WI. She holds a PhD in urban education with a specialization in educational administration from the University of Wisconsin–Milwaukee. Prior to entering higher education, she served in a variety of roles in K–12 public school administration.

G. Williamson McDiarmid has helped create or revise teacher preparation programs at five universities, including the Michigan State University, the University of Washington, and the University of Alaska. Most recently, he served as dean and alumni distinguished professor at the University of North Carolina at Chapel Hill. He currently serves as the University Chair

Professor in Education at East China Normal University in Shanghai, China, and coaches early-career deans as part of the Deans for Impact organization. He is the author or co-author of over 60 research articles and monographs, 4 books, and 14 book chapters.

Benjamin Ngwudike was educated in Nigeria and the United States of America. He obtained his PhD from the Department of Educational Administration, Foundations, and Research at Jackson State University, where he is now a professor. Dr. Ngwudike's areas of research include student achievement, closing the achievement gap, and teacher quality.

Tabitha Otieno earned her PhD in the field of social science education from Ohio University, Athens. She is currently serving as professor for social science at Jackson State University, Mississippi. Her research interest includes issues in teacher education, online teaching, and gender.

Linda A. Patriarca is a retired professor in the Department of Special Education, Foundations and Research and the former dean of the College of Education at East Carolina University. Her research interests revolve around teacher education, specifically teacher assessment and teacher development.

Jennifer Scalzo is a lecturer and coordinator of the MEd in the teacher education program at the Gevirtz Graduate School of Education at the University of California, Santa Barbara. She received her PhD in education with an emphasis on cultural perspectives from UCSB. She currently teaches courses in teacher education focused on multilingual learners and teacher inquiry.

Marcelo Schmidt is an educational psychologist with interests in curriculum development, program assessment, and data-use practices in higher education. He has a master's degree in education from the University of Texas–Pan American and a PhD in educational psychology from Texas Tech University. He has experience in teaching physical education and sports, has served as an administrator for outcomes assessment and accreditation, and is currently an assistant professor of curriculum and assessment in the Texas Tech University School of Veterinary Medicine.

Joy Stapleton is an associate professor and the elementary program director in the Department of Curriculum and Pedagogy at Winthrop University. She currently teaches elementary social studies methods, teaches/supervises field experiences and internships, and collaborates with other elementary faculty in facilitating the senior year edTPA process. Her research publications and presentations focus on increasing the effectiveness of teacher preparation programs through curriculum innovations. Examples of publication topics include using video coaching software to support teacher candidate development, co-teaching, and the Inquiry Design Model.

Christina Tschida is an associate professor in the Department of Curriculum and Instruction at Appalachian State University. Her research centers on improving teacher education through critical, equity-centered, anti-racist pedagogies; quality online instruction; and clinical practice reform through the use of co-teaching and coaching.

Jahnette Wilson, EdD, is a clinical professor at the University of Houston. Her primary role includes the supervision and training of site coordinators who work with student teachers. Additionally, Dr. Wilson teaches undergraduate courses. Her research interests are focused mainly on field supervision and program improvement.

Chase Young is an associate professor and director of the literacy EdD program in the School of Teaching and Learning at Sam Houston State University. He earned his PhD in reading education from the University of North Texas. Previously, he taught elementary school and served as a literacy coach.

Aaron Zimmerman is an assistant professor of curriculum and instruction in the College of Education at Texas Tech University. He earned his PhD in curriculum, instruction, and teacher education from Michigan State University. His research focuses on the experiences of teacher educators and early-career teachers.

Index

The letters *f*, *n*, and *t* after a page number indicate a figure, note, or table, respectively.